# LEADERSHIP 2030

# LEADERSHIP 2030

The **Six Megatrends** You Need to Understand
to Lead Your Company into the Future

**GEORG VIELMETTER**
**YVONNE SELL**

**:AMACOM**
**American Management Association**
New York • Atlanta • Brussels • Chicago • Mexico City • San Francisco
Shanghai • Tokyo • Toronto • Washington, D. C.

This publication is designed to provide accurate and authoritative information in regard to the subject matter covered. It is sold with the understanding that the publisher is not engaged in rendering legal, accounting, or other professional service. If legal advice or other expert assistance is required, the services of a competent professional person should be sought.

**Library of Congress Cataloging-in-Publication Data**
Vielmetter, Georg.
    Leadership 2030 : the six megatrends you need to understand to lead your company into the future / Georg Vielmetter, Yvonne Sell.
    pages cm
    Includes bibliographical references and index.
    ISBN 978-0-8144-3275-4
1. Business forecasting. 2. Business planning. 3. Management. I. Sell, Yvonne. II. Title.
    HD30.27.V54 2014
    658.4'092--dc23                                                                              2013033729

**About AMA**
American Management Association (www.amanet.org) is a world leader in talent development, advancing the skills of individuals to drive business success. Our mission is to support the goals of individuals and organizations through a complete range of products and services, including classroom and virtual seminars, webcasts, webinars, podcasts, conferences, corporate and government solutions, business books, and research. AMA's approach to improving performance combines experiential learning—learning through doing—with opportunities for ongoing professional growth at every step of one's career journey.

Printing number
10 9 8 7 6 5 4

*To my wife, Elena Nancu, and my son,*
*Jan Lenhard, for sharing their lives with me*
**—Georg**

*To my parents, for all their foresight*
*in raising me to always face forward*
**—Yvonne**

*"In the past, even the future was better."*
**—Karl Valentin, Bavarian comedian**

# Contents

For more information on the evolving role of leaders in 2030, as well
as the many challenges created by the six megatrends, please visit:
www.haygroup.com/leadership2030/

\* \* \*

More information about the book, as well as the Bibliography, can
also be found at: www.amacombooks.org/go/Leadership2030

# Acknowledgments

As with every book that is based on true collaboration, many people contributed to making it happen. Our thanks and gratitude for their help go to:

Hay Group, the global management consultancy we work for, for granting us time and resources to work on this book.

The team at the foresight company Z_punkt in Cologne, whose members collaborated with us in the early research phase: Vanessa Watkins, the team leader; Cornelia Daheim, Klaus Burmeister, and Tim Volkmann, our research assistants in Berlin; Markus Gunnesch and Caroline Mallien, as well as Hay Group's corporate librarian, Claire DiPardo, in Philadelphia.

Hay Group's Global Practice Council, Mary Fontaine, Ruth Malloy, Nick Bolter, and David Derain, who supported the initiative right from the beginning; the team in Europe working on the Leadership 2030 survey, Lucy Traynor, David Barnard, Magdalena Magusiak, Alexandre Ledu de Nesle, Marta Wojcik, and Chris Hayley; our marketing and PR colleagues in Europe and the United States, Jen Scharff, Anna Patterson, Luke Lacey, Octavia Walton, and Mitch Kent; our team at AMACOM in New York, our editor, Christina Parisi, our managing editor, Andy Ambraziejus, and our copyeditor, Jacqueline Laks Gorman.

Finally, this book would not be as rich and as personal without all the colleagues and personal and business friends all over the world who discussed the issues with us, shared their stories, passed on articles, read parts or all of the manuscript, or contributed otherwise: Juha

Äkräs, Kirsta Anderson, Meike Bahr, Marcel Brenninkmeijer, Gavin Brown, Gina Byrne, Wayne Chen, David Derain, Claude Dion, Jürgen Erbeldinger, Mary Fontaine, Ron Garonzik, Donna Gent, Frank Höffgen, Stuart Hyland, David Jennions, Ville Karkiainen, Harriet Kirk, Ruth Malloy, Gillian McNamara, Ashwin Mohee, Thomas Muhr, the NLMC, Timis Rallis, Andreas Randebrock, Stefan Rasdorfer, Jörg Rumpf, Jan Schmidt-Dohna, Jeff Shiraki, Mohinish Sinha, Carl Sjöström, Signe Spencer, Scott Spreier, Philip Spriet, Manik Surtani, Holm Tetens, Ruth Wageman, and Graeme Yell. Our special thanks go to Daryl Newman, who during the composition of this book did a tremendous job in polishing and aligning our writing.

# Introduction: Empire and Manure

*"Prediction is very difficult, especially about the future."*
—**Mark Twain,**[1] humorist

Name the following country: It is the richest nation in the world, with the world's highest standard of living, largest military force, and most developed education system. It is the global center of business, finance, innovation, and invention, and its currency is the international standard of value.

The answer is: Great Britain.

Actually, we misled you a little. More precisely, the answer is the British Empire *in the year 1900.*

Even more recently than that, in 1922, the British Empire was still the largest empire the world had ever known. It spanned 12.7 million square miles (33 million square kilometers), roughly a quarter of the earth's land mass, with 456 million people, a quarter of the world's population.

At that time, few could have imagined how the world was going to change within just 100 years. Nobody could have forecast the ebb and flow of world power that would follow: the emergence of the United States as the world's dominant superpower, the rise and fall of the Soviet Union, and now the ascendency of China to threaten America's hegemony. And many people have no idea that Britain's supremacy was ever the global status quo.

But then, prediction is very difficult, especially about the future of superpowers.

## IN THE MIRE

Nevertheless, people dare to predict. Let us return to the days of the British Empire for a moment and consider the great horse manure crisis of 1894.[2]

Imagine London in 1894: the world's largest city, a hectic, densely populated metropolis, and the commercial center of the world. Transportation was its lifeblood. And in the nineteenth century, as it had for thousands of years, transportation meant horses. Just about every product made relied on horsepower for distribution. No large city could have functioned without horses.

In 1894, therefore, London was home to tens of thousands of horses, each of them consuming, according to one calculation, the produce of five acres of arable land per day. And each produced between 15 and 35 pounds of manure. *Per day.*

This was a problem. More than a problem: It was a crisis. Horse manure was piling up on London's streets. It was reaching intolerable levels, polluting the environment and attracting billions of flies, which spread fatal diseases such as typhoid. The stench was abominable, and the effect of rain on all that waste does not bear thinking about.

The abundance of horses led to other problems, too: road congestion (horses were slow), accidents (they were given to panic in crowded conditions), mistreatment of the animals, and a growing demand for valuable land to house and feed them.

Scientists and politicians were at a loss as to what to do. An urban planning conference addressing the topic broke up prematurely when no solution could be found. This was the context in which the *Times* of London dared to predict in 1894 that by 1950, every street in London would be nine feet deep in horse manure. Of course, London was not the only modern city facing a horse manure nightmare. Another forecaster warned that New York would be plagued by droppings three stories high by 1930.

But then, prediction is very difficult, especially about the future of horse manure.

## THE TIMES THEY ARE A-CHANGIN'

The fact is nobody knows what the future will look like. It is all too easy to focus on one single trend, development, or incident, then extrapolate and jump to the wrong conclusion. But there comes a time when people have a feeling that change is in the air. We live in such a time.

This is the impression we have gleaned from hundreds of conversations with business leaders, academics, colleagues, and clients. They perceive that the way we do business will be dramatically different in the future, as will the way we lead people and organizations. It is a perception born of thousands of experiences, observations, and trends, all of which add up to a sense that we are in an era of far-reaching change.

It is a perception born of economic growth booming in unexpected parts of the world and stagnating in old economies, and of China being on the verge of surpassing the United States as the world's largest economy.

It is a perception born of nanotechnologies and biotechnologies advancing in ways that most of us do not really understand.

It is a perception born of younger generations operating in the virtual world as comfortably as in the physical one, and expecting to be allowed to spend time on Facebook while working.

It is a perception born of employees becoming as concerned about living fulfilling lifestyles as they are about how much they earn—if not more so. Of talented individuals being able to change jobs at will. Of top managers in Brazil, Russia, and China earning more than their colleagues in Germany, the UK, and the United States. Of companies struggling to find young talent, while older employees continue to work past 60, 70, and even 80 years of age.

And so on …. It is a perception born of all of these things and many, many more.

In early 2013, an iconic symbol of London—the onetime global center of commerce—came under Chinese ownership. The company Manganese Bronze, which makes the famous London black cab, was bought by Chinese car manufacturer Geely. (There is more on Geely in Chapter 1). In fact, after its bankruptcy a few months before, Manganese Bronze was rescued by Geely.[3]

The fate of Manganese Bronze is deeply symbolic of the fact that times are changing. The prospect of the last car company in British hands being saved by a Chinese buyer was not bemoaned as a national catastrophe. Rather, it was warmly welcomed by London's mayor, Boris Johnson, who declared himself "delighted" that Geely had secured the company's future.[4]

We too get the feeling that change is afoot. A few weeks ago, we interviewed a chief financial officer as part of the due diligence process for a private equity deal. She told us that she had been working three days a week for the past two years to give her more time with her young family. The investors were only vaguely surprised—and largely unconcerned—to learn about this. A decade ago, however, a senior executive working a three-day week would have been unimaginable. Now it barely merits a mention.

The European head of a global financial services company recently complained to us that his organization struggles to recruit the best talent. This is not because the best do not apply but because "they expect good salaries, but are totally unwilling to put in the long hours we had to ten years ago."

In addition, a recent hire informed us—while in the process of signing his contract—that he planned to go on paternity leave just a few weeks later. And one job candidate asked about our company's "carbon policies."

We've seen numerous senior managers from emerging markets leave careers in the West to return to their native countries of India, China, and Indonesia to work for local companies. At the same time, Anshu Jain, an Indian who hardly speaks German, became co-CEO of the German financial giant Deutsche Bank in 2012.

All of this led us to the same conclusion as the leaders that we and our colleagues at Hay Group, the global management consulting firm we work with, talk to: Something is in the air. But it is difficult to get a grip on exactly what is changing, how and why, and what the future will look like as a result.

**Figure I-1** ■ The Leadership 2030 Research Process

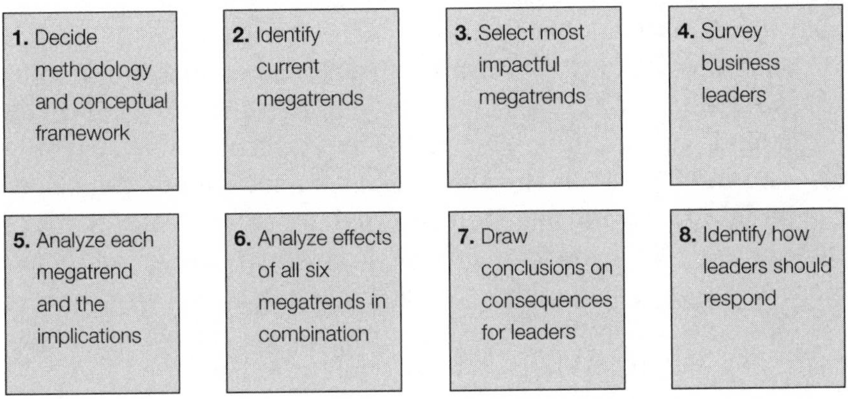

| | | | |
|---|---|---|---|
| **1.** Decide methodology and conceptual framework | **2.** Identify current megatrends | **3.** Select most impactful megatrends | **4.** Survey business leaders |
| **5.** Analyze each megatrend and the implications | **6.** Analyze effects of all six megatrends in combination | **7.** Draw conclusions on consequences for leaders | **8.** Identify how leaders should respond |

This motivated us to dig deeper. We asked ourselves: Exactly what is changing? What are the implications for organizations and their leaders in the immediate and longer term? How will this affect the way that leaders lead? What will leadership look like by the year 2030?

We wondered if it would be possible to identify the main drivers of change. How could we systematically analyze these drivers and their implications? What would be the right framework for such a study? Figure I-1 shows our entire research process.

## THE BENEFIT OF FORESIGHT

The answer lay in in the science of foresight analysis (sometimes called future research). Foresight analysis is robust, cross-disciplinary, scientific research that focuses primarily on social science. The same rigorous criteria apply to this field as any other science: relevance, logical consistency, simplicity, clarity of premise, narrative and presuppositions, and a practical value to everyday life.[5]

Once we knew that we would be using foresight analysis, the next task, which began three years before writing this book, was to find the right conceptual framework to investigate the questions we wanted to answer. After extensive research, we decided that the most fruitful way to analyze the changes occurring would be to identify the current *megatrends* in global society.

The concept of a megatrend was first introduced by John Naisbitt in his 1982 book *Megatrends*.[6] It is important to understand that a megatrend is not a short-term trend of the sort that characterizes the clothing and FMCG (fast-moving consumer goods) industries. These can be short-lived and are often localized in nature. Rather, a megatrend is a *long-term, transformational process with global reach, broad scope, and a fundamental and dramatic impact*.[7]

More specifically, there are three dimensions that define a megatrend: time, reach, and impact. See Figure I-2.

**Figure I-2** ■ The Three Dimensions Defining a Megatrend

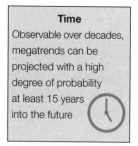

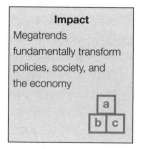

| Time | Reach | Impact |
| --- | --- | --- |
| Observable over decades, megatrends can be projected with a high degree of probability at least 15 years into the future | Megatrends affect all regions and stakeholders, including governments, individuals, and businesses | Megatrends fundamentally transform policies, society, and the economy |

We recruited a research partner to help with the early analysis, which would identify the global megatrends driving the changes being perceived by the business leaders we work with. We chose as our research partner Z_punkt, a German foresight company regarded as a European leader in the field of long-term foresight analysis.

Working with Z_punkt, we initially identified around twenty megatrends, all regularly cited in academic papers and credible studies as having a significant impact on societies and economies. As we honed our understanding of these, we zeroed in on six megatrends that are creating—and will continue to create—the greatest shifts in the business environment.

This took us into the next phase of our research: canvassing business leaders for opinions about and insight into these six megatrends. We analyzed the views of thousands of employees around the world on their organizations' leadership practices from a variety of Hay Group data sources. We also conducted hundreds of informal conversations with business leaders and academics about the megatrends, as well as presented dozens of speeches, lectures, and workshops in which we discussed the issues at hand. In addition, we analyzed hundreds of articles and studies on each megatrend.

We carried out our analysis megatrend by megatrend. This enabled us to understand the causes and consequences of each one in great detail, on three important levels: the business environment, organizations, and leaders and their teams. In this book we focus primarily on the implications for leaders.

The next stage was to analyze the six megatrends in combination. What do they have in common? Where do they cross over? To what extent do they reinforce or contradict each other, and how? And again, what are the implications of the megatrends taken together?

This led us to an important discovery. Not only does each megatrend have huge implications for organizational leaders, but combined they result in five "reinforcers" and four dilemmas that will make life even tougher for business leaders in the future.

Finally, based on this exhaustive analysis, we drew our conclusions about what leaders need to do to survive and thrive in a world shaped by the megatrends.

## THE SHAPE OF THINGS TO COME

So despite the difficulties of prediction, we are daring to predict. In this book, we predict the changes, challenges, and environments that leaders will encounter in a future shaped by the six megatrends, as well as the attributes they will need to cope with an altered landscape.

It is important to put this into perspective, however. Our aim is not to extrapolate hard numbers into the future, as people tried to do when faced with rising levels of horse manure in the streets. That would be attempting the impossible.

And we don't have a crystal ball. We are not trying to set down in stone exactly how the future will unfold. That would also be attempting the impossible. We have no way of knowing whether "black swans"[8] might occur: unforeseeable, disruptive episodes with far-reaching effects that radically alter the course of world events and the direction of one or more of the megatrends. Examples of such events are the recent financial crisis, the revolutions in Eastern Europe, the invention of the Internet, and World War I.

Rather, we are forming a view of the shape of things to come. What this book *does* attempt to do is to investigate the early indicators of long-term, fundamental change, then draw conclusions from this analysis.

In some ways, this is a counterintuitive exercise, for human beings tend not to question the world around them. Rarely, if ever, do we ponder how the complex normality we have constructed for ourselves might be different. Rather, we take as self-evident everyday life as we know it. We unthinkingly accept our physical environment, societal structures, and the cultural norms, common values, and belief systems that give us identity, belonging, and meaning.[9] To question all of this at the same time would be to place ourselves under an unbearable mental and emotional strain.

So we go about taking everyday life for granted. We trust that the world is round, that the sun will come up in the morning and set in the evening, and that there will be oxygen to breathe. We assume that the building we work in will be there when we arrive each day. And we believe without doubting it that the United States is the world's greatest superpower (or at least, we did until very recently).

In 1900, people took for granted that the world's dominant power was Great Britain. And they took for granted that the main means of transportation was the horse and that they just had to put up with all the manure.

But overreliance on our known world leads to inertia. The blithe acceptance that things are as they are brings about a reluctance to recognize and embrace change, even when it is staring us in the face. This is understandable. But it can blind us to the inevitable, and to the need to adapt to change.

In 1907, this type of blind acceptance led the U.S. National Association of Teachers to believe that "students today depend too much upon ink. They don't know how to use a pen knife to sharpen a pencil. Pen and ink will never replace the pencil."[10]

But then, prediction is very difficult, especially about the future of pencils.

Overreliance on the known world also blinded our horse manure forecasters to the solution to their problem. The internal combustion engine had been in existence for thirty years or more by 1894, and it underwent numerous advances and improvements throughout the 1890s. Perhaps most significantly, Carl Benz patented his *Motorwagen* in 1886, and in 1894 he began production of his first series. Another significant factor was the use of asphalt, which had been employed to create smooth roads in the United States from around 1870.

The writing was on the wall for horse-drawn transportation. Yet the eminent scientists, politicians, and urban planners who came together to tackle the horse manure crisis failed to understand the changes going on around them. To them, horses and manure were the status quo.

The fact is that sometimes we need to face up to change, because change is coming whether we like it or not. Now is one of those times.

In this book, therefore, we question the status quo because the business world will soon be very different.

## ABOUT THIS BOOK

The book begins by analyzing the hard facts of each megatrend and examining the implications that each has for leaders. We then explore the consequences of all six megatrends and set out what leaders need to do in response.[11]

The six megatrends, shown in Figure I-3, are:

1. *Globalization 2.0.* A new economic world order is emerging. Power is shifting to fast-developing markets in Asia (China in particular) and away from "old" economies. This will result in numerous opportunities and threats from highly localized market dynamics as a new middle class materializes in emerging markets.

2. *Environmental crisis.* Critical natural resources are becoming scarcer and climate change more threatening as a result of human activity. In the face of accelerating costs and social and market pressures, leaders will need to fundamentally rethink their operations if they are to continue to compete.

3. *Individualization and value pluralism.* Growing affluence in emerging markets will drive increasingly individualistic attitudes in more parts of the world. People will come to expect their individual needs to be catered to, as both customers and employees. This will create niche opportunities for customized offerings, greatly diversify the demands of employees, and require far greater sensitivity and agility from organizations.

4. *The digital era.* Living and working with digital technology is becoming the norm. Digital platforms are shifting power from organizations to consumers and employees—particularly younger "digital natives"—and breaking down old divisions between personal and professional life. This generates unprecedented transparency, which will oblige leaders to act with sincerity and authenticity or see their reputations plummet.

5. *Demographic change.* A burgeoning and rapidly aging world population will transform markets and place enormous pressure on social structures and welfare systems. This will result in a shrinking global workforce, sparking a war for talent among organizations on an unprecedented scale. Leaders will need to cope with the demands of an increasingly intergenerational workforce, in which each age group has vastly diverse attitudes and requirements.

6.  *Technological convergence.* Scientific progress in fields such as nanotechnology and biotechnology will transform many areas of our lives, the greatest advances resulting from the combination of these technologies. This wave of innovation will create untold new product markets. It will also place huge demands on companies to stay ahead of the curve and to collaborate closely with competitors on complex R&D programs.

**Figure I-3** ▨ The Six Megatrends

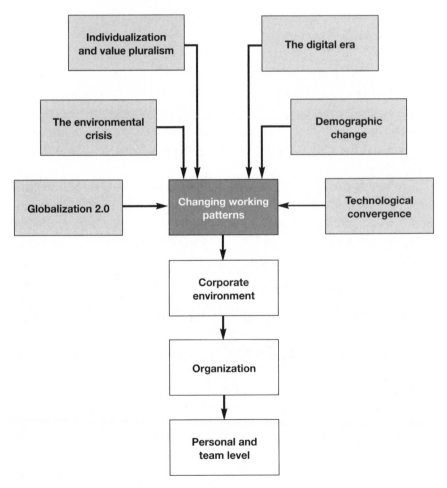

In our study of the megatrends and in compiling this book, we have made every effort to take a truly global perspective. The mega-trends are, after all, global in nature, and we have considered in detail their implications for large, global organizations.

However, we are a German and a Canadian; our nationalities, backgrounds, cultures, and social education are unavoidably Western. To an extent, therefore, we cannot help but address the issues at hand with Western perspectives, mindsets, and thought processes.

## TO BE CONTINUED

As the Greek philosopher Heraclitus observed, change is the only con-stant: No man can step in the same river twice. And like Heraclitus's river, the megatrends are in constant flux. They continue to progress as we write this book and as you read it. But as their effects are to be felt over the long term, we can confidently examine their impact fif-teen years hence.

However, our study does not cease with the completion of this book. If you want to participate in our ongoing study of the mega-trends and understand how they will affect your organization and your leaders, please visit www.haygroup.com/leadership2030/ where you can fill in our Leadership 2030 survey and find a wealth of additional material relating to our research, as well as the Bibliography to this book. You can also read about which trends will impact your organi-zation most, and what you might consider doing to cope with them.

**Georg Vielmetter** and **Yvonne Sell**
Berlin and London

# 1 Lost in Translation: Globalization 2.0

*"It has been said that arguing against globalization is like arguing against the laws of gravity."*
—**Kofi Annan,** former Secretary-General of the United Nations

## AT A GLANCE ■ GLOBALIZATION 2.0

**Five Essential Points**

1. *Globalization 2.0 is fundamentally different from version 1.0.* The East will progress from just being the workplace of the West; Western companies will still operate in the East, but under different circumstances. Goods, people, and capital will flow in multiple directions, not just from West to East, but also very much from East to West.

2. *Traditional trade patterns will be disrupted.* As economic power shifts eastward, trade between emerging markets will flourish. The East will rely less and less on the West for goods and services. Organizations will need to think differently about marketing.

3. *Beware of "glocalization."* New middle classes will emerge in more and more countries, each with its own set of consumer demands, thereby "glocalizing" the market. A single, centralized strategy and operating model will no longer be adequate for multinational organizations.

4. *The burden of complexity will intensify.* Globalization 2.0 will demand a complexity of thinking that few organizations or leaders have encountered—significantly intensifying the cognitive and, in particular, the conceptual and strategic demands on already overstretched leaders.

5. *Contextual awareness will be critical.* Organizations will need to be more adaptable and encourage diversity of thought, in order to enhance their contextual awareness and ensure that communication is truly two-way.

**Five Questions Business Leaders Should Ask**

1. How agile is my organization?

2. Are our strategy and operating model adapted to the demands of different regions?

3. How nimbly can we react to local demands?

4. Will the next generation of leaders come from the local population, or will we need to import talent?

5. How can we ensure that our leaders are equipped with the conceptual and strategic demands required for the demands of the new globalization?

---

Ten years ago, this book would have been written on American laptops, designed and engineered by IBM. But the company that revolutionized computing in the 1980s famously sold its PC manufacturing arm to Lenovo in 2004. So now here we are, tapping away on Chinese-made machines.

Three or four years back, one of us drove a Volvo, the other a Land Rover. Once the pride of the Swedish automotive industry, Volvo sold its car division to Ford in 1999. Ford also acquired Land Rover from BMW in 2002. The American manufacturer subsequently sold Land Rover to Indian carmaker Tata Motors in 2008, and Volvo to China's Geely in 2010.

And a year ago, when one of us needed to replace an old Grundig TV, friends recommended Philips, a European leader in technology, design, and engineering. The day the new set was delivered, the Dutch electronics giant announced the divestment of its TV division to a joint venture with Hong Kong's TPV Television. Philips now has a 30 percent minority share.

So only recently, between us we owned American computers, Swedish and British cars, and a German TV—all decidedly Western. Today, these appliances are Chinese and Indian. What happened?

Welcome to the world of Globalization 2.0.

## THE HISTORY OF GLOBALIZATION

Before examining what happened, let's briefly refresh our memories of what has characterized globalization until now. We'll call this Globalization 1.0.[1]

Under Globalization 1.0, West went East. Western corporations sought cheaper production in less developed markets. They transferred labor and manufacturing facilities to distant locations, exporting their products back to their home markets at a fraction of the cost of domestic production. These distant locations were principally in the East: India, China, and the Far East (and in the case of some U.S. companies, Latin America). To put it crudely, the East became the sweatshop of the West.

Globalization 1.0 is nothing new. The process is hundreds of years old at the very least, possibly older. We might argue that it goes back to the Silk Road or the sea traders of ancient times. The International Monetary Fund (IMF) calls it "an extension ... of the same market forces that have operated for centuries at all levels of human economic activity."[2]

The phenomenon really took hold during the second half of the twentieth century, when technological innovation and international liberalization created the conditions for it to flourish. The twentieth century was, of course, a time of great technological advancement. Global travel, international freight, and long-distance communication became considerably easier, not to mention cheaper. And the advent of information technology enabled organizations to systemize and manage work, processes, and transactions happening thousands of miles away. Innovation decimated the time, cost, and practical barriers associated with doing business across borders.

At the same time, bureaucratic barriers also crumbled. The liberalization of international regulation occurred on an unprecedented scale. The peace that followed two devastating world wars allowed the creation of international pacts and free trade areas, such as the European Economic Community that was formed by the Treaty of Rome in 1957. Hurdles to cross-border trade fell away. Commerce, labor, and capital were able to flow between countries at hitherto unseen levels.

However old Globalization 1.0 may be, like it or not, it's a given. We cannot choose whether or not to accept or participate in it. The world is globalized, and it has been for some time. But globalization as we know it is changing.

## What Is Globalization?

In its widest sense, globalization isn't a single topic. It's several all at once. As the *Stanford Encyclopedia of Philosophy* points out, globalization covers a "wide range of political, economic, and cultural trends." It can be defined variously as the pursuit of liberal, free market policies in the world economy; the dominance of Western forms of political, economic, and cultural life; the proliferation of new information technologies; and even the grand notion that humanity stands at the threshold of realizing one single unified community.

But thankfully, social theories have in recent years converged on a generally agreed upon definition. Broadly speaking, globalization is the compression of space and distance as the time it takes to connect geographical locations is reduced.[3] This is the force that gave Globalization 1.0 a turbo-boost during the last century (see above).

In other words, the world is getting smaller.

This definition has been discussed by philosophers for 200 years or more. It may come as a surprise to learn that Karl Marx viewed this compression as, at least in part, a positive force. In the *Communist Manifesto* of all places, he and Friedrich Engels predicted that it would bring about the "universal interdependence of nations."[4] The German philosopher Martin Heidegger was less welcoming. He bemoaned this "abolition of distance," issuing a bleak warning that "everything gets lumped together into uniform distancelessness."[5]

More recently, the IMF provided a more strictly economic definition, one very much aligned with our concerns in this book. In 2000, an IMF paper described globalization as "the increasing integration of economies around the world, particularly through trade and financial flows." The term also encompasses the movement of people, knowledge, and technology across international borders, the report pointed out.

The paper also defines four "basic aspects" that make up globalization. These are trade and transactions; capital and investment movements; the migration and movement of people; and the dissemination and exchange of information, knowledge, and technology.[6]

The IMF report also brings an economic logic to the compression of time and space described by our philosophers and social theorists. Globalization, it says, is the "result of technological advances that have made it easier and quicker to complete international transactions—both trade and financial flows."

In other words, the world is getting smaller.

## THE MEGATREND: GLOBALIZATION 2.0

The twenty-first century is witnessing the emergence of a parallel phenomenon to Globalization 1.0: Globalization 2.0. East is now also going West. Everything we thought we knew about the economic, commercial, and financial world is being turned upside down.

An important point to note here is that the new model does not replace the old. Globalization 1.0 goes on. Western multinationals will continue to operate from distant, low-cost bases. In June 2012, as the UK geared up for the Queen's Diamond Jubilee, *The Times* of London reported that souvenir tea towels were on sale in London at £4.25 per pair, sourced in China for just 9.1 pence (about 15 cents) each.[7]

Though the locations are changing, many of these low-cost bases will still be in the East. However, of the so-called Next 11 emerging countries identified by Goldman Sachs in 2005, seven are in Asia (Bangladesh, Indonesia, Iran, Pakistan, the Philippines, South Korea, and Vietnam). The list contains only one European nation (Turkey), as well as Mexico, Nigeria, and Egypt.[8]

But Globalization 2.0 is a different beast compared to its predecessor. It is not model 1.0 in reverse. Rather, it is characterized by two unique and interrelated attributes: (1) the shift in the economic balance of power to Asia, and (2) the rapid expansion of the middle class in the emerging nations.

## The Asian Century

There is a wealth of statistical evidence documenting the rise of Asia as an economic power. China has been the fastest growing economy for the last thirty years, growing nineteen-fold in real terms over three decades since 1980.[9] Market saturation and the economic crisis in the West are causing growth prospects there to practically stagnate—or, in many cases, leading to out-and-out recession. Meanwhile, Asian policy makers are frustrated that growth in the East is struggling to regain the double-digit acceleration it was experiencing before the financial crisis of 2008. The chart below summarizes GDP growth in 2016, as estimated by the Economist Intelligence Unit's *World Economy Forecast* of March 2012.

**Figure 1-1**  Estimated GDP Growth in 2016

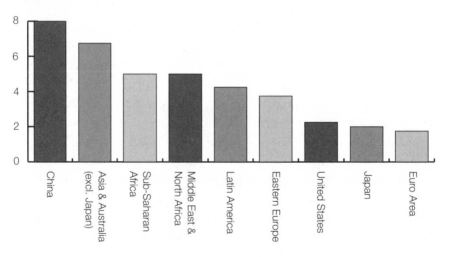

In the race for economic growth, East is beating West hands down. But simply outperforming Western economic superpowers does not equate to a power shift. The tipping of the balance can be seen in the comparative scale and influence between East and West resulting from this reversal of economic fortunes.

In April 2011, the IMF provoked dramatic headlines across the world by forecasting that China would surpass the United States as the world's largest economy in purchasing power terms as soon as 2016.[10] According to PwC, India is on course to overtake the United States on the same basis by 2050, at which point China's economy will outstrip America's by some 50 percent. Come this time, just three of the world's top ten economies will be from the West: the United States, Germany, and the UK.[11]

With scale comes influence; with economic scale comes financial influence. China's foreign exchange reserves totaled $3.2 trillion in February 2012.[12] In May of the same year, the country's state-owned investment fund, the China Investment Corporation (CIC), was sitting on assets worth $440 billion.[13] And inevitably, the capital is flowing West. Chinese foreign direct investment (FDI) in Europe totaled $12.6 billion (€9.6 billion) in 2012.[14] In 2011, for the first time, more Chinese companies than U.S. companies invested in business locations in Germany, and by a significant number: 158 compared to 110.[15] This would have been inconceivable twenty years ago.

### Red Lights, Green Lights: The Geely Story

*"There is nothing mysterious about making cars... I am determined to do this, even at the risk of losing everything I have."*
—**Li Shufu,** Chair, Geely Automobile Holdings Limited, 1997

China's largest private car manufacturer is in many ways the very model of Globalization 2.0. The company's rapid rise from humble beginnings culminated in its takeover of Volvo in March 2010.

The Volvo deal is a sign of the economic power shift from West to East. As if to underline this, Geely bought Sweden's most recognizable auto

*(continued)*

brand from none other than American icon Ford—the very first company to mass-produce affordable cars. What's more, it did so at a bargain price: Ford paid $6.65 billion to acquire Volvo in 1999, while Geely paid Ford a mere $1.8 billion.

Geely's Chair, Li Shufu, had courted Volvo for three years, a determination he demonstrated many times over before Geely's meteoric rise. For example, in what has become a well-known story, when Li graduated school, he invested the money he received as a graduation gift in an old camera and bike. Then, he cycled around tourist spots, taking photos of tourists for cash. The enterprise made him ten times the money that his equipment and transportation had cost.

A successful foray into refrigerator manufacturing came to an abrupt end in 1986, when the company closed down after failing to obtain a license to operate under new government rules. Frustratingly for Li, several competitors simply kept going without licenses.

But his experience planted the seed from which Geely grew. With an analogy to driving that proved to be prophetic, he said at the time: "As long as you don't give up, you can always bypass red lights, or wait for them to turn green."

Li's move into car production was initially blocked by the same official hurdles he'd previously faced. But by this time, Li had learned his lesson. Having bought a factory in Zhejiang province licensed to make only two-door autos, he nevertheless pressed ahead with production of four-door sedans. He then set about traveling tirelessly between Beijing and Zhejiang to lobby national and regional ministers for the authorization. Each successive refusal was met with a renewed attempt, earning him the nickname "the car maniac" in government circles. In 2011, the "maniac" finally gained his license to produce sedans. And the rest is Globalization 2.0 history.

Geely's first car rolled off the production line in 1998. Just six years later, the company was producing 100,000 cars a year. In 2011, sales reached 422,000 cars, earning revenues of almost 21 billion yuan ($3.3 billion) and 1.54 billion yuan ($241 million) in net profit, up 13 percent from the previous year.[16] The company plans to turn out 2 million models annually and complete the construction of fifteen overseas production bases by 2015.[17]

## Out of the Loop

A side effect of the shifting balance of economic power under Globalization 2.0 will be a sea change in world trade patterns. Increasing levels of commerce between emerging nations will present another significant threat to Western economies and corporations. Business relationships, strategic alliances, and economic agreements that exclude the West altogether are increasingly being struck.

The China Investment Corporation, for example, announced in May 2012 that it was looking to move its investments in the United States and Europe to emerging markets. Ominously, the CIC's president, Gao Xiqing, described this as a "natural shift."[18]

Driven in part by the fast-expanding East's hunger for commodities, trade between Latin America and China expanded sixteen-fold in just ten years between 1999 and 2009. During the same period, trade between the United States and Latin America grew by just 50 percent.[19] In 2009, China replaced the United States as Brazil's prime export destination.[20]

Chinese trade and investment in Africa are also mushrooming. China became the continent's largest trading partner in 2009, overtaking the United States, and Chinese FDI in Africa soared from less than $100 million in 2003 to in excess of $12 billion in 2011.[21]

Economic allegiances are also being formed within and between the Asian, African, and Latin American continents. The four BRIC countries (Brazil, Russia, India, and China)—originally no more than an acronym coined by Goldman Sachs[22]—signed an alliance in 2006. The German newspaper *Die Zeit* heralded this as "the first major world forum without Western involvement."[23] The group has since held five official summits, the latest in March 2013, welcoming South Africa into the fold along the way (which necessitated the change in acronym to BRICS).

The group has lofty ambitions. On the agenda at its 2012 summit was a potential development bank to invest in infrastructure and development projects within the BRICS and other emerging economies. The group also created the BRICS Exchange Alliance, allowing the five nations to inter-invest directly, overcoming the need to use an intermediate Western currency.[24]

Another hugely significant example is the China-ASEAN (Association of Southeast Asian Nations) free trade area. The world's largest economic bloc by population came into being in 2010. The area covers some 1.9 billion people and regulates around $4.5 trillion of trade annually. Its combined GDP totals a gigantic $6 trillion.[25] By the terms of its agreement, 90 percent of products traded between the eleven member states are no longer subject to import tariffs.[26] For Chinese companies, the treaty inevitably means cheaper and easier access to raw materials and rapidly growing markets across Southeast Asia.

## Middle Class Spread

With dizzying economic expansion and strengthening corporate success comes the growing wealth of the local population. To state the obvious, companies cannot operate without people, and to employ people, they must pay them. As a country's corporate and sovereign wealth grows, so too does the affluence of the population. Per capita income follows the same upward trajectories of a nation's GDP and its companies' profits.

Under Globalization 2.0, this means improving purchasing power for hundreds of millions of people in low- and middle-income economies: Between 2010 and 2050, per capita income is forecast to increase 800 percent in China, 600 percent in India, and around 400 percent in Thailand and Indonesia—compared to just 50 percent in the United States.[27] The result will be the emergence of a burgeoning middle class, with differing tastes and demands in different geographies.

In 2008, Goldman Sachs estimated that the number of people worldwide with middle incomes (defined as $6,000 to $30,000 annually) was growing at an unprecedented 70 million per year. This is a staggering growth rate, considering that the banking firm estimated the total global population of middle earners to be just 472 million at the time. Yet Goldman Sachs forecast that this would accelerate to a growth rate of some *90 million* a year by 2030, pushing an astonishing 2 billion people into the ranks of middle income.

As a result, middle income earners will be receiving some 40 percent of global income by 2050, up from the current 30 percent.[28] According to McKinsey, consumption in emerging markets will total $30 trillion annually by 2025, a growth the firm describes as "the biggest growth opportunity in the history of capitalism."[29]

The logic of the Asian Century dictates that a large proportion of these new middle class consumers will be concentrated in the world's largest continent: 66 percent of the world's middle class will be in the Asia-Pacific region in 2030.[30] This will create a series of rapidly expanding new markets for companies from both developed and emerging economies. In effect, the sweatshop is rapidly becoming a gold mine, and the gold rush is already on. As the media love to report, Asian consumers are developing an apparently insatiable appetite for luxury Western goods. McKinsey estimates that China will account for a fifth of worldwide luxury purchases by the year 2015.[31]

Western companies are lining up to feed the dragon. Over the last few years, dozens of luxury goods manufacturers have seen their results inflated by demand from Asia, particularly China. The British fashion retailer Burberry posted a 21 percent sales boost for the last quarter of 2011, compared to the previous year, seeing earnings in Chinese outlets soar by 30 percent. In addition, sales of Johnnie Walker Scotch whiskey jumped 9 percent in China during the first half of 2011.[32] And Porsche enjoyed a staggering 500 percent upswing in sales in China for July 2011, compared to the previous year, despite a 4 percent drop worldwide during the same month.

Luxury cars are a surefire barometer of spending power. Tellingly, sales of luxury car brands are predicted to grow faster than the mainstream car market in China. Demand for luxury vehicles is predicted to grow cumulatively by a rate of 139 percent between 2010 and 2015.[33]

Clearly, rising disposable incomes across Asia and Latin America will present untold market opportunities for local and global players from both developed and emerging markets. Demand will explode for luxuries that many millions of Western consumers take for granted: vacations, cars, designer clothes, laptops, MP3 players, wines, and nights out in restaurants, bars, and nightclubs. The new middle classes will indulge the very human desire for a better quality of life.

However, it's important to recognize that we are not talking about a globally homogenous group of increasingly affluent workers with identical consumption patterns. Significant cultural differences and unique local preferences will drive demand for different products and services in each local market. As we shall see, it will be vital for companies—and their leaders—to understand these idiosyncrasies if they are to succeed under Globalization 2.0.

## Eating the West's Lunch

As noted, the emerging middle class will create significant opportunities for companies from both the developed West and the emerging East. But for Western corporations, there is a threat inherent in Globalization 2.0: the end of their market dominance.

Under Globalization 1.0, Western multinationals enjoyed decades of unchallenged control of their markets, allowing them to command premium prices and the pick of talent wherever they operated. But the game is changing. This dominance is being challenged at every turn. Some of the world's biggest brands are now being outperformed, locally and globally, by Asian challengers.

The cell phone market provides a textbook example. In the early 2000s, Nokia took a stranglehold on the global handset market. As mass cell phone ownership took off in the developed world, the Finnish manufacturer launched successive models that would become fondly remembered icons. The famous—some might say infuriating—"Nokia tune" was heard on streets and public transportation all over the globe.

In 2007, Nokia was the world's number one smartphone provider, with a global market share of almost 51 percent. By the second quarter of 2012, this share had shrunk to a once inconceivable 6.6 percent.[34]

Nokia has been beset by a competitive onslaught unimaginable before the advent of smartphones. Korean producer Samsung replaced Nokia as the world's largest handset manufacturer in the first quarter of 2012,[35] posting record quarterly profits—up 42 percent from the previous year on the back of smartphone sales—twelve months later. In 2011, Taiwan's HTC surpassed Nokia in terms of market capitalization.[36]

Even Apple cannot breathe easily. HTC handset sales now match those of iPhones in the Asia-Pacific region. Meanwhile, Huawei has grand plans to become the "Chinese Apple."[37] Ranked the world's fifth most innovative company,[38] Huawei has launched a smartphone for just $30 in the United States, where the iPhone 5 retails for up to $850 without a contract.[39] In this context, U.S. government accusations that China might use technology made by Huawei (and rival ZTE) for espionage purposes were met by accusations of protectionism, even by the American media.[40]

This competitive rebalancing is being replicated in market after market—home appliances, for example. China's Haier has replaced Whirlpool as the world's leader in global refrigerator sales.[41] The same development can be seen in home computing. In South Korea, local producers Samsung and LG now have a combined share of the PC market of more than 50 percent, squeezing out Western competitors such as Dell and HP.[42]

Even fast food is not immune. For every hamburger that McDonald's sells in the Philippines, local favorite Jollibee sells two. (We'll have more to say on Jollibee shortly.) This is an industry created and virtually monopolized for decades by some of America's most globally recognized brands: McDonald's, KFC, Burger King. Yet in Asia, local competitors are—in executive parlance, and forgive the pun—eating their lunch.

---

**CASE STUDY** ▪ Jollibee—Would You Like Pineapple with That?

The success of Jollibee in the Philippines illustrates yet another threat to the hegemony of Western corporations as a consequence of Globalization 2.0: so-called glocalization (or re-regionalization, as some prefer to call it).

As mentioned, the emerging middle class is not one uniform group. As we shall also see in Chapter 3, increasing affluence in countries across Asia will result in markets re-regionalizing. Unique, localized demand patterns will emerge in response to cultural norms, local preferences, and domestic fads. Local players will be better

*(continued)*

placed, geographically and culturally, to identify and exploit these opportunities. They will be more readily attuned to local market peculiarities. And being smaller and more agile than their centrally controlled, multinational competitors, they will be able to react more swiftly to them.

This is how Jollibee has managed to eat McDonald's lunch in the Filipino market. Just consider that for a moment. McDonald's versus Jollibee: Surely that's not even a fair fight. In the red-and-yellow corner is McDonald's, the world's largest food service organization: a chain of more than 33,000 restaurants, employing 1.7 million people and serving almost 68 million people daily across 119 countries (at the time of writing). To give a sense of the scale of McDonald's operations, it is the world's largest distributor of toys—a product it doesn't even sell.

In the other red-and-yellow corner (with a bit of white thrown in) is Jollibee. The Filipino contender has around 2,300 stores, the great majority in its domestic market.[43]

No contest, right? Wrong. Jollibee has captured more than 65 percent of the Filipino hamburger market, around twice that of McDonald's. *The Economist* called Jollibee's success "a huge embarrassment to McDonalds."[44]

Jollibee is a Filipino success story, with 16 percent revenue growth in 2010 and almost 18 percent in 2011.[45] Net profits for the second quarter of 2012 were up an impressive 33 percent from the previous year.[46] Capitalizing on the growing middle class in Asia, the company is expanding across the continent from its home base: More than 17 percent of its stores are in international markets, including twenty-six in the United States, at the time of writing.[47] And there are plans for more of the same: Jollibee aims to grow its proportion of overseas revenues from 20 percent in 2011 to 50 percent by 2014.[48]

So how has Jollibee floored the heavyweight? The answer is deceptively simple: with pineapples and rice.

The *New York Times* attributes Jollibee's achievement to "the fact that it respects local tastes."[49] In other words, the chain has exploited precisely the sort of localized opportunity that glocalization makes possible. Jollibee's success is the result of the company's making small but crucial tweaks to the tried-and-tested fast-food restaurant concept to suit local preferences.

Its restaurants, for example, offer an Amazing Aloha Burger. This is nothing more sophisticated than a hamburger with a slice of pineapple. The menu also offers a burger meal with rice, sauce, and vegetables instead of a bun and fries, plus a number of local dishes. These apparently minor adaptations to the conventional fast-food menu have achieved the unthinkable. By localizing the offer, David has out-competed Goliath. It has restricted McDonald's to just one-third of the Filipino market.

The company has taken a similarly localized approach to its marketing. Advertisements are in the local language, Tagalog, whereas McDonald's' are in English. And then there's the mascot. Move over, Ronald McDonald, and step forward, Jollibee: a giant, jolly-looking—you guessed it—bee, dressed in—you guessed it—red and yellow.

The company has clearly done its homework in designing the character. According to the organization's founders, Jollibee was designed to reflect the Filipino spirit.[50] A huge success locally, he is one of the most recognized characters in Filipino popular culture, with a far higher profile than Ronald McDonald. He even has his own children's TV show.

The smart niching strategy behind Jollibee's success—simple additions to a standardized offering—raises some fairly fundamental questions about the ability of a large and centralized multinational to respond when glocalization strikes.

The solution may seem obvious: Add pineapple to *your* burgers; offer a rice-and-burger dish; use your global scale to undercut the competition. But there's the rub: It is precisely McDonald's scale that counts against it when faced with the effects of glocalization. McDonald's is not only a corporate giant; it is also highly centralized. And its margins depend on the efficiencies that result from ruthless standardization. Under this structure, adding a component to one of your products is anything but a simple decision.

For a start, who makes the decision? Where in the structure does the authority lie? Is it the local general manager? The global head of product? Is the decision led by supply or marketing considerations? How will the pineapple be sourced? How long will it take to implement such a decision? Ultimately, how profitably can be it done?

This last question takes the decision to a strategic level. If the pineapple cannot be sourced profitably, should it be introduced as a loss leader to regain market share? How great a share can be recaptured—and at what cost? How vital is the Filipino hamburger market in the bigger strategic picture?

Suddenly, that humble slice of pineapple begins to look like a prickly thorn in McDonald's side. McDonald's has been, as the *New York Times* put it, "constrained by its obligation to remain faithful to its core products. Jollibee was flexible."[51] *The Economist* concurs: "McDonald's, perhaps hidebound by its global standards, never quite seems to get it right [in the Philippines]."[52]

Of course, this isn't to suggest that McDonald's is not capable of such decisions. The company does localize menus, offering a salmon burger in Norway, beer in

*(continued)*

France, and even temporary fasting menus to suit certain markets' religious festivals. In the movie *Pulp Fiction*, John Travolta waxes lyrical about the McDonald's menu in France as an example of what he calls the "little differences" between Europe and the United States. Yet for whatever reasons, the company has not seen fit or been able to challenge Jollibee's two-thirds share of the Filipino market. In the Philippines, for the time being at least, glocalization has slayed the giant.

In contrast, however, one of McDonald's biggest rivals has had quite some success at capitalizing on the glocalization effect. In China, KFC has not only added the local breakfast favorite congee to its menu,[53] but it has adapted the dish to meet a demand among China's growing middle class for a healthier diet, offering a lower-fat version. Other localized KFC menu options include a Beijing Chicken Roll (served with seafood sauce) and Sichuan-style Spicy Diced Chicken.[54]

An American chain adapting a Chinese dish to suit changing local tastes—this is glocalization in action. When entering the Chinese market, KFC sourced its leadership team predominantly from Taiwan, providing an "intuitive knowledge of the market context," in the words of one former vice president, Warren Liu.[55] In his book about what he calls the "improbable success" of KFC in China, Liu points out that "strategy is context-dependent; a strategy that works well in a stable and mature market economy would most likely not work well in China."[56]

The result: KFC has more than 2,000 stores in China and is the country's most popular breakfast destination.[57]

---

## Blink and You'll Miss It

Such are the opportunities and threats that glocalization will present. The Jollibee story holds a sobering lesson for Western corporations: *Blink and you'll miss it.*

Centralized control and standardized operations will not succeed in the new world. Globalization 2.0 demands the flexibility to identify, understand, and react with speed and agility to local market developments.

The inability to respond in this way contributed to Nokia's recent woes (described above). Around 2008, the company missed an opportunity to consolidate its position as the most trusted mobile phone brand in the burgeoning Indian market. A decision was made at Nokia headquarters in Finland not to provide a "dual-sim" device in India, where users frequently switch sim-cards to navigate the country's web of regional network providers.[58]

In contrast, companies sensitive to the quirks of local markets, and nimble enough to respond, will reap the rewards of glocalization, at times even pursuing openings outside their core offerings.

The Walt Disney Company did precisely that by identifying a growing demand for English education in China. Disney English was founded via a partnership with an established local education company, and its first center opened in Shanghai in 2008. At the time of writing, there are twenty-nine such centers around China.

And the laws of glocalization apply equally to the virtual marketplace. Tianji, which is China's answer to LinkedIn, is glocalization in microcosm. The success of the country's largest professional social network is the result of adapting the model to local customs (see the section *Virtual Glocalization*).

### Virtual Glocalization

"The Internet is different in China."[59] The words of Tianji founder Derek Ling hint at the local knowledge behind the social network service dominating the Chinese market.

Understanding the cultural norms that govern business networking in China is what has enabled Tianji to flourish. In April 2012, while the service was hitting 10 million members and growing by 500,000 new users per month,[60] Western rival LinkedIn had chalked up only 2 million users in the world's most populous country.[61]

According to the Chinese-born, American-educated Ling, LinkedIn's search-based model does not sit easily with Chinese businesspeople, who insist on personal interaction before doing business.[62] As a result, the loose connections forged on LinkedIn fail to drive commercial relationships in China.[63]

Tianji provides platforms for members to get to know each other through groups, forums, and online and offline events.[64] "When you create

*(continued)*

an environment where people can interact and get to know each other, the business part takes care of itself," Ling says. "[Chinese] people are good at leveraging their relationships once they feel comfortable."[65]

The network was established in 2005 and bought just two years later by the French company Viadeo, the world's second largest professional social network provider behind LinkedIn. Acquiring a product developed specifically for the Chinese market reflects what Viadeo calls its "multi-local" approach to global expansion.[66] Crucially, Viadeo stayed true to its glocalization strategy when taking over Tianji, retaining Ling to lead an operation that is based, run, and staffed 100 percent locally.

*Tianji* means "worldly connection" in Mandarin. But the network's connection to local values is the secret of its success.

# IMPLICATIONS OF GLOBALIZATION 2.0

We have already encountered some the consequences of Globalization 2.0 for Western companies: intensifying competition, dwindling global influence, the challenges of glocalization, and increasing exclusion from economic and commercial alliances. Now let us look in more detail at the implications of the new global environment for multinational organizations and the demands that these implications will place upon their leaders.

## A New Balance

International corporations have long been advised to "think global, act local." This maxim has never been more apt. But Globalization 2.0 has nudged the strategic dial, subtly but perceptibly, toward the local end of the scale. Global companies need to think and act more locally than ever before.

One size no longer fits all. As we've seen, centralized decision making risks being too slow to allow organizations to spot and exploit local opportunities. More than ever, businesses will need to develop global and locally adapted strategies *in parallel*.

Local strategies should be developed at local levels, with regional operations drawing on corporate resources to enable cheap and effective execution. The view from local markets will be essential to strategic decision making, prompting the need for greater cross-country and cross-functional collaboration. Teams will need to become more diverse as organizations seek a broader range of perspectives.

Organizations will also need to create processes to strengthen their contextual awareness. They will need to develop a finely tuned sensitivity to the complex web of unique influences shaping each local market. These influences consist of the availability of resources and skills and the impact of cultural norms, behaviors, and preferences. They also include both the official and sometimes less official rules and regulations governing different localities.

## Strategic Focus

Globalization 2.0 will place exceptional cognitive and strategic demands on the leaders of organizations. The new globalization means a more complex, varied, and unpredictable business environment, characterized by a myriad of localized opportunities and threats. It will also create a greatly expanded ecosystem of internal and external stakeholders to manage across multiple territories and cultures. This is unchartered territory for many organizational leaders, and it will raise the intellectual challenge for business leaders to new heights.

The new world will also require a renewed focus on strategy. Conventional wisdom dictates that for leaders, strategy isn't the hard part—execution is. But the shift in economic power, the expansion of the middle class, and the demands of glocalization may require new strategies and new operating models.

Companies will need to develop local sensitivity and enable higher agility, without losing the ability to take advantage of global scale. Getting strategy right will become exponentially more difficult in the world of Globalization 2.0.

# THE DEMANDS OF GLOBALIZATION 2.0

Organizations and their leaders are grappling with unprecedented complexity in the macro-business environment brought about by Globalization 2.0. Here is a summary of the key challenges businesses are facing and the demands these challenges will place on leaders.

1.  *Contextual awareness and conceptual thinking.* More agile structures will be necessary to enable localized strategic decision making in order to take advantage of glocalization. Strategies, business models, and operating models will need to be adapted to the demands of different markets. Leaders will require highly developed contextual awareness and conceptual thinking to identify and implement the right structures for their organizations.

2.  *Cross-collaboration.* Deeper and more frequent collaboration will be required between functions and across regions and countries to fine-tune businesses' local radars. And not only internal collaboration. Glocalization will demand more collaboration with external partners in order to enter local markets. For leaders, this means being able to manage effectively across multiple functions, regions, countries, nationalities, cultures, and markets.

3.  *Diversity.* Stronger contextual awareness, improved local sensitivity, and greater cross-country collaboration will necessitate more diverse teams. And they must be diverse in all senses of the word: nationality, ethnicity, culture, age, gender, function, career background, etc. Intercultural sensitivity and adaptability will be essential attributes in leaders.

4.  *Loyalty.* The global war for talent will be transformed by Globalization 2.0. Loyalty will be at a premium. Talented employees and future leaders will be able to take their pick from among employers the world over, as competitors spring up throughout the emerging regions to challenge established Western corporations. Only the most compelling and inspiring leaders will be able to attract, retain, and engage the best people in a talent market devoid of loyalty.

# 2 Less Is More: The Environmental Crisis

*"You cannot have well humans on a sick planet."*
—**Thomas Berry,** cultural historian

## AT A GLANCE ■ ENVIRONMENTAL CRISIS

### Five Essential Points

1. *Climate change is real and almost irreversible.* Global warming as a result of economic activity has caused extreme weather events around the world, leading to death, displacement, and considerable economic damage. The earth's temperature is approaching catastrophic levels.

2. *Critical resources are being depleted.* Peak oil supply from conventional sources was reached in 2006. Yet global energy consumption is rising, as millions of consumers worldwide join the ranks of the middle class. Water shortages are becoming increasingly drastic. Rare earth minerals—essential to modern technology—are becoming scarcer, more expensive, and more difficult to reach.

3. *The implications are potentially catastrophic.* This creates a recipe for, at best, drastically reduced margins for organizations, and, at worst, deep global recession, famine, and widespread social turmoil.

4. *Carbon footprint moves from corporate social responsibility to the bottom line.* Carbon reduction will become essential to market competitiveness. Organizations

will need to embed environmental awareness into their processes and decision making in order to create a culture and operations that minimize environmental impact.

5. *Transformational thinking and operations will be necessary.* Leaders will need to think transformationally to achieve this, communicate a clear rationale for such radical change, and ensure that they execute the vision. New kinds of collaboration, including joint ventures with competitors, will be required to find the innovative solutions needed.

### Five Questions Business Leaders Should Ask

1. To what extent are environmental issues recognized within my organization?

2. How will margins be impacted by the rising costs of fossil fuels and rare minerals?

3. How much further do we need to go to embed an environmentally friendly culture and create sustainable operations?

4. What contingency plans do we have in place for business disruption caused by environmental disasters?

5. Where can we seek collaborations to help find solutions to such intractable issues?

---

"The door is closing .... If we don't change direction now on how we use energy ... the door will be closed forever."

This drastic warning on the future of the environment was not the partisan rhetoric of an environmental activist organization or renewable energy lobby group. These are the considered words of the chief economist of the International Energy Agency (IEA), Fatih Birol.[1]

According to the IEA, new power stations that burn fossil fuels are being built around the world at an alarming rate. At this rate, the global warming effect will be beyond 2°C (3.6°F) by the year 2017.[2] Two degrees Celsius is thought by scientists to be the "safety limit" for avoiding truly catastrophic climate change. The goal is to prevent average global temperatures from rising more than 2°C.

This stark conclusion comes from the IEA's annual *World Energy Outlook,* widely recognized as the authoritative source of global energy projections and analysis. According to the 2011 edition, climate change is on the very verge of becoming irreversible. The last hope of containing it is about to be lost forever.[3]

## THE MEGATREND: ENVIRONMENTAL CRISIS

It is difficult to discuss the environment without occasionally lapsing into hyperbole and resorting to apocalyptic scenarios. The environmental crisis is perhaps the most profound of the megatrends we shall examine. It calls into question the very fundamentals on which economic prosperity and development are based. And at its heart are grave implications for global society and prosperity, and therefore for businesses and their leaders.

Yet surprisingly, the issue is rarely considered in the context of business leadership, perhaps because the implications for organizations are simply too mind boggling—and the human implications too frightening. Beyond ticking off the boxes for CSR (corporate social responsibility) efforts and paying to offset carbon emissions, companies tend to put the environment in the "too-difficult-to-deal-with" category.

But the ostrich approach will not be an option for much longer. The environmental crisis facing the earth comprises a complex web of factors. We will look at two of these in detail in this chapter: the changing climate due to global warming, and a growing scarcity of natural resources (principally oil, water, and rare earth minerals). As we shall see, these developments are closely and dynamically interrelated. But first, let us examine each of them on their own terms.

### An Incontestable Truth

Before looking in detail at the environmental crisis megatrend, let us put to rest the debate on whether or not climate change is actually happening. For the purposes of this book, we will assume that human-caused climate change is real. Like globalization, it is a given.

*(continued)*

That the planet is getting warmer is undisputed. Studies from highly credible, independent, nonpolitical, and—in many cases—nonenvironmental organizations provide mounting evidence that the climate is changing.[4] Few, if any, serious independent scientists or academics challenge this.

However, a small but influential minority of dissenting voices (especially in the United States) continues to refute the conventional wisdom that climate change is the result of human activity, as opposed to natural variations in weather patterns. It is widely accepted that these voices count among them very few credible scientists or climatologists. Rather, they are for the most part conservative lobbyists and political campaigners.[5]

Here is the fact of matter: The average temperature of the earth's surface has risen by approximately 0.8°C (1.4°F) over the past 100 years. And here's the really scary part: *Around three-quarters of this increase has occurred during the past thirty years.*[6]

The Intergovernmental Panel on Climate Change (IPCC), which shared the Nobel Peace Prize in 2007, concluded six years previously that "most of the observed warming over the last 50 years is likely to have been due to the increase in greenhouse gas concentrations." The Panel was founded by the World Meteorological Organization and the United Nations (UN) Environmental Programme with the specific duty to monitor global warming. The IPCC was in no doubt about the source of the greenhouse gas concentrations: "Human activities ... are modifying the concentration of atmospheric constituents."[7]

In 2007, the Panel declared it "90 percent likely" that climate change is human-made,[8] pointing out that the energy supply—by definition, a human-made source—puts the greatest proportion of carbon into the atmosphere.[9]

More recently, a joint study by the U.S. National Oceanic and Atmospheric Administration (NOAA) and the Met Office (the UK's national weather service) actually managed to attribute individual weather incidents to human-made climate change.[10] And in 2013, a report from the U.S. National Climate Assessment and Development Advisory Committee stated plainly that "human-induced climate change" is resulting in a litany of climactic events: hotter weather, rising sea levels and temperatures, increasingly frequent and intense winter storms, as well as reductions in snow cover, glaciers, permafrost, and sea ice.[11]

## Slow Cooking

In the summer of 2012, the United States experienced what many media commentators dubbed a second Dust Bowl. According to official figures, almost two-thirds of the mainland United States—an area engulfing *eight entire states*[12]—were under drought conditions. Almost a quarter suffered extreme drought.[13]

Temperatures actually topped records set during the Dust Bowl era of the 1930s. July 2012 was the hottest month on record in the United States, registering average temperatures 0.2°C (0.36°F) higher than those reached at the height of the Dust Bowl in July 1936.[14] In fact, 2012 proved to be the hottest year in U.S. history.[15]

Of course, a single extreme weather event does not necessarily indicate a changing climate. But in the United States alone, there were an unprecedented twelve weather disasters in 2011 that cost more than $1 billion each. What's more, the previous high of nine such incidents in a year had been set as recently as 2008.[16]

In addition, the last ten years has witnessed a disturbingly high incidence of such weather extremes across the globe. In 2003, for example, a prolonged heat wave caused 70,000 deaths across Europe. Hurricane Katrina devastated New Orleans two years later. The year 2007 was marked by unprecedented wildfires in Greece. And in 2009, drought and record temperatures caused bushfires that killed more than 100 people in Australia.

The following year, Russia's worst heat wave on record caused wildfires that choked Moscow and burned dangerously close to a number of nuclear installations. Also during 2010, flooding in Pakistan claimed more than 1,000 lives and displaced millions of people. Flash floods in China had similarly disastrous consequences. Germany, Poland, and the Czech Republic also suffered serious flooding.[17]

In the UK, 2012 was, in the words of the *Sunday Times* newspaper, "the year the weather went crazy" with an unprecedented "juxtaposition of extremes." There was near-record heat and cold *and* rainfall, while the second wettest year on record followed drought conditions. The Met Office warned of more extremes to come.[18]

In autumn of the same year, the largest Atlantic storm on record rampaged across large parts of the United States. Hurricane Sandy caused an estimated $50 billion in damage, making it the second most costly hurricane in U.S. history.[19] Then in 2013, as bushfires again raged in Australia, Sydney suffered its hottest day ever: Temperatures touched a frightening 45.8°C (114.4°F).[20]

Scientists are now beginning to prove that there is a link between such extreme weather occurrences and human-made climate change. A study published in *Science* in 2012 suggested that global warming is dramatically accelerating the cycle of evaporation and rainfall over the oceans, causing drought in some areas and flooding in others.[21]

About the same time, the study by NOAA and the Met Office (mentioned above) claimed that certain notable weather events had almost certainly been caused by human activity (see the section *An Incontestable Truth*). The organizations studied the UK's warmest November since records began being kept around 150 years ago, concluding that this was at least sixty times more likely to have been human-made than the result of natural weather patterns. Similarly, they found that the heat wave that decimated crops in Texas in summer 2010 was around twenty times more likely to have been caused by human-made climate change.[22]

The fact is that we have been slowly heating the planet since fossil fuels first stoked the Industrial Revolution in the mid-1700s. Since that time, technological progress has enabled us to innovate and manufacture a dazzling array of products, heat hundreds of millions of homes and workplaces, and travel farther, more easily, and more cheaply by an expanding range of choices. This, of course, has all meant burning ever greater amounts of fossil fuels, pushing more greenhouse gases into the atmosphere.

Over the last 200 years, the developed world has consumed more energy per capita than throughout the rest of recorded history.[23] Global carbon emissions from fossil fuels increased more than sixteen-fold between 1900 and 2008, and by around 150 percent between 1990 and 2008 alone.[24] This has led to a 0.8°C (1.4°F) rise in the temperature of the earth's surface over the last century. And the UN predicts that current emission levels will likely generate a *further* 2.5°C to 5°C (4.5°F to 9°F) of warming, taking global warming far beyond the accepted 2°C safety limit.[25]

The World Bank makes the same prediction. A comprehensive study it commissioned in November 2012 from the Potsdam Institute for Climate Impact Research concluded that the planet could warm by 4°C (7.2°F) by the year 2100, even if nations fulfill international agreements on carbon reduction. This would result in more extreme heat waves, a reduction in global food supplies, the loss of ecosystems, reduced biodiversity, and devastating rises in sea levels.[26]

Yet even maintaining current emission levels will prove a massive challenge, let alone reducing them in accordance with international treaties. As noted, the greatest source of greenhouse gases today—responsible for just over a quarter of the current output of carbon—is the energy supply.[27] And as we shall see, industrialization in the emerging world is set to turbo-boost global demand for energy. Left unchecked, rising energy consumption will push carbon dioxide emissions up by 1.6 percent annually through 2030 (carbon dioxide being a key greenhouse gas linked to global warming).[28]

Even without the effect of growing industrialization, greenhouse gas emissions are already rising at unprecedented rates. In 2012, the Global Carbon Project (GCP) recorded a record high of 39.2 billion tons (35.6 billion tonnes) of carbon dioxide emissions worldwide. In an echo of the IEA's dire warning the previous year, the GCP signaled that the likelihood of restricting warming to 2°C was diminishing. Achieving this would mean "relying on technologies that are yet to be developed," according to one of the study's authors.[29] In the face of such evidence, some leading scientists are beginning to predict the direst consequences for humanity.[30]

## The Oil Paradox

American golfers lose an estimated 300 million balls a year.[31] Almost every one of those balls contains polybutadiene, a petrochemical synthetic rubber.[32] That's 300 million of just one oil-dependent product, in one year, in one country. Now extrapolate from that to annual global golf ball production. Now go further, to the 90 percent of worldwide industrial output that necessitates the use of oil.[33]

It is impossible to overstate the dependence of human economic activity on oil. Oil fuels production, transportation, and travel. It heats homes and workplaces. It is the basic ingredient in plastic, itself the base material for millions of products. And it is running out.

According to the IEA, peak oil—the point at which the rate of global conventional oil production begins to fall—was reached in 2006.[34] If this is true,[35] then the amount of conventional crude oil being extracted from the ground each year is already dwindling.

The consequences of peak oil defy underestimation. On the wholly unrealistic assumption that global consumption levels remain static, existing conventional reserves would last less than forty years.[36] In 2010, a leaked report from the Department of Future Analysis of the German Army's Transformation Center—an organization with no ax to grind in the climate change debate—predicted a catastrophic global economic meltdown as a result of peak oil.[37] (See the section *Pain Reaction.*)

Frightening stuff. Yet peak oil is only half the problem. The world may have reached its oil *supply* zenith, but it is very far from its *demand* peak. The IEA forecasts that global energy consumption will increase by 36 percent between 2008 and 2035.[38]

In a cruel global paradox, peak oil has been reached just as Globalization 2.0 is taking off in the East (see Chapter 1). Economic acceleration across an enormous part of the world is creating an ever greater thirst for oil. The emerging markets are craving more and more of the lifeblood of industrial production, at the very point at which it is beginning to diminish.

Several billion people across Asia, Latin America, and Africa are enjoying burgeoning wealth and demanding a multitude of products in huge quantities, which require oil for production and transportation. As a result, energy demand among non-OECD countries will account for almost two-thirds of the world's total by 2030, compared to just under half in 1990.[39]

## An Unconventional Problem

Dwindling supplies of conventional crude oil have turned the world's attention to alternative supplies.[40] Unconventional oil is that which is extracted by means other than well drilling. The two most common sources of unconventional oil are oil sands, which contain a mix of bitumen, water, and clay, and oil shale, which is sedimentary rock containing kerogen, a material that yields oil when heated.

These sources are not without their problems. First, unconventional oil production is far less efficient and far more costly than conventional oil production, as the methods used do not produce oil that is ready to refine. Substances like bitumen and kerogen require intensive processing before they can be refined into petroleum. This uses around 30 percent of the amount of energy eventually produced.[41]

The additional cost places a question mark over the economic viability of these sources, at least for the time being. Unconventionally sourced oil requires elevated crude prices for a sustained period in order to be commercially viable. Of course, the specter of peak oil may mean that this is a realistic prospect in the longer term.

A second problem with unconventional sources, somewhat ironically, is that the process of extracting these oils devours large amounts of conventional fuel, as it requires intense heat. Kerogen, for example, must be heated to 500°C (932°F).[42]

Finally, there is the environmental impact of unconventional oil extraction techniques. The clue is in the names: Steam injection and steam gravity–assisted drainage are two such methods. These use enormous quantities of water, thus depleting available sources of safe drinking water because once used, the water becomes highly poisonous. In Alberta, in Canada—the only country where oil sands are commercially exploited[43]—the water used in oil sand production comes primarily from the Athabasca River. Wastewater and other pollutants from the oil sands seep into the groundwater.

Also, the processes involve burning conventional fossil fuels—for example, the heating process for kerogen uses natural gas. As a result, greenhouse gas emissions resulting from oil sand extraction in Alberta are three times higher than for conventional oil. More air pollution is produced in Alberta than anywhere else in Canada.[44]

Yet even if these challenges can be efficiently resolved, unconventional energy sources are unlikely to be a panacea for the increasing scarcity of fossil fuels. They will only delay the decline in supply, and not necessarily for very long. In America, oil production from shale fracking (hydraulic fracturing) is expected to peak as soon as 2020.[45]

## A Drop to Drink

Our vision of life after oil, though bleak, is still only imagined. But we are all too familiar with the tragic human impact of life without water.

The United Nations International Children's Emergency Fund (UNICEF) and the World Health Organization (WHO) estimate that 11 percent of the world's population—around 783 million people—had no access to safe drinking water as recently as 2012.[46] According to the UN, in 2006, a disturbing one-fifth of the global population was facing an extreme water shortage.[47] Staggeringly, this is forecast to grow to two-thirds by 2025, based on present consumption patterns.[48]

And as with oil, water scarcity is being exacerbated by exploding demand. Population growth will fuel a 300 percent increase in worldwide drinking water consumption between now and 2030.[49]

## A Rare Monopoly

"Rare earth element" is, in one sense at least, a contradiction in terms. Rare earth elements occur abundantly in the earth's crust, roughly on a par with more commonly known resources such as copper, nickel, and zinc. But while they are abundant in quantity, rare earths are scarce in terms of economically viable deposits. Only 138,000 tons (125,000 tonnes) of an estimated global stock of 125 million tons (114 million tonnes)—little more than a tenth of 1 percent—are mined each year.[50]

And they are rarer still in terms of geographic distribution. Active mines are found in very few parts of the world. In effect, they are found in only one part of the world. China currently produces some 90 percent of global output.[51] As Deng Xiaoping once said, "The Middle East has its oil. China has its rare earths."[52]

As with oil, the developed world is completely dependent on rare earth minerals. They are a vital component in hundreds of everyday products, from cars to computers and cell phones. They also have highly technical applications in numerous fields that are essential to modern life, such as aerospace, medicine, and nuclear energy (see the section *All Too Common*). Reuters warned in 2009 that worldwide demand for rare earths would exceed supply by some 44,000 tons (40,000 tonnes) annually within just a few years.[53]

Soaring demand for a commodity of which nine-tenths comes from one source: by the laws of supply and demand, this can mean only runaway price inflation. Chinese export prices of two rare earths—neodymium and dysprosium, used to make magnets—rocketed by close to 6000 percent in just six years between 2005 and 2011. The price of neodymium increased tenfold in the eighteen months to the end of 2011, while the price of dysprosium increased fifteen-fold during this time.[54]

### All Too Common

Most of us would probably struggle to name a single rare earth element.[55] Names like ytterbium and praseodymium hardly trip off the tongue or crop up in conversation over a beer. Yet we use rare earths every day. Though we may not realize it, as consumers we are addicted to rare earths. We quite simply could not live our modern lives without them.

Rare earth elements are found in baseball bats, bicycles, light bulbs, LED screens, TV tubes, cell phones, cars, camera and telescope lenses, colored glass, ceramics, magnets, cigarette lighters, microphones, loudspeakers, headphones, computer hard disks, and fluorescent lighting. They are present in an equally bewildering array of specialized and technical equipment, including aerospace components, carbon-arc lighting (used in film production), lasers, nuclear reactors, marine propulsion systems, fiber-optic cables, high-temperature superconductors, wind-turbine generators, and stress gauges. They also have a wide range of medical applications, for example, in medicines, MRI imaging, X-ray systems, and even the treatment of cancer.

*(continued)*

They crop up in curious places, such as inside handguns. The 330 million-plus people living in the Eurozone carry an appropriately named rare earth around with them every day in their wallets and purses: Europium is contained in the anti-counterfeiting phosphors on Euro notes.

And somewhat ironically in the context of this chapter, rare earth metals are at the heart of the car industry's efforts to minimize environmental impacts. They are found in catalytic converters and are central to efforts to maximize fuel mileage.[56] They also feature prominently in hybrid cars. In the Toyota Prius, for example, rare earths can be found in the battery, electric engine and generator, catalytic converter, twenty-five electric motors throughout the vehicle, glass and mirrors, LCD screen, and additives to the diesel fuel the car runs on.[57]

## Surface Tensions

Growing shortages of the essential resources found on and beneath the earth's surface threaten to generate massive international tensions and even potential conflicts—a concern signaled by the UN in its above-mentioned report on water scarcity.

And the imbalance in the supply of these dwindling resources will in all probability intensify this risk. Developing countries possess approximately 85 percent of oil and 93 percent of natural gas reserves.[58] And post–peak oil, remaining crude reserves will eventually lie almost entirely in the Middle East.[59]

The shift in global power relationships that these scenarios imply has focused the attention of economists and military strategists alike. In his book *The Hydrogen Economy,* economist and political adviser Jeremy Rifkin warned that it could threaten the economic and political stability of every nation on the planet. The German military report on peak oil discussed earlier analyzes these risks in alarming detail.[60] (See the section *Pain Reaction.*)

As for the present, China's domination of the rare earth supply is already causing international disputes. China has at times closed mines, capped production, restricted exports (cutting quotas by 40 percent in 2010 alone[61]), and halted shipments to Japan, Europe, and the United States, citing declining stocks and environmental concerns. The World Trade Organization has gone as far as to declare some of these policies illegal, a ruling that China rejects.[62]

And to heighten the potential for geopolitical tensions still further, certain governments and global financiers stand accused of "land grabbing." In the wake of the financial crisis, the activist group GRAIN alleged that cash-rich governments from the Middle East and Asia, along with global financial institutions, were obtaining agricultural land in poorer, resource-rich nations.[63] A subsequent report by the World Bank detailed similar developments.[64] To stabilize their own food security, certain nations were attempting to buy farmland and water sources in other countries—in effect, outsourcing their food production. For banks, hedge funds, and pension companies, the goal was simply to maximize returns from a relatively safe investment haven amid the turbulence caused by the credit crisis.

### Pain Reaction

Famine, national bankruptcies, the collapse of the entire capitalist system, and unending security implications: Such dystopian visions are not what we might expect from the sober analysis of military strategists. But these are just some of the more eye-popping consequences of peak oil spelled out by the German Federal Defense Force Transformation Center in 2010.[65] It envisions a terrifying, long-term chain reaction, *if no viable alternative is found to the oil that lubricates the world's economic and social systems:*

- Increasing oil prices reduce consumption and economic output, causing widespread recession. Rising transportation costs inflate the prices of *all* goods and services, depressing global trade and severely reducing the capacity to travel, intensifying the economic downturn. Unemployment soars in all developed societies.

- The production and distribution of food becomes problematic. With government budgets under severe pressure, spending on securing food supplies competes with investment in conventional oil substitutes. Famines strike as some countries are no longer able to afford essential food products.

*(continued)*

- With no end to global economic contraction in sight, commercial investment dries up in the absence of any likely profit. Banks are left with no commercial basis on which to trade. Financial markets, stock exchanges, and the entire banking system—"the backbone of the global economy"—all implode.

- Confidence evaporates in the value-preserving function of money, resulting in the collapse of value chains, hyperinflation, and black markets. Localized barter economies spring up.

- National revenues disappear. Infrastructures crumble as the resources to maintain them no longer exist.

- Political instability and extremism flourish as a result of a crisis of confidence in national institutions and their ability to solve problems.

The study warns that this "highly unstable" state of affairs, accompanied by "intensified competition for dwindling and unevenly distributed resources," will complicate and heighten the prospect of civil and international conflict. Policy clashes will erupt between warring oil importers, between exporters jockeying for position, or between buying and selling nations. Civil strife will also become common.

Beyond these, the report effectively admits, the consequences of peak oil are anybody's guess. As the authors put it, "All other security consequences would be imaginable."

## A Vicious Spiral

Each of the trends outlined above—climate change, extreme weather, and shortages of oil, water, and rare earths—are deeply worrisome in their own right. But of course, they do not operate in isolation. They are closely interlinked, each feeding and intensifying the others to exacerbate and accelerate the environmental crisis. And each is being inflated by a growing world population and increasing wealth and consumption in emerging markets.

Global demand for food, water, energy, and production will continue to climb. Growing demand for food will require increased agricultural production, which will use more water and result in greater deforestation—another major contributor to greenhouse gas emissions. And deforestation also presents its own threats. Climate experts believe that deforestation in the Amazon could alter the pattern of the so-called trade winds that influence the flow of the Gulf Stream. This may result in even greater weather extremes, plunging Europe into harsher winters while Brazil would suffer from drought.[66]

Increasingly affluent consumers will drive more manufacturing, which will require more energy and heighten the need to burn fossil fuels and use oil and rare earth metals. This will pour more greenhouse gases into the atmosphere, further heating the planet's surface, intensifying droughts and floods, destroying crops, and threatening factories and power stations, including nuclear facilities.

Spiraling production and consumption will also generate mountains of additional waste. This will need to be disposed of in ways that inevitably pollute the land, waters, and air. Air pollution levels in China, for example, are more than five times higher than WHO guidelines. In 2007, at the Chinese government's request, the World Bank estimated the total cost of air and water pollution to China's economy at some 5.8 percent of GDP.[67]

The resulting warming effect also threatens to melt polar ice. Thawing has already pushed sea levels up almost 8 inches (20 centimeters) since 1880. An increase of 20 inches (50 centimeters) could displace the 10 percent of the world's population that lives on low-lying coastal land.

Ice cover in the Arctic Ocean's fabled Northwest Passage has been shrinking for many years, making the strait increasingly passable and leading to international tensions. In 2010, Arctic sea ice reached the lowest level ever recorded for June.[68] The Canadian military has "renamed" the strait "Canadian internal waters," making clear the government's proprietary claim over this strategically and commercially important crossing between the Atlantic and Pacific Oceans. This has put Canada at odds with most other nations, which consider the Passage to be international waters.[69]

Climate change is having a similar effect on the Northeast Passage above Russia. In August 2013, a cargo vessel set sail from China for Holland, taking advantage of disappearing ice to attempt China's first commercial crossing of the channel. The company responsible claims the route could cut shipping times between China and Europe by up to fifteen days.[70]

Yet the consequences of the polar ice melting go far beyond political disputes and even catastrophic sea levels. Melting ice also threatens to wreak yet more havoc on global weather systems, as well as making a huge contribution to the greenhouse effect. It would change ocean temperatures, further skewing the evaporation cycle. It would release large deposits of carbon dioxide and methane trapped in the permafrost, a development that could wipe out the commercial benefits of more accessible shipping lanes. A study published in *Nature* magazine in July 2013 and reported on by *The Guardian* warned that methane release from thawing Arctic ice would result in greater climate change, with an estimated cost to the world's economy of some $60 trillion.[71]

## IMPLICATIONS OF THE ENVIRONMENTAL CRISIS

The consequences of the environmental crisis are almost unfathomable in their scale, gravity, and complexity. But business leaders must fathom them. In time, consumers will demand that the crisis be dealt with. The markets will demand it, governments will demand it, and the logistical implications of climate change will necessitate it.

### A Clean Slate

Ultimately, companies need to make a significant change in their integrity where the environment is concerned. How one deals with the carbon footprint will no longer be merely a CSR matter. Rather, it will determine a business's competitiveness and therefore its bottom-line performance. The imperative will be to genuinely slash carbon usage, rather than simply pay for planting trees to offset emissions. Businesses will need to adopt radically different ways of working in order to minimize their environmental impact, and they will have to seek new, sustainable technologies to replace the fossil-based sources that currently fuel their operations.

There are signs that this may be starting to happen. According to KPMG, two-thirds of large corporations were publishing dedicated sustainability reports by 2011, with a further 12 percent planning to do so within two years.[72] In 2009, Dow Jones launched the Sustainability Indexes, which analyze stock performance of the world's largest corporations through an environmental, social, and economic lens.

More significantly, the global market for so-called clean energy is booming. Global sales of biofuels, solar energy, wind power, and photovoltaic (PV) electricity generated from solar radiation grew by almost a third in 2011, totalling $246 billion compared to $188 billion the year before.[73] Interestingly, China, despite its voracious appetite for fossil fuels, became the world's biggest investor in renewable energy in 2011, according to a joint study by the UN and the Frankfurt School of Finance.[74]

In addition, organizations as large and diverse as Ford and the Chinese government are experimenting with green design and manufacturing approaches such as "cradle to cradle," which goes beyond recycling, aiming to eliminate waste altogether and ensure that products have a regenerative effect on the environment. (See the case study *From Recycling to Regeneration.*)

---

**CASE STUDY** ■ From Recycling to Regeneration

*"Growth is good. The question is, what are you growing ... poverty or prosperity?"*[75]
—**William McDonough,** co-founder of the Cradle to Cradle Products Innovation Institute

A Ford executive once described the company's aging River Rouge factory complex in Michigan as "what the twenty-first century is no longer willing to accept."[76] Once America's largest industrial site, much of the facility was obsolete and contaminated with carcinogenic toxins by the 1980s.[77]

That was then. Since being overhauled in the late 1990s, the 600-acre center is very much of its time, and the *Architectural Record* called it "a 21st-century model of manufacturing." It features a 10-acre "living roof" made from sedum, which retains

*(continued)*

and cleans rainwater and moderates the internal temperature of the building. The result is 7 percent lower energy costs and 40 percent better air quality.[78] The roof forms part of an $18 million rainwater treatment system, which cleans some 20 billion gallons (75 billion liters) of rainwater each year. This overcomes the need for mechanical treatment facilities, saving Ford $50 million annually.

The River Rouge complex is an example of an emerging approach to design and production, one of several that go further than merely minimizing environmental impact. Cradle to Cradle (C2C) is a sustainable design methodology that aims to create things that not only avoid environmental damage altogether but actually give back to the earth by having a regenerative effect.

C2C is a rigorous set of design principles by which production is reformulated to emulate biological processes. All materials used must decompose in the local natural environment, providing nutrition to the soil, or else must have a neutral impact on the environment and be reusable with no loss of quality or integrity.

The concept is the brainchild of German scientist Michael Braungart and American architect William McDonough. Via the Cradle to Cradle Products Innovation Institute they founded, C2C is now a formal certification program. The Institute claims to have certified around 400 products, eliminating more than 14.3 million tons (13 million tonnes) of carbon emissions and 1 million pounds (450,000 kilograms) of toxic waste.

Following the successful regeneration of the River Rouge complex, Ford also embraced C2C in its car product designs. In its centennial year (2003), the automotive giant unveiled its Model U concept car. The Model U is run by a hydrogen-powered internal combustion engine with hybrid electric transmission. Soy-based materials are used to fill the seats and in the construction of the tailgate. The car could be described as Cradle to Cradle in terms of utility as well as production. Highly adaptable, it can transform from SUV to pickup, evolving with the owner's changing lifestyle and thereby reducing the need to regularly buy a new car.

As a design philosophy, C2C can be applied to almost anything: products, buildings, even whole communities. Swiss company Rohner Textil, for example, has developed a range of fabrics using a substitute for cotton that is made from natural fibers, eliminates the need for pesticides, and drastically cuts water usage. The manufacturing process uses no toxins, and the material biodegrades 100 percent in soil.

Educational institutes have also been designed according to C2C principles—including the Lyle Center for Regenerative Studies in California and the Netherlands Institute of Ecology—as have several homes and communal buildings in Holland. The Chinese government has shown keen interest in C2C, though an attempt to build an entire sustainable village in Huangbaiyu (in collaboration with McDonough) did not succeed.[79]

Of course, 400 certified products do not equate to an environmental revolution in design, manufacturing, and construction methods. But while C2C is just one of many approaches to reducing environmental damage, it is potentially a great leap forward in the search for clean technology. Theoretically at least, it holds the power not just to reduce but to reverse the impact of human activity on the planet.

---

## Moral Dry Ground?

Clean technologies will present new opportunities for organizations to operate more sustainably. But ultimately, businesses will be driven by one of two clear motives: inherent eco-ethics or the laws of market economics.

Some businesses are undoubtedly driven by the desire to operate as sustainably as possible, minimize ecological impacts, and safeguard the future of the planet. Eco-ethics are the founding norms of these companies. To them, environmental protection is a guiding principle, not a CSR exercise or market response. Green is in their DNA. As we've seen, some organizations design products and operations to actually regenerate the local environment (see the case study *From Recycling to Regeneration*). Others are set up as low-profit organizations, putting social good—not only in the environmental sphere—above maximizing profits. Several states in the United States have passed laws to make the low-profit "L3C" (low-profit limited liability company) a legal form of business entity.

But it would be naive to expect every company to be motivated by inherent eco-ethics—tantamount to asking them to forsake the rules of capitalism. And to neglect these rules would be to commit organizational suicide.

There are basically two arguments for organizations to become more ecologically aware. One is the moral standpoint: If they do not adapt, then, as we have seen, living conditions for future generations will be catastrophic. This is sufficient justification for eco-ethical organizations, and in many cases it is the reason why they exist.

The second argument is the logic of capitalism, which puts price competition and financial performance above all else. The moral case alone is not sufficient for most businesses. Until society accepts a different kind of market economics, where the profit motive is no longer all-consuming, the market will determine the need for sustainable operations for most companies.

As human beings, we crave the opportunity to improve the quality of our lives as best we can, and not just in financial and material terms. (This is discussed in greater depth in Chapter 3.) And we expect future generations to be able to do the same. In market economics, companies chase profits by responding to this not unreasonable desire.

As the signs of the environmental crisis become frighteningly clear, we can expect this self-interest to begin pushing ecological priorities up the consumer agenda. This will ratchet up the pressure on organizations to behave more sustainably and to act with credibility and integrity as they do so.[80] Businesses will need to respond to this evolution in consumer (and employee and investor) demand if they wish to remain competitive in their markets. Eco-friendliness may come to be business-critical.

There is evidence that this shift in priority may already be beginning to take hold. In 2010, the Bertelsmann Foundation surveyed 2,000 Germans and Austrians about their views on the environment, and the results are enlightening. The think tank found that in the wake of the financial crisis, around 90 percent of respondents expected a future in which protection of the environment and responsible use of resources will be taken into greater consideration. Four-fifths believed that growing wealth can go hand-in-hand with more efficient use of resources and better treatment of the environment. Three-quarters felt that material wealth was less important than protecting the environment for future generations.[81]

Germany, of course, is famed as a society for its environmental awareness. But a green consciousness is not limited to Europe. According to *National Geographic*'s Greendex survey of sustainable consumer behavior, South Korean consumers displayed the greatest increase in environmentally sustainable behavior between 2010 and 2012. German consumers were in second place, followed by Spanish and Chinese consumers. Among those mostly likely to feel guilty about their environmental impact were the BRIC countries (Brazil, Russia, India, and China, with India in the top place and China second), South Korea, Mexico, and Argentina.[82]

Pressure to "green up" will also come from the political domain. Politicians, of course, have their own motives for being responsive to changing consumer demands: Consumers are, after all, electors. Fiscal and regulatory systems will increasingly encourage sustainable practices and tighten the knot around businesses that fail to adapt. What were considered radical green doctrines two or three decades ago will become—indeed, are already becoming—mainstream political policies.

There are also indications that companies are starting to respond to these pressures. In 2011, the KPMG report mentioned earlier found that 95 percent of companies either had or were developing a corporate sustainability strategy. Almost two-thirds already had such a strategy in place, up from just over half three years previously.[83]

And in 2012, the French company Total became the first major oil company to warn against drilling in the Arctic. Tellingly, the company's reputation was chief among CEO Christophe de Margerie's reasons. An oil leak in Greenland would, he said, "do too much damage to the image of the company."[84]

## Catalyst for a Conversion

Remodeling an organization along sustainable lines requires a holistic and complex transformation. This paradigm shift will necessitate wholesale strategic and operational innovation on an extremely high level.

Companies will need to become far more strategically agile: Disruptive threats to markets and operations must be anticipated, and adaptive strategies must be put in place. It may prove necessary to pursue multiple and sometimes contradictory objectives, to reconcile commercial, economic, ecological, and social aims.

Businesses should consider how to embed a deep environmental awareness within their decision making, cultures, structures, processes, and procedures. Creating an internal eco-brand will mean making corporate social responsibility one of the most important assets of the business.

In addition, operational solutions that make both sustainable and economic sense will need to be identified and implemented. These include, for example, optimizing energy use, changing to renewable resources, moving IT to greener solutions, achieving paperless offices, hosting meetings virtually (as business travel becomes undesirable), and adopting cradle-to-cradle design. Water and carbon footprints—including those of suppliers—will need to be monitored, as will compliance with environmental standards.

This degree of change and the innovation challenge it presents are likely to prove beyond the capability of any single organization or its leaders. Businesses will need to learn to "collaborate across boundaries,"[85] externally as well as internally. They will need to seek joint solutions to sustainable operations by entering into new forms of collaboration with more eco-effective, leading-edge companies, and at times even with competitors. BMW and Peugeot's joint venture to design components for hybrid and electric engines is a case in point.

## Change Agents

Leaders inevitably face huge challenges whenever business transformation is on the agenda. Major organizational change programs are among the most difficult initiatives to get right. And the environmental crisis will force change of unprecedented complexity.

Leaders will need to be the agents of this change. They will need to innovate it, implement it, find partners to help them, and communicate it to their workforces. They will need to clarify not only the practicalities (structures, roles, responsibilities, tasks, and targets) but also the greater good behind the transformation. They must achieve all this in a way that engages employees behind sustainable strategies, without the business losing sight of intended results.

Such deep and intricate change will demand outstanding cognitive and decision-making skills from leaders. The pressure to innovate will require them to think beyond their organization's immediate environment, for example, when identifying the right collaborative partners to help them create a sustainable organization, and communicating the value of this to external stakeholders.

## THE DEMANDS OF THE ENVIRONMENTAL CRISIS

How do leaders create sustainable operations and cope with rising costs as resources dry up? Here is a summary of the main challenges for businesses and their leaders.

1. *Transformational thinking.* Strategies, structures, decision making, operations, cultures, processes, and procedures must all evolve to minimize environmental impact. Innovation will be necessary on a massive scale. Creative, strategic, and conceptual thinking will be critical leadership skills.

2. *Execution.* Change initiatives rarely fail at the conception stage; successful execution is what so often eludes organizations. Leaders with a track record in delivering business change will be prized.

3. *Visionary communication.* Organizations invariably suffer from a natural state of inertia. As agents of transformation, leaders will need to inspire employees to strive to achieve the new, sustainable organization. And they will need to spell out with total clarity what it means in practical, everyday terms for individuals' roles and performance.

4. *New forms of collaboration.* The intellectual power to deal with climate change will be beyond any one leader or even organization. Collaborations across functions and with external partners will become essential. Competitors will be forced to come together to find shared solutions.

# 3 Power to the Person: Individualization and Value Pluralism

> *"Wealth is not about having a lot of money;*
> *it's about having a lot of options."*
> —**Chris Rock,** comedian

## AT A GLANCE ▪ INDIVIDUALIZATION AND VALUE PLURALISM

### Five Essential Points

1. *Mounting affluence will drive growing individualism in emerging societies.* Greater income levels will give people easier access to cultural influences, which will expose them to a wider range of life and career options.

2. *People's values will increasingly pluralize.* Higher incomes will also grant individuals the freedom to follow their unique priorities and tastes when choosing between these new options.

3. *Niche opportunities will emerge in local markets.* Societies will individualize at different paces. Agile businesses will be able to identify and capitalize on local market opportunities created by individualization.

4. *Organizations' internal and external environments will fracture.* As the expectations of individuals are transformed by increased wealth, companies will need to

consider every employee and every customer as an individual. Failure to do so will mean loss of talent and business.

5.  *Greater flexibility and sensitivity will be essential.* With loyalty at a premium, organizations must get closer to their markets and workforces than ever before. More flexible, less centralized, and flatter structures will be needed to understand and respond to customers' and employees' needs.

**Five Questions Business Leaders Should Ask**

1.  Do our structure and management information enable us to sense changes in our market dynamics and corporate environments?

2.  Can our strategy be adapted to take account of the varying rates at which different local markets individualize?

3.  Are our leaders ready to treat our employees as individuals?

4.  Are our employees ready to treat our customers as individuals?

5.  How do we foster loyalty in a highly individualized world?

---

What do the following facts all have in common?

■   The number of car models on the world market increased by more than 40 percent between 1990 and 2006.[1]

■   In China, students enrolling in higher education topped 30 million in 2010, up 35 percent from 2005.[2]

■   In the first half of 2009, 23 percent of German male employees took the paternity leave to which they were legally entitled,[3] up from 3.5 percent in 2006.[4]

■   In the UK, annual enrollment in a government apprenticeship program was reported to be up 900 percent in 2011—among those over 60.[5]

Behind this odd assortment of data is a significant underlying trend. These statistics signal the widening range of life choices that individuals around the world are taking advantage of.

The world is not only globalizing. It is individualizing.

## THE MEGATREND: INDIVIDUALIZATION AND VALUE PLURALISM

In the 1979 spoof biblical epic *Monty Python's Life of Brian*, the eponymous hero addresses a gathered throng that has mistaken him for the Messiah. The crowd is hanging on his every word. Brian attempts to convince them to stop following him en masse. "You're all individuals," he pleads. "Yes," they parrot in unison, "we're all individuals."

Our hapless protagonist tries again: "You're all *different*," he urges. Again, the crowd choruses as one: "Yes, we *are* all different .... "

To the crowd's annoyance, a lone voice protests: "I'm not .... "

Brian might have had more luck convincing the emerging consumer classes we saw in Chapter 1. For as societies industrialize and their citizens become wealthier, everyday life becomes increasingly governed by more individualized choices and decisions.

With more money in their pockets, people find that they can leave behind the economic strictures of the past. Prosperity frees a society from scarcity of the basic requirements of human existence, such as food and shelter.

As a result, people's priorities move up through Maslow's hierarchy of needs[6] as they look to improve other aspects of their lives. As Professor Ronald Inglehart of the University of Michigan identified during the 1970s, this leads individuals to focus on more complex, postmaterialistic values.[7] When the next meal is no longer a pressing concern, people look to satisfy more cerebral needs, such as belonging, autonomy, self-realization, and self-expression. (Witness the illegal use of Twitter in China; see the section *Access All Areas*.) These people are driven by more profound values, like humanism, religious faith, social justice, and protection of the environment. And they are at liberty to indulge in more emotionally fulfilling activities, seeking intellectual challenge and pursuing their aesthetic preferences.

Repressive governments notwithstanding, people discover the freedom to make choices that are guided by such values. They begin to make decisions driven by their own sets of ethics, priorities, and tastes. These shape the choices they make about almost everything, from family, career, and politics to the car they drive (and whether they choose to drive at all), the cell phone they carry, and the fashion brands they wear. Previously unthinkable goals, such as work-life balance, fulfillment, self-improvement, and self-expression, come into the frame.

Values-driven engagement—choosing your work, lifestyle, interests, and purchases according to your personal values—gradually becomes the norm. As a consequence, people make decisions that challenge traditional societal structures and the cultural status quo.

In addition, as increasing numbers of people move into the ranks of the middle class, societies undergo a growing pluralism of these values. The result is an unprecedented proliferation of demands—not just for previously unaffordable products and services but also for previously unimaginable professions, careers, and lifestyles.

As we saw in Chapter 1, Globalization 2.0 is set to boost the material standing of some 2 billion people around the world, providing them with access to the cultural capital that informs choice. For perhaps the first time in human history, choice is going global.

## A Wider Angle

As a society's wealth grows, so does its citizens' access to education and a diverse range of media—newspapers, books, TV, films, and of course the Internet (as we shall see later in this chapter, and in more detail in Chapter 4). Exposure to this cultural capital opens their eyes to new lifestyle options.

In the digital era, this effect is intensified by enhanced global communication and greater exposure to media from all over the world. In the 1976 Wim Wenders film *Im Lauf Der Zeit (Kings of the Road)*, the character Robert Lander observes that America has "colonized our subconscious." The film was released at a time when modern American culture had been distributed worldwide for several decades. People across the globe were exposed to U.S. values, or at least a version of them, via movies, TV, and music. No other country exported its cultural output to anything like the same extent.

Skip to the present and the availability of Internet connectivity, voice-over IP, file sharing, streaming media, social networking, mobile communications, satellite TV, and 24/7 news media. We are no longer necessarily exposed to predominantly American or, for that matter, Western values.

For the swelling ranks of the middle class today, access to global cultural influences, and to direct communication with people the world over who have like minds and similar values, is just a few clicks away. There is an almost limitless range of cultural capital out there for individuals to draw their influences from: Witness the growing global popularity of Bollywood[8] and Nollywood[9] cinema over the past decade or so.

We need to look only at our online behavior (which we will do in more detail in Chapter 4) for evidence of individualization and the pluralization of values being driven by digital technology. The Internet is both a means of access to information (including cultural capital) and an outlet for the human desire for self-expression. The world's top ten websites are therefore dominated by those that quench the thirst for information—for example, search engines Google (ranked number 1), Yahoo! (ranked number 4), and Baidu in China (ranked number 5), and online encyclopaedia Wikipedia (number 6). Social media also dominate the top sites, such as Facebook (number 2), YouTube (number 3), and Twitter (number 8). These provide platforms for people to share their news, views, likes, and dislikes with the world (see the section *Access All Areas*).

### Access All Areas

Given that social media is a vehicle for self-expression, we might expect the spread of individualism in emerging economies to drive rapid adoption of Internet access and social networking in these markets. Sure enough, Internet users numbered 2 billion worldwide in 2011, almost half of them (45 percent) in Asia.[10] And social platforms such as Facebook and Twitter are experiencing soaring growth in Asia (with the exception of China, where neither site has launched) and South America.

Here are the statistics on Facebook:

■ Facebook's Asian user base grew by more than 48 percent from March 2011 to March 2012, compared to 26 percent growth worldwide.[11]

*(continued)*

- The number of Facebook users in Brazil and Thailand was estimated to have doubled in the twelve months leading to September 2012.[12]

- India registered almost 52 percent growth in the same period.[13]

- South America had 135 million Facebook users in October 2012—more than a third of the population of the entire continent, and a higher penetration than in Europe.[14]

Here are the statistics on Twitter:

- Brazil is Twitter's second biggest national market after the United States.

- Brazil is also the second-largest market after the United States in terms of number of profiles, and it has the most active user base, generating more than 10 percent of all tweets.

- Indonesia may soon overtake the UK in fourth place in the Twitter rankings: The UK has 32.2 million user profiles, Indonesia 29.4 million. But the Asian country is experiencing faster growth.

- Jakarta is Twitter's most active city worldwide.[15]

- Reports surfaced in September 2012 that China is Twitter's most active nation—despite the service being blocked in the country.[16]

The power of individualization knows few bounds.

## Culture Clubs

A global rise of individualism may appear to contradict the conventional wisdom on national cultures, which has tended to portray Eastern societies as generally more collectivist than the individualistic West.[17] For example, in his renowned studies among tens of thousands of IBM employees worldwide, management researcher Geert Hofstede ranked countries according to their levels of individualism. Sure enough, his ten most individualistic nations were without exception North American, Western European, or Australasian, while Asian countries were found almost entirely in the bottom half of his list.[18]

It should be noted, however, that the top individualistic regions also boast a disproportionate concentration of the world's most industrially advanced nations, such as the United States, Canada, and the UK. The citizens of these countries have enjoyed a level of wealth that has granted them freedom of choice, economically speaking at least, for far longer than in many other parts of the world.

And it is telling that Japan, one of Asia's richest nations, was ranked in the top half of Hofstede's ranking.[19] Although Japanese culture is renowned for putting the needs of the group firmly before those of the individual, Japan ranked far higher for individualism than we might expect. In a society where a common proverb reminds the population that "the nail that sticks out is hammered down," high levels of wealth have driven surprising levels of individualism.

This is not to suggest that national culture is irrelevant to individualization. On the contrary, it is deeply influential. A society's place on the individualist-collectivist spectrum to some extent dictates the pace at which its values pluralize. And cultural norms inherently affect people's values and choices. But the reality is that given the opportunity, people make choices that best suit their own values. And what is important to each of us differs. An individual's unique set of values plays a leading role in shaping the choices that he or she makes.

## A Shattering Effect

On the surface at least, growing wealth and increased freedom of choice for billions of people around the world would seem to be a wholly positive development (see the section *Too Much of a Good Thing?*). But for organizations, the consequences are likely to be deeply perplexing. Individualism and value pluralism will fracture companies' external and internal environments, shattering established structures and existing market dynamics.

As we shall see, these developments will change the nature of markets, channels, and customer behaviors, challenging the agility of large corporations and creating opportunities for niche suppliers. And they will cause a seismic shift in the nature of relationships and networks, affecting organizational structures, employee expectations, and career patterns.

## Too Much of a Good Thing?

In 2008, Starbucks ran ads boasting that its outlets offered a staggering 87,000 varieties of coffee.[20] Four years later, UK department store chain Debenhams did just the opposite. The retailer announced a new, simplified coffee menu, written in plain English. Out went cappuccino, mocha, latte, and espresso, and in came frothy, chocolate, "really, really milky" coffee, and "a strong shot." Old-fashioned mugs and cups replaced tall, grande, and venti sizes. The company had declared war on "coffee confusion."[21]

Debenhams may have been unwittingly helping customers navigate the "paradox of choice." In his book of that name, psychology professor Barry Schwartz challenged the assumption that more options always mean greater satisfaction, and he warned of the perils of excessive choice. Schwartz pointed to the bewildering array of alternatives that face modern-day consumers when they are making the most mundane or the most significant decisions: from ordering a coffee, buying jeans, or selecting a cell phone to applying to college, buying life insurance, or choosing an investment plan.

This explosion of choices sets unrealistic expectations, he contended, causing confusion, uncertainty, and nagging doubts once a selection is made. These feelings eat away at our satisfaction. Choice becomes a problem, rather than a hallmark of the individual freedom and self-determination that comes with material wealth.

Paradoxically, option overload can even lead to choice paralysis. Schwartz cites the example of a specific retirement savings plan in the United States. The more fund options the plan offered, the lower the enrollment among employees—despite the fact that the employer was matching employee contributions. Schwartz's argument is that reducing choice would actually alleviate the stresses, anxiety, and clutter of modern-day life.[22] In other words, be careful what you wish for.

# Any Product You Want

Henry Ford famously offered his Model T in "any color [any customer] wants, so long as it is black."[23] In the early twentieth century, the needs of mass production superseded any notion of customer choice.

A hundred years later, the guiding principle of the values-driven marketplace will be "learning to regard customers as individuals."[24] The twin forces of individualism and value pluralism will demand a level of product diversity at the extreme end of the spectrum from that imposed by Ford's system of standardized mass production.

As the emerging middle class flexes its new-found financial muscle, freedom of choice will splinter demand patterns, creating the need for an ever expanding array of products and services to satisfy increasingly varied tastes. Individualization will give rise to niche opportunities—some fleeting, some more sustained—on an unprecedented scale.

An example of this is the "long tail" market. The long tail is the potential for e-commerce players such as Amazon and Apple to sell small numbers of a vast range of less popular books and music, in addition to the big, volume-shifting hits and bestsellers. In the online world, where "the tyranny of physical space"[25] is no longer a constraint, long tail exponents can stock almost everything, exploiting the fact that "everyone's taste departs from the mainstream somewhere."[26]

Another manifestation of this market fragmentation is the growing demand for customized and personalized offerings. A 2008 study on customization pointed to an "exploding interest" in products and services tailored to the precise preferences of individual customers.[27] It presented an array of examples: custom-printed T-shirts and greeting cards, user-curated photo albums, cookbooks compiling the user's chosen recipes, customized breakfast cereals, and made-to-order blends of tea. Reebok even launched a sneaker that could be styled to reflect the wearer's favorite song.

Another example is German chocolatier Ritter Sport, which allows consumers to create their preferred chocolate flavors. In addition, Canadian company My Virtual Model provides personalized avatars and virtual dressing rooms for downtown fashion brands, allowing shoppers to find exactly the right color and fit. The company website displays a constantly updating counter of the number of sales its service has helped close. At the time of writing, it was steadily ticking higher, having topped 125 million.

However, this fragmentation of markets is a double-edged sword. The study cited above sounded a warning for corporations that lack the agility to respond: "In the end, it is the customer who drives the business, and customers just want to get what they want."

The subtitle of a book about the long tail—*Why the Future of Business Is Selling Less of More* [28] encapsulates the challenge for organizations. As the experience of glocalization demonstrates (see Chapter 1), large organizations can be ill equipped to exploit the law of small numbers. Their scale and structure can hamper their ability to identify and capitalize on niche opportunities, leaving the way clear for smaller, nimbler, often local players.

## Ties That Don't Bind

While playing havoc with the external environment, individualization will also skew the internal landscape for organizations, bending attitudes to work and careers and changing the structure, quantity, and quality of people's relationships—with each other, and with their employers.

As people embrace social networks as showcases for individual expression, they are becoming increasingly reliant on them for both personal and professional communication. Facebook topped 1 billion users worldwide in September 2012,[29] up by an estimated 33 percent from the previous year.[30] Twitter passed 500 million users in June 2012,[31] and at the time of writing, U.S. Twitter users totaled 54 percent of the nation's entire population.[32] As of June 2012, professional networking site LinkedIn claimed two new sign-ups every second.[33]

This blurs the boundaries between our private and working lives (more on this in Chapter 4). It is also forging wider but by necessity looser personal and professional networks: The average Facebook user had 245 "friends" as of February 2012,[34] surely far more people than any individual can meaningfully know.

The digital sphere also engenders a more spontaneous attitude to forming relationships, as contacts can be activated and deactivated at will. These loose ties create a major headache for businesses when it comes to creating valuable loyalty. Customer loyalty means repeat business, while employee loyalty means higher engagement and better performance. But how do you foster loyalty among people who run their friendships and professional relationships on a laptop or smartphone?

## Moving the Goals

As noted, individualization encourages people to seek previously unattainable personal goals. Nowhere does this resonate more profoundly, or more disruptively, than in the workplace, where the rule book is being ripped up.

Conventional career decision-making criteria such as pay, benefits, and prospects for promotion are becoming no more than basic expectations. Instead, employees are seeking "soft" factors like fulfillment, social recognition, self-realization, personal development, self-expression, and the all-important work-life balance.

According to a 2011 Hay Group study, Malaysian Generation Y graduates place work-life balance at the top of a list of factors important to their working environment[35] (see the section *Y, Us?* for more on Generation Y). A survey by Ernst & Young found that Singaporean workers rank salary only third among their work goals, with the balance between work and family life taking priority.[36]

The sudden spike among German employees to sign up for paternity leave (noted at the beginning of this chapter) is a further case in point. Tellingly, this was triggered by a relatively minor legislative tweak. Extending the permitted leave period by two months signaled an increased social acceptance of paternity leave (which had to be taken by the other parent) to fourteen months, challenging the conventional logic that it is "unmale" and harmful to career prospects. The effect was to unleash a pent-up demand among German fathers eager to prioritize family considerations. In recent years, Germany has seen a spate of major corporations build their own kindergartens, among them Adidas, BASF, Commerzbank, Daimler, RWE, SAP, Siemens, and ThyssenKrupp.[37]

In addition, workers no longer expect to have to put in long hours to achieve career success, as the expectations of Malaysian graduates interviewed by Hay Group demonstrate. Despite their emphasis on work-life balance, the majority of workers still anticipate a promotion after just a year in the workplace.[38]

Changing expectations among workers lead to accelerated staff turnover, as workers move around in search of their life goals. Perpetual motion is becoming a global workforce phenomenon. More than 90 percent of American Generation Y employees expect to stay in a position for less than three years.[39] And according to the 2012 Kelly *Global Workforce Index*, more than half of workers worldwide prefer to change jobs frequently rather than remain with one employer, while almost half admit to constantly job searching, even when they are happy in their current role. Both of these trends were more marked in the fast-developing Asia-Pacific region than elsewhere.[40]

Changing expectations also attract more people to careers in professional, service, and creative industries, which are perceived as being more fulfilling—as well as more lucrative.

In a thought-provoking book[41] (which drew criticism from some quarters[42]), Professor Richard Florida of the University of Toronto pinpointed a new "creative class" as the key driving force for postindustrial economic development in the United States. According to Florida, this socioeconomic group comprises some 40 million American workers, or 30 percent of the workforce, earning twice the average wage in the United States. These workers occupy roles in fields as diverse as science, education, engineering, IT, research, healthcare, law, business, and finance. Florida lists individuality and self-expression among their fundamental values.

## Y, Us?

"These kids in the office today...." A familiar refrain? Possibly, among some over-40s in the workplace. To them, Generation Y (aka Millennials, broadly defined as having been born in the 1980s and 1990s[43]), is a different breed, let alone a different generation.

They possess attitudes, ambitions, and expectations that seem at odds with corporate convention. Long hours, responsibility, loyalty, and traditional career paths are not high on their agendas. Work-life balance, fast promotions, and decent salaries are. And they have a totally different view of the power relationship with employers.

The expectations of Malaysian graduates studied by Hay Group in 2011 are an illuminating example. Graduates in nine of thirteen industries were earning less than they had anticipated, while more than three-quarters of those leaving their first position within a year did so for a better opportunity elsewhere.[44] Similarly, a global study by Ashridge Business School found that only 57 percent of British Gen Y employees intended to stay in their current job for as long as two years.[45]

As the Ashridge study points out, younger and older generations "view the workplace through different lenses."[46] While managers admire the intelligence and energy that Gen Y brings to the workplace, they can resent the younger generation's desire for recognition, as well as their self-focus, overconfidence, dislike of teamwork, and lack of respect that some older workers perceive.[47]

Another item not on Millennials' to-do list—perhaps most worryingly for organizations—is leadership. As the Ashridge study discovered, "Generation Y... does not want its managers' jobs."[48] Only 38 percent of Malaysian graduates said they want to experience decision-making opportunities. Undesired and unexpected job responsibilities were the second biggest reason for leaving their first post within a year (cited by 54 percent).[49]

The European School of Management and Technology (ESMT) also noticed a growing reticence to take on responsibility among young talent. Rising stars being primed for leadership and sent to the school as part of their development were increasingly asking: "Is it OK not to strive for a leadership position?" Intrigued by this, the school polled 900 participants in its leadership development program. The conclusion was overwhelming: "The avoidance of responsibility is a huge phenomenon, which companies must find a way to address." Work-life balance was a primary reason for it, along with an unwillingness to take on responsibility for people and to get involved in personal politics.[50]

A study of Gen Y by the German Leaders' Association (Deutscher Führungskräfteverband) came to similar conclusions. More than two-thirds of respondents told the association that higher levels of responsibility and remuneration fail to counterbalance the accompanying work pressures and impact on family life. Some 83 percent were more concerned about the con-

*(continued)*

tent of their work than their position in their organization's hierarchy. And just 27 percent considered promotion their main career objective.[51] This is especially worrying given the impending leadership exodus facing the developed world in particular, as the baby boom generation approaches retirement (see Chapter 5).[52]

However, it is all too easy to fall into the trap of assuming that Millennials are afraid of challenge. On the contrary. A survey by Audi of its Generation Y employees found that they actively seek challenge. They just define it differently. Audi's HR officer told the German newspaper *Der Spiegel*: "Working on the content and on factual issues is more important to them than leadership and responsibility for employees."[53]

## Changing Lanes

Individualization also drives the desire to shape not just our careers but our entire working lives, as we see fit. The traditional three-phase life cycle—youth, professional life, retirement—is no longer the rigid template it once was. People question the conventional wisdom that they should begin working immediately after completing their education and retire at a set age. As a result, careers are gradually expanding from three to five stages. Economics permitting, some people choose to delay the onset of professional life, building a "postadolescence" phase into their life pattern before their professional lives begin, which might consist of a period of travel or volunteering. When Germany did away with military service in 2011, a civilian Federal Voluntary Service (Bundesfreiwilligendienst) was established in its place. Immediately, too many people applied for the available places, and some had to be placed on a waiting list.[54]

At the other end of the scale, people are increasingly postponing their retirement phase until beyond the age of 60 or 65. This may be an economic imperative, brought on by pension plans crashing with the markets or the prohibitive cost of eldercare. But it is also being driven by improving health and life expectancy, which present older people with the opportunity to take on a new direction later in life by retraining for careers that align with their values as mature adults. The experience of the older apprentices in the UK mentioned near the beginning of this chapter is a case in point, as is Germany's Federal Voluntary Service, where 20 percent of applicants are over 50 years old.[55]

## IMPLICATIONS OF INDIVIDUALIZATION AND VALUE PLURALISM

Organizations like structure: a body of people brought together into a logical formation to achieve a common purpose. For companies, of course, the purpose is the production of goods and services for distribution to customers at a profit. To achieve this objective as effectively and efficiently as possible, companies organize people into structures, and customers into market segments.

Individualization is at odds with structure, and value pluralism runs counter to the very nature of organizations. As noted, this force requires businesses to consider every single employee and every single customer as an individual, a unique being with his or her own agenda, distinct from each other and separate from that of any organization.

This is not how organizations like to think.

The challenges are daunting. How do companies retain all of their customers and all of their talent when each has his or her own agenda? And in doing so, how do companies design and execute different strategies for markets with stronger individualistic or collectivist traditions, which will individualize at varying speeds?

The answer is that they must get closer to their customers and employees than ever before. This creates a baffling level of complexity. Organizations will need to understand the rapidly proliferating value sets of potentially thousands of employees and millions of customers. They need to identify what individuals consider important, and they must work out how to connect their brands and cultures to this. Otherwise, customers and employees will exercise their freedom of choice and vote with their feet.

## A Higher Purpose

When it comes to engaging employees, money is no longer the solution for everybody. As we've seen, workers with economic choices are not looking for the best financial offer when making career decisions. And as Globalization 2.0 progresses apace, more and more people will be in a position to afford this luxury. More important than financial gain will be meaningful work and the right lifestyle.

Such is Generation Y's understanding of work-life balance. Indeed, it is worth considering that the term *work-life balance* has taken on different meanings for each generation.

For the baby boomers (and earlier generations), work-life balance basically meant reducing working hours to free up more time for family obligations. There was little expectation that work should provide anything more than the ability to earn a living. The next generation (often termed Generation X) demanded that phases of work were followed by periods of leave or sabbaticals. Nowadays, Millennials are blurring the distinction between their personal and working lives. To them, time is to be used for the combination of professional and personal activities that suits them best. They demand meaning from their work, and they expect it to be compatible with their personal identity and values.

As such, career choices are increasingly influenced by personal values. Take the example of a friend of ours who is a structural engineer. Shocked to discover that a potential employer in the mining industry had no CSR policy, she turned down a job offer, despite the company's being based in the precise part of the UK where she wished to relocate.

In response to this tendency, organizations will require less rigid, more flexible structures. They will need to fundamentally redesign their work processes and procedures if they are to accommodate the desire to reconcile personal and professional lives and goals.

Employees will demand greater autonomy over their work and time, as well as the scope to move their own projects and ideas forward. To attract high performers, businesses will need to create working environments and offer employment conditions that encourage self-development and the achievement of life goals—for example, offering sabbaticals or external study. Childcare and flexible work arrangements will be considered a basic right. HR departments will need to balance these demands with the skills required by the organization.

## Open Relationships

In this highly individualized world, employee loyalty and retention—at least in the traditional sense—will be considerably more difficult to achieve. Accessing necessary talent will depend on an organization offering compelling opportunities to work on fulfilling tasks and allowing people to do so in ways that satisfy the demands of their lifestyles.

This will mean moving beyond relying on conventional, employer-staff contractual relationships. Businesses will also need to establish loose networks of talent to enable them to draw on the right skills at the right time. Establishing and maintaining long-term relationships with this network will be essential if companies are to have the necessary resources on tap.

## Leading in a Loose World

Making organizational structures looser will fundamentally impact the role of the leader. On top of the agenda for leaders will be the need to secure commitment from their teams, in a world where people's loyalty is to their social and professional networks as much as to any one organization.

Loyalty will no longer be judged by length of service but by length and quality of relationships. Leaders will need to establish enduring relationships across an ever expanding network of current and former team members, and they will have to consider how to access social networks and leverage company values to create these relationships.

Facing accelerated churn, leaders will need to carefully consider whom to invest in developing. They will increasingly need to make judgments based on not only potential but also on personal ambitions and objectives. Which team members actually want to progress? Which are happy simply doing a good job, then moving on? How can leaders keep both engaged?

To further complicate the challenge, teams will be made up of increasingly heterogeneous personalities, all with different motives, goals, priorities, and working styles. This will demand carefully tailored development goals and more subtly personalized performance evaluation. In addition, leaders will need to display heightened sensitivity in order to assess individual contributions.

Managing diverse teams will also demand highly developed conflict prevention and resolution skills. Leaders will be required to rapidly reorganize teams and provide stability to prevent a domino effect as members leave.

They will also be expected to enable greater autonomy and self-organization among their teams. This will mean setting objectives, ensuring a shared understanding of them, and expecting teams and individuals to find the solutions. And it will require a difficult balancing act: Individuals may need to play the dual role of manager and leader. Too much micro-managing risks stifling the creativity that workers crave, while too free a rein may lead to disunited teams and uncoordinated efforts.

---

## CASE STUDY ▪ Get with the Programmer

Meet Arvi. A friend of the authors, Arvi (this is not his real name) is a programmer for a multinational technology company. He is a classic example of why organizations need to think beyond traditional employer-employee relationships to attract the best talent. He is a member of the new global middle class, whose talents allow members to negotiate working conditions on their terms.

At 30, Arvi has never had what has traditionally been considered a "real" job. He doesn't do nine to five. Instead, he chooses his own working hours, he chooses where he works, and he chooses how he communicates. And it is Arvi—not the company—who retains the patents on his work.

If you ask him where home is, you'll get a strange look. His apartment is in London, but only because of its prime travel connections. He's been known to write code while lying on a beach in Bali or at a music festival on the Black Sea. Most of his communication is virtual.

But ask him about his ambitions for leadership, and he'll give you a straight answer: "Who'd want *that* responsibility?"

He may be one of his company's most skilled programmers (he has just published his first book on the subject), but he has no desire to climb the corporate ladder. He knows that top talent can afford not to pursue traditional career paths.

Fortunately, his employer realizes this too, and the company has allowed the flexible working arrangements to provide the work-life balance that talented individuals like Arvi demand. The company knows that treating these employees as individuals is the only way to recruit the skills they need in a global, tech-savvy, highly mobile, increasingly individualized marketplace.

---

## THE DEMANDS OF INDIVIDUALIZATION AND VALUE PLURALISM

Individualization and value pluralism will likely lead to fragmenting employee and customer values, more diverse teams, less centralized structures, flatter hierarchies, flexible working practices, and greater employee turnover. As a result, organizations and leaders will need to:

1. *Display intellectual openness and curiosity.* Sensitivity to individuals' needs and the flexibility to respond accordingly will be crucial to generating loyalty. Leaders will need to be curious about and open to employees' and customers' pluralistic drivers, so as to understand what motivates people and be able to attract, engage, and retain them.

2. *Provide bounded autonomy to unite diverse teams.* Leaders will need to draw on the appropriate leadership styles in order to make staff members appreciate each other's strengths while respecting differences, and to manage and engage diverse teams and highly individualized team members. Providing autonomy within a clear set of boundaries to create stability and direction will be necessary to foster the right conditions for teams to perform.

3. *Redefine loyalty and manage extended networks.* When staff retention can no longer be expected, loyalty will depend on leaders' ability to develop and maintain lasting relationships with current and former employees, within and beyond the organization.

# 4 Remote Possibilities: The Digital Era

*"The Internet is the first thing that humanity has built that humanity doesn't understand."*
—**Eric Schmidt,** Executive Chair, Google

## AT A GLANCE ▦ THE DIGITAL ERA

**Five Essential Points**

1. *The digitization of our lifestyles is becoming the norm.* With ubiquitous Internet connectivity, the proliferation of mobile devices, and the popularity of social networking, we are now "always on," at home and at work. This is eroding traditional boundaries between our personal, private, and professional lives.

2. *Digital natives have increasing influence.* The inexorable progress of digital technology is creating a divide between younger, tech-savvy "digital natives" and older generations. Younger people have a technological edge over their more senior colleagues, yet in many cases lack the attitudes and social skills expected in the corporate world and tend to challenge authority. Organizations must find ways to accommodate and cross-skill both groups.

3. *Virtualization is disrupting power relationships between companies, customers, and employees.* The digital era has given rise to new virtual business models and platforms, enabling consumers to pick and choose more easily and trade among themselves instead of with commercial providers. This gives customers unprece-

dented levels of choice. In addition, reputations are at risk as disgruntled employees can publicly hold employers to account online.

4. *The workplace is fragmenting.* When employees are always on, the concepts of work and the workplace become fluid. In many cases, employees can perform tasks anywhere, anytime, challenging the need for a central, bricks-and-mortar location and traditional organizational hierarchies. This will appeal in particular to digital natives, who readily embrace virtual working methods and tools and have little respect for orthodox structure and hierarchy.

5. *Leadership will need to "go remote" and prioritize loyalty and reputation management.* Leaders need to get a grip on managing diverse, loose-knit teams whose members are dispersed around the world and have varying degrees of digital competence. In order to create loyalty, leaders must foster a sense of unity, engagement, and collaboration among people who rarely meet, and ensure that there is effective decision making among these groups. Openness, integrity, and reputation management will be key in a transparent, virtual world.

**Five Questions Business Leaders Should Ask**

1. How do we attract digital talent and harness the innovation and creativity of the unconventional digital generation?

2. How can we cross-fertilize younger generations' technical expertise and more senior workers' corporate skills?

3. How do we reap the cost and productivity benefits of virtual working practices, and what are the implications for our current organizational structure?

4. What are the leadership competencies required to manage and engage remotely—and how do we equip our leaders with them?

5. How will leaders manage reputation in a transparent, virtual world?

---

At the time of writing, an unusual petition is gathering momentum in Sweden. The campaign aims to change the dictionary definition of the word *nörd*—"nerd" in English—to give it a more positive meaning.[1]

Not so long ago, to be called a technology nerd—to be enthusiastic about IT—was wholly disparaging. But in an increasingly digital age, to be a nerd is becoming normal. The shift in connotation occurred during the 2000s. According to an associate editor of the *Merriam-Webster's Dictionary*, as more people learned HTML and built their own websites, the word began to lose its pejorative connotation.[2]

Nowadays, you don't even need to be a nerd to carry out all sorts of advanced technological processes that were unimaginable just a decade ago. People routinely take photos and videos with their phones, upload them to websites, and make video calls on voice-over IP (VoIP) networks, as well as watch videos, listen to audio, or play games on their laptops, tablets, and cell phones.

More than 25 million items of content are shared across social media every month.[3] A staggering 250 million photos are uploaded each day to Facebook alone, and 500 million minutes are spent on the site each month.[4] Users of the VoIP service Skype logged a startling 115 billion minutes of calls in one quarter of 2012.[5] In addition, every minute, twenty-four hours of video are uploaded to YouTube.[6] And just one game in one video game franchise—*Call of Duty: Black Ops*—logged a staggering 68,000 *years* of playing time worldwide within only a month of its launch in 2010.[7]

To millions of people, such technical operations are by no means "nerdish": They are simple, everyday activities, an integral part of their personal and working lives.

## THE MEGATREND: THE DIGITAL ERA

Digitization is a booming worldwide phenomenon. As noted in Chapter 3, Internet and social media use, already commonplace in the developed West, is growing rapidly in emerging markets across Asia, Latin America, and Africa. Indeed, digitization is intricately linked with the individualization megatrend examined in Chapter 3. As we shall see, the two megatrends overlap to a degree. However, the profound implications of the digital era for leaders merit separate investigation.

Relentless digitization is not only changing the way we communicate; it is also transforming the way we work and the nature of our professional and personal relationships. It is opening up new divides, blurring long-established boundaries, and turning traditional hierarchies upside down.

## Always On

Since the first email was sent in 1971,[8] the Internet has become a hugely pervasive medium of communication, commerce, and cooperation and a widespread channel of access to education and culture. It has spawned countless industries, business models, products, services, and companies that could not have existed before its invention: ISPs, search engines, security software, website design and hosting, VoIP technology, web conferencing, online dating, social and professional networks, streaming media ... the list is endless.

And over the past fifteen years, as digital technology has progressed, the web has gone mobile. This has enabled anytime, anywhere access, via ever faster mobile and Wi-Fi networks and on increasingly powerful and sophisticated devices. This leaves us "always on"—constantly accessible to friends, colleagues, and bosses; continually available to talk, text, instant message, email, video call, access information, and view content. Google's Latitude mobile application even lets users know where their contacts are at any given time. In effect, the digital age has no off switch.

And the future will likely be even more digitally enriched. By 2020, all cell phones will be Internet enabled.[9] What's more, devices such as augmented reality glasses will enhance the world around us, constantly providing real-time information and effectively using our entire environment as a life-size, 3D computer screen.[10]

## Cyberspace Cadets

This state of technological affairs is producing a new breed of digital citizens. Younger generations have never known life without the Internet and mobile technology.[11] These digital natives have grown up online, happily sharing files, being active on social networks, blogging, tweeting, playing massively multiplayer games, and so on. They instinctively live digital lifestyles: Some 95 percent of this generation are members of a social network.[12] To them, the digital world is as comfortable as the real world; in fact, there is little distinction between the two. As a report from corporate IT network provider Cisco put it, "there are 206 bones in the human body, and the smartphone could plausibly be considered the 207th for Gen Y."[13]

As they live life online, digital natives create their own form of virtual social capital. They are streamlining work processes and practices, managing their personal and professional relationships, and transacting, collaborating, and socializing with people across the globe.

## Public Lives

An aspect of the digital era (alluded to in Chapter 3) is people's growing dependence on online networking to keep in touch with friends, family, and work contacts, and the blurring of our public and private lives that this results in. According to the Cisco study mentioned above, more than half of people state that they "could not live" without the Internet. The research demonstrated that online communication is now challenging face-to-face contact as people's primary method of maintaining their personal relationships.[14]

Cisco unearthed some remarkable views about life online, particularly among students—the next generation of workers. For two-thirds of college students worldwide, online access is more important than owning a car. Two-fifths consider the Internet more important than dating or friends, and more than a quarter say the same about Facebook.[15]

On social sites like Facebook, LinkedIn, and Twitter, we choose to live our lives in a virtual goldfish bowl, continually posting and tweeting status updates, social arrangements, our latest news, photographs, videos, "likes," new jobs, promotions, meetings, events we are attending, and so on. We willingly put a regularly updated history of ourselves into the public domain, merging our public and private selves. In addition to being always on, in the digital age, we are "always on the record"[16] (see the section *Chasing Shadows*).

Living life in such a public and always-on manner breaks down the barriers that traditionally divided people's personal, social, and professional lives. Cisco found that some 70 percent of employees now "friend" their managers on Facebook. Almost as many (68 percent) follow managers and coworkers on Twitter. Startlingly, less than a third say that they prefer to keep their personal life private.[17]

## Chasing Shadows

In the 1994 movie *The Shawshank Redemption,* protagonist Andy Dufresne quotes a supposed Mexican proverb that states that the Pacific Ocean "has no memory." The very opposite can be said of the Internet: It has no capacity to forget. A *New York Times* headline once declared that "the web means the end of forgetting."[18]

The newspaper cited the case of Stacy Snyder, a student teacher who was denied her college degree just weeks before graduating in 2006. Her misdemeanor: posting a photo of herself on her MySpace page, drinking from a plastic cup at a costume party, captioned "Drunken Pirate." Snyder's college considered this behavior to be promoting drinking to her underage students. Snyder sued—and lost.

Her fate is a troubling illustration of the visible traces we voluntarily leave as we go about our personal and professional business in cyberspace. This "web shadow" is made up of all we do online, each link to us, and every mention or inclusion of us in content posted on websites.[19] As a *Times* of London journalist found to his frustration, to be "unGoogleable" is all but impossible.[20]

As web search techniques become more intelligent, this digital footprint becomes all the more detectable, and all the less deletable. Germany's largest credit agency, for example, now mines Facebook pages when assessing creditworthiness.[21] According to the *Harvard Business Review*, more than 75 percent of employers evaluate job candidates' digital presence. More than 70 percent have actually rejected applicants based on what they found.[22]

Recruitment service TalentBin is a search engine that claims to scan the entire web, finding candidates wherever they are active online and analyzing their skills, interests, and activity. A poll by a similar company, Jobvite, suggested that 89 percent of American employers intended to use social networks to source job candidates in 2011.[23]

Clearly, this online transparency has massive implications for our professional lives. In a world where the public and the private are one, your whole life becomes your résumé. And as the TalentBin website claims, "it seems nobody is out of reach."

## Peer Pressure

The digital era is also disrupting conventional power relationships between companies and their customers, fragmenting traditional market structures and value chains, and creating a constantly shifting kaleidoscope of opportunities and threats.

The proliferation of virtual business models and platforms has not only given rise to new business models and new ways for companies and their customers to transact. It has also provided consumers with unprecedented choice and power. Individuals can now compare providers' prices and service quality on comparison and review sites before buying just about anything. This has a major influence on their purchasing behavior: Only 14 percent of consumers claim to trust advertisements, compared to 78 percent who trust peer recommendations.[24]

A study from Cornell University concluded that online reviews can inflate or depress hotel room rates by more than 10 percent.[25] Similarly, the University of California found that a mere half-star improvement in online restaurant ratings makes an establishment up to 49 percent more likely to be fully booked during peak times.[26]

Virtualization has even provided the means for consumers to avoid transacting with commercial entities altogether, instead trading among themselves, and in huge volumes. Online marketplace eBay had almost 120 million active users as of June 2013.[27] Almost two-thirds of payments on the site during 2011 resulted from peer-to-peer (P2P) sales.[28] In addition, classified ad service Craigslist covers more than 700 cities in 70 countries, attracting in excess of 50 billion page views worldwide each month.[29]

The P2P philosophy behind sites like eBay and Craigslist also threatens to transform the very lifeblood of business growth: the lending, borrowing, and raising of capital. Described as the "eBay of banking,"[30] P2P lending is the direct lending and borrowing of money online, without the involvement of banks. The model has the potential to transform both the business funding and consumer credit markets beyond recognition, at the expense of the traditional banking sector. (See the case study *Credit Where It's Due*).

Potentially as disruptive is crowdfunding, the crowdsourced approach to raising money. Crowdsourcing brings together large numbers of people for a common goal, usually over online platforms. The most commonly cited example of crowdsourcing is Wikipedia (despite its founder's objections to the term).[31] Crowdfunding uses this model to enable private individuals to contribute as much or as little as they want to projects, be they commercial, political, charitable, or not-for-profit. Businesses usually offer investors a small share in the business in return. An example of this approach is Kickstarter, which specializes in crowdfunding for creative ventures. As of August 2013, Kickstarter claimed that more than 4.7 million people had used its platform to donate in excess of $757 million to over 47,000 projects since its launch in 2009.[32]

---

## CASE STUDY ▦ Credit Where It's Due

The venerable old Bank of England is the last place you might expect to hear gushing hyperbole over the latest online business model. Yet Andy Haldane, the bank's director of financial stability, predicted in 2012 that peer-to-peer lending could one day actually replace conventional financial institutions.[33]

P2P lending takes place on virtual credit marketplaces. Lenders and borrowers connect directly over sites such as Zopa, Funding Circle, RateSetter, ThinCats, Lending Club, Prosper, and Smava. Individuals and small businesses agree on the rates at which to loan and borrow, bypassing established banks.

The model emerged in the mid-2000s, and its attractiveness since the financial crisis has been evident, as banks have squeezed credit availability hard. Though building from a low base, P2P funding is on the rise. British provider Zopa may have arranged only around £185 million in loans since its inception in 2005, but this shot up by an impressive 800 percent in the four years prior to 2012.[34] Lending Club and Prosper loaned about $1 billion between them in the United States during the six years leading up to 2012.[35]

In the UK, the sector has even become a focus of government economic policy. Business Secretary Vince Cable announced at the end of 2012 that half of a £110 million government plan to help fund small businesses would go to P2P lenders instead of traditional banks.[36]

The model is not without its risks and challenges. Awareness remains low. In addition, the industry is unregulated, offering no protection to lenders from default.[37] One lender, Quakle, closed down under an almost 100 percent default rate.[38]

Yet in essence, as Andy Haldane pointed out, there is "no reason why end-savers and end-investors cannot connect directly." In his view, the hegemony over personal and business lending enjoyed for decades by traditional financial institutions is "in retreat" as a "much more diverse ecosystem" evolves.

And Haldane warns that the endgame may be a stark one for the banks: "The banking middlemen may in time become surplus links in the chain."[39]

---

Virtualization is also driving two important trends set out in Chapter 3. First, there is the increasing customization of products: Online platforms are what enable consumers to design their tailor-made clothes, cards, chocolate flavors, tea blends, photo albums, cookbooks, and calendars. These platforms also provide access to the "long tail" of niche and minority entertainment products exploited by the likes of Amazon and Spotify, which are impossible to commercialize in a bricks-and-mortar environment.

Second, digital technology is also challenging the status quo between corporations and their "suppliers." As BlackBerry manufacturer RIM discovered, companies are finding themselves unable to control the supply ecosystem that produces mobile applications. In 2011, Google ceased providing and supporting its Gmail app for use on BlackBerry devices.[40] Though the search firm gave no reason for the decision, it is difficult to avoid speculating that BlackBerry's declining market share may have been a factor.

## Everything Everywhere

A further characteristic of the virtual era is the "fluidization" of work and the workplace. As previously noted, in today's always-on culture, people and data are accessible anytime, anywhere. In this climate, the workplace no longer needs to be a single bricks-and-mortar location to which staff are obliged to travel. (This is a boon for organizations' sustainability strategies.) Once connected to the corporate intranet, workers can perform tasks wherever they wish. In addition, with the adoption of cloud technology—estimated by Merrill Lynch to have generated $160 billion in global revenues in 2011[41]—the corporate data center can be hosted anywhere in the world.

As a result, work becomes more fluid. And work patterns shift in terms of time as well as space. If there is no longer a reason to be in one place, and people are always on, then the rationale for a rigid working day falls away.

This move from conventional working structures will appeal greatly to digital natives—the same leadership-shy, younger workers we call Generation Y (see Chapter 3). Already reluctant to work beyond their contracted hours, these workers' digital lifestyles call into question the very need for a nine-to-five, office-based regime. As the experience of our friend Arvi demonstrated in Chapter 3, talent can choose how, when, and where it works in the virtual age.

Sure enough, a growing legion of creative workers is taking control of its economic fate by abandoning permanent employment. These "digital bohemians," identified in the book *We Call It Work*,[42] opt for a new form of working lifestyle, using the Internet as their primary mode of communication, information gathering, and self-promotion. The book cites numerous studies suggesting that digital bohemians are more satisfied "working from the comfort of their own computers" than working as permanent employees, even if they earn less money. In the words of the book's coauthor, "the map of how we work in the future is a great deal less charted than many ... might imagine today."[43]

Charting this new map of the world of work is spawning a whole global industry. Sites such as oDesk, Elance, and Fiverr are virtual marketplaces that connect creative and technical freelancers with organizations needing their services, anywhere in the world.[44] The CEO of oDesk, Gary Swart, describes this as a new wave of globalization, claiming that 80 percent of orders commissioned on the site are cross-border.[45]

## IMPLICATIONS OF THE DIGITAL ERA

For businesses, future success will depend on digital capabilities in an online world. Digital knowledge will become the currency of the global economy, placing a huge premium on innovation and intensifying the war for tech talent.

To remain competitive, companies will need to unleash the cost and productivity benefits that digital tools and skills offer, that is, cheaper, easier, and faster communication, cooperation, organization, decision making, and production. And they will need to know how to respond to the opportunities and threats that the digital era will present. Meeting these challenges will take organizations and their leaders into unchartered waters. Equipping companies for the digital age will turn their worlds upside down.

Existing power relationships will be reversed. We have seen how this is happening to market structures, transforming the pecking order between corporations and their customers. The same is true of the traditional chain of command between generations in the workplace, and between employees and employers.

### Young Pretenders

Whether the brave new virtual world sounds like digital heaven or a bewildering technological dystopia depends to some degree on when you were born, for digitization is creating a specific demographic divide.

In contrast to younger generations' inherent ease with technology, for older people, the virtual realm can feel much less like second nature. It can be a struggle to comprehend the virtual world—a mysterious, confusing, and even daunting domain.[46] In an inescapably digital environment, this gives younger employees a clear competitive edge in the workplace, contrary to traditional organizational hierarchies. Younger, tech-savvy individuals find themselves with more influence, and able to have more impact, than 50-something managers, who may lack technological skills and essential knowledge of the sphere in which so much business is done.

## Integrity and Reputation Management

What's more, given the transparency of the virtual domain, employees have the power to hold their managers and organizations accountable as they see fit. Organizations are finding it much more difficult to keep company business, confidential information, and staff misdemeanors behind the firewall. Two of the Big Four global accountancy firms found this out, to their acute embarrassment, when internal emails were leaked in the Republic of Ireland. In remarkably similar and widely reported cases, male employees at PwC and KPMG were revealed to be discussing in emails female colleagues in overtly sexual (and in some cases extremely crude) terms.[47]

Under these conditions, the risk to reputation is magnified. Transgressions and grievances can immediately be posted to the world, instantly damaging corporate and individual credibility.

With their reputations placed in a virtual shop window, organizations will need to be above reproach in their conduct and ethics. This will require openness, sincerity, and integrity from leaders, who will be expected to act as role models, living these values in their every statement and behavior. This is especially true since providing transparency is a role that the online world has been only too happy to embrace.

The people behind the TalentBin search service (see the section *Chasing Shadows*) previously ran the site Unvarnished, which was later rebranded as Honestly.com. This controversial site invited anonymous users to create online profiles of coworkers, past or present, then submit frank, warts-and-all reviews of them.[48] In the face of initial media disapproval,[49] site founder Pete Kazanjy protested that his aim was simply to bring transparency to the issue of reputation, by generating a "productive conversation" and providing an "honest and candid window into a person's professional identity." As he told ABC News: "Professional reputation resides in the brains of all your colleagues and coworkers, and it's very hard to access that."[50]

At the time, many people clearly bought into his view. Honestly.com attracted tens of thousands of active users and postings in its opening months, catching the attention of recruiters and raising $1.2 million in investment capital.[51]

Cubeduel, a sort of rapid-fire version of Honestly.com, proved equally popular when it first appeared in 2011. Cubeduel simply asked visitors to vote for their favorite between two colleagues selected at random via LinkedIn. Users could also see how they themselves rated.[52] Within days of the launch, LinkedIn had to temporarily suspend the "game" because of excessive traffic.[53]

While this online transparency will demand impeccable conduct from companies and their leaders, paradoxically, it might have the opposite effect on workers—especially when they can hide their identities and post criticisms anonymously.

Expectations of reputation will evolve as life is lived increasingly in the digital domain. Our "web shadow" will most likely become less important to our professional futures. As the founder of online technology journal *Tech Crunch* theorized, it will come to "carry less weight" as just about everybody's youthful indiscretions are posted online (often by the individuals themselves). As society adjusts, private behavior that is irrelevant to a person's job will be looked upon more leniently. Drunken photographs from our college days will no longer count against us when we apply for jobs. If pictures of almost every candidate smoking pot can be found online, then to employers, "it just won't be a big deal anymore."[54]

This will not, however, give people carte blanche to behave in any way they please. Integrity will remain the foundation on which reputation is built—and it will still be judged according to a person's sincerity and consistency of values, words, and deeds. Frivolous behavior away from the workplace may be tolerated, but a lack of integrity will not. And in the era of digital transparency, a lack of integrity will be at much higher risk of being exposed (see the section *A Lesson in Integrity*).

### A Lesson in Integrity

The importance and vulnerability of integrity in the digital age were illustrated by a case in Germany that had repercussions among the highest levels of government. In 2012, Education Minister Annette Schavan found her thirty-

*(continued)*

year political career at an end when an anonymous blog exposed apparent plagiarisms in her Ph.D. thesis—written some thirty-three years before.

The allegations were based on software developed to spot plagiarism in doctoral dissertations. Schavan's alma mater, the University of Düsseldorf, launched a nine-month investigation, eventually agreeing with the blogger and revoking her degree. Despite vigorously denying the charge (and announcing that she intended to sue the university), Schavan resigned in February 2013.[55] Until that point, Schavan had enjoyed a long, successful, and scandal-free career. She had carved an impeccable reputation as a passionate and knowledgeable advocate of the scientific community.

No matter. Her integrity was suddenly in question, especially as education minister, and in a culture where academic achievements and titles are highly respected.[56] (There was also the complication of an education minister taking legal action against a university.) So Schavan had to go. Tellingly, she said in an interview about the incident that the damage to her integrity was the most hurtful aspect of the whole episode, far more so than the removal of her degree and title.[57]

## Digital Wisdom

The consequences of digitization will force leaders out of their comfort zones, possibly more than any of the other megatrends we examine. It will oblige them to be open to concepts, ideas, and developments that rely on technology that at times they do not fully comprehend.

Though they may lack technological expertise, executives will need to acquire "digital wisdom." It will be their responsibility to judge the commercial potential of proposed strategies, without necessarily understanding their technical implementation. They will also need to grasp the implications of the execution of these proposals for their organization and its leadership.

## Restless Natives

One of the most pressing questions for leaders will be how to manage the recalcitrant digital generation. These Millennials boast vital technological skills, which will in some ways better equip them to lead in the virtual age than their more experienced senior colleagues. In addition, their digital prowess enables them to multitask more effectively,[58] search and filter large quantities of data quickly and effectively, and make fast decisions based on this information.[59]

Yet for all their crucial knowledge, they have a tendency to over rely on technology, as a result often lacking the social skills and awareness required of corporate leaders. Research by UCLA demonstrated that heavy use of the Internet is changing the way the brains of digital natives work, engendering antisocial attitudes and a heightened tendency toward an inability to concentrate.[60] Successive studies have found that this leaves them insensitive to the subtleties of nonverbal communication (body language, tone of voice, facial expression) during face-to-face contact and less able to develop empathy and interpersonal relations. As the *Harvard Business Review* put it, "young people may be under-stimulating and under-developing the neural pathways necessary for honing social skills."[61]

Not only are these abilities essential in the corporate environment, but they are also critical leadership skills. (And as we shall see in Chapters 7 and 8, they shall become even more vital in a future shaped by the six megatrends discussed in this book.) In addition, as well as lacking these attributes, younger employees have little ambition to take on leadership responsibility in the first place, as noted in Chapter 3. This has the potential to create a worrying leadership vacuum for organizations in the coming years. As we shall see in Chapter 5, up to half of the current crop of senior managers will be due for retirement in the coming few years.[62]

Yet whatever their social skills, younger employees' tech talents are critical assets that will contribute significantly to the success of the businesses they work for. It is crucial that leaders leverage this potential by embracing these workers' creativity, innovation, curiosity, and open-mindedness. It will be necessary to create conditions that encourage them to integrate into the corporate environment their knowledge and unconventional approach to work.

At the same time, leaders will be called on to provide guidance to younger generations, to help steer them through the corporate milieu that is so alien to them. Leaders will need to put the right frameworks in place and give advice on issues such as corporate confidentiality, the boundaries between private and professional life, and how to adopt a professional attitude.

### News Kid on the Block

Since the dawn of the Internet, the multimillion-dollar sale of a promising on-line start-up has periodically hit the headlines. But in March 2013, it was more than the $30 million price tag Yahoo paid for news aggregator service Summly that enthralled the world's media.

Summly's founder, Nick D'Aloisio, was a mere 17 years old at the time of the deal, and he was just 15 when he created the app.[63] While his achievement is undoubtedly impressive, are his fortunes really such a surprise, when the story of D'Aloisio and Summly perfectly encapsulates life in the digital era?

Summly is the perfect app for an always-on, ever-on-the-move gener-ation of people who have never known life without a smartphone. The soft-ware aggregates news stories, condensing them into summaries for display on mobile devices. The 100-word format is ideal for digital natives used to communicating by text, instant messaging, and 140-character tweets.[64]

Indeed, Adam Cahan, a senior vice president at Yahoo, described D'Aloisio as representing "a generational shift" for his ability to "think about what it means to be truly mobile." D'Aloisio's generation, Cahan said, "is not just mobile-first, they are mobile-only. That's a different point of view."[65]

D'Aloisio himself is a prime example of the tech talent that will be es-sential in a digitized world. Cahan called the teenager an "exceptional prod-uct thinker." Not only did the deal make him extremely rich, it also landed him a job at Yahoo's London office. And it was seen as part of the Internet business's strategy to boost its struggling performance by focusing on mo-bile.[66] Expect to see a few more D'Aloisios as the digital era progresses.

## Push Me, Pull You

Incorporating the skills of digital natives presents an opportunity to implement a two-way, cross-generational knowledge transfer.

Younger workers must be encouraged to demystify technology for older colleagues, as the rapid proliferation of digital tools outstrips the development of any formal training on how to use them. This will ne-cessitate new, collaborative learning processes. Early adopters will need to show those less comfortable with technology not only how new devices and applications function but how to use them as pro-ductively as possible.

At the same time, processes should be put in place for more experienced employees to instruct their younger, less socially adept colleagues on navigating corporate life.

## Left to Their Own Devices

Managing the fluid workplace will present two enormous challenges to leaders: (1) ensuring the robustness of the organizations' IT systems, and (2) leading remote teams.

Leaders will be increasingly responsible for securing the corporate IT architecture. Unremitting digitization has triggered a rapid proliferation of the technologies and tools deployed in the workplace, giving rise to a "bring-your-own-device" (BYOD) culture that would have been unthinkable ten years ago. Unable to keep up with the ever expanding range of smartphones and tablets on the market, companies are simply allowing employees to use their own gadgets for work purposes. Telecoms analyst Juniper Research predicted that employee-owned personal mobile devices used in the workplace would reach 350 million globally by 2014—double the total in 2012.[67] This creates a huge security headache for corporations, which need to ensure the confidentiality of sensitive information.

According to a study by IT security company McAfee and Carnegie Mellon University, only 10 percent of businesses describe formulating and enforcing mobile policies as an easy task. As a result, less than a third of employees have a good level of awareness of their company's policy.[68] According to the Cisco study discussed earlier in this chapter, 70 percent of employees knowingly break their organizations' IT security policies on a regular basis.[69] And analyst Ovum found that 28 percent of IT departments ignore workers' BYOD habits, while a further 18 percent are unaware of them—leaving their "own" devices completely unmanaged in almost half of organizations.[70]

It will therefore fall to leaders to establish and communicate clear policies for the use of hardware, software, apps, web tools, and cloud computing in the workplace, to ensure legal compliance and protect privacy and corporate data.

## Wish You Were Here

Leaders also face the challenge of managing remotely. With more and more work done wherever and whenever employees choose, face-to-face contact will increasingly be replaced by virtual communication.

In this context, leaders will need to foster a sense of unity and engagement among staff they seldom see. They must also make possible effective collaboration, knowledge sharing, and decision making between dispersed teams whose members are rarely in the same place at the same time. This will be made all the more difficult by the increasing diversity of team members and elevated staff turnover rates as a result of growing individualism (see Chapter 3).

In an age in which life is lived online and there is little distinction between the public and personal, social media will be a key environment in which to engage remote teams that are increasingly made up of digital natives. Yet surprising numbers of organizations persist in banning access to social networking sites, despite evidence of the damage this can do to motivation and productivity (see the section *In Your Facebook*).

### In Your Facebook

"Humans have a natural proclivity to want what they cannot have." This was the conclusion of a technology journalist and college lecturer observing the behavior of his students in lecture halls where Internet access is barred.

On entering the room, he would see students "hunched over cell phones," updating their Facebook pages. He would find them gathered around the very edges of the hall, trying to log onto a weak Wi-Fi signal emanating from elsewhere. Efforts to block social media are doomed, he blogged, in the face of "our insatiable appetite for sharing information, combined with the nearly limitless ways to access the web."[71]

It is a futility that organizations seem slow to accept. As recently as 2009, more than half of companies still banned the use of social networking sites in the office. A further third allowed only restricted use.[72] It goes without saying that in the digital era, this is a shortsighted and hopelessly outdated approach. Worse, it is potentially damaging.

Contrary to employers' intentions, banning social networking may actually hamper productivity. The University of Copenhagen found that people who were allowed to watch an amusing video then performed better at a simple counting task than others who had been knowingly barred from watching it. The study suggested that willpower is a finite resource: Expending it obeying "no Facebook" policies in the office reduces the ability to focus on work tasks.[73]

If so, the last thing an employer wants is staff investing time and energy in finding ways around the ban and covering their tracks. Research by KPMG found that more than a third of staff working for companies that blocked access had found ways around the firewall.

Barring social media use at work also erodes engagement, further decreasing productivity. KPMG found that 63 percent of workers at organizations that allowed access to social media considered themselves satisfied in their jobs, compared to just 41 percent of those with restricted access.[74]

In addition, such bans place companies at a distinct disadvantage in the coming war for vital digital talent. A further study claimed that 39 percent of 18- to 24-year-olds would consider quitting their job if Facebook was barred from their workplace. A further fifth agreed that they would be annoyed by such a ban.[75]

Perhaps organizations should give careful thought to what Oscar Wilde told us more than a century ago: "The only way to get rid of a temptation is to yield to it." [76]

## Round the Houses

What will be the cumulative effect of remote working, flatter organizational structures, and a virtual and more individualized world that is increasingly dominated by tech-savvy, antiauthoritarian Millennials? Might the absence of the physical trappings of hierarchy instill less respect for the corporate chain of command in younger generations? Will having virtual access to one's managers and peers dilute accountability, encourage more micro-management, or allow people to push decisions up the ladder?

Or will the overall effect be to democratize decision making, opening it up to informal groups that frequently change? This may have advantages, enhancing engagement and encouraging innovation. But will it also render decision making slower and more laborious?

To address this, leaders will need to establish the right conditions for effective group decisions. This will require absolute clarity over each team member's objectives and responsibilities—that is, the bounded autonomy described in Chapter 3.

## THE DEMANDS OF THE DIGITAL ERA

Here is a summary of the key challenges organizations and their leaders are facing in the digital era.

1. *Bridging the gap.* Organizations will need to address the digital divide between younger and older generations in the workplace, as well as digital natives' less traditional attitudes toward corporate life and leadership roles. Organizations will need to embrace the creativity, curiosity, and innovation that digital natives bring, while providing frameworks, guidance, and coaching to help them cope with corporate life and acquire the necessary social skills.

2. *Virtual working.* New structures, hierarchies, and IT infrastructures will be required to enable work to be carried out anywhere in the world, at any time, and to allow dispersed teams to collaborate effectively. Organizations will also need to figure out the infrastructure and security implications of an ever increasing proliferation of devices, many of them owned by employees rather than the company.

3. *Digital wisdom.* Leaders will face the challenge of making decisions on and rolling out programs that they may not fully comprehend. They will need to understand the implications of these decisions in terms of structures and processes and the skills and abilities required.

4. *Remote leadership and loyalist management.* Leaders must find ways to organize, manage, and motivate teams that rarely meet and are located all over the world. Leading disparate groups will demand new decision-making processes and new ways to foster loyalty.

5. *Integrity and reputation management.* In a transparent world, where reputations can be publicly trashed at the click of a mouse, organizations will need to behave impeccably. For leaders, this will demand high levels of openness, sincerity, and integrity, which will mean consistency of values, words, and deeds.

# 5 Social Insecurity: Demographic Change

> *"If [population growth] continued at this rate ... by 2600
> we would all be standing literally shoulder to shoulder."*
> —**Stephen Hawking,** physicist and cosmologist

## AT A GLANCE ■ DEMOGRAPHIC CHANGE

### Five Essential Points

1. *The world's population is expanding and aging in parallel.* The global populace is expanding, particularly in developing and emerging markets, and rapidly maturing, especially in the industrialized world. Both trends are forecast to continue and even intensify well into this century. International migration is also on the rise and will be magnified by an array of "push" and "pull" factors in the coming decades.

2. *Demographic change is placing great pressure on social structures and (especially Western) companies.* National welfare systems are being stretched to the breaking point by growing populations, as well as by faltering support ratios (numbers of working-age adults to dependent citizens) as a result of aging. In addition, many Western societies (and also China) are maturing beyond the point at which they will begin to perform less effectively in socioeconomic terms.

3. *The war for talent will intensify.* An aging global population will mean a shrinking global workforce, stepping up the competition for specialized skills, high perform-

ers, and effective leaders. Corporations and even nations will find themselves in a global war for key talent.

4. *Workforces will diversify as companies adapt.* Successful organizations will need to develop an increasingly diverse workforce to ensure an adequate talent pipeline. This will mean recruiting men and women of all ages and from a variety of cultural backgrounds, relying on migration where necessary. Working practices, employment conditions, and HR procedures will evolve to reflect the varying needs of different ages, ethnicities, and genders.

5. *Managing diversity will be a core leadership competency.* Leaders will need to display exceptional sensitivity to their employees' needs and abilities to earn the loyalty and maximize the performance of diverse teams. This will demand a thorough knowledge and depth of understanding of their teams.

## Five Questions Business Leaders Should Ask

1. Is our employer brand competitive in the global talent market?

2. Do our recruitment drives attract as diverse a pool of candidates as possible?

3. Will we be able to create the tangible and intangible conditions to attract and retain talent of all ages and ethnicities? Will these conditions be compelling to male and female employees alike?

4. How do we equip our leaders to manage and inspire an increasingly diverse workforce?

5. How do we ensure that older and younger employees learn from each other?

---

It took from the dawn of humanity until the early 1800s—tens of thousands of years—for the number of human beings on earth to reach 1 billion.[1] It then took little more than two centuries for the number to soar an amazing sevenfold. On the first day of 2013, the U.S. Census Bureau's online world population counter put the total at 7,056,700,180.[2] As if that wasn't startling enough, in less than four decades from now, it is estimated that there may be up to 3 billion more people added to the global population.[3]

And as rapidly as the world's population is expanding, it is also maturing. By 2030, half of the people in Western Europe will be over age 50—a quarter of them over 65. Life expectancy across the continent will average 90 years.[4] And the aging of the population is not merely a Western phenomenon. In Japan, adult diapers already outsell children's.[5]

The world's demographic makeup is changing in other ways, too. In 2011, the National Geographic Society produced the composite face of the planet's "typical" person: a 28-year-old Han Chinese male. At the same time, the organization forecast that by 2030, the average human will be Indian.[6] A few decades from now, humanity will look very different from the way it looks today.

## THE MEGATREND: DEMOGRAPHIC CHANGE

Demographic analysis is a vital component of organizational intelligence. Businesses invest enormous amounts of time and money in understanding the size and structure of the markets for their products and services and the nature of their target customers. Similarly, public bodies plan their provision of services around the demographics of their localities. Yet in developed and emerging societies alike, these profiles are changing before our very eyes.

Demographic change is primarily a combination of three concurrent phenomena: population growth, aging societies, and increasing migration. As these trends alter the dynamics of the world's populace, they will wreak havoc on organizations' product and employment markets.

### The Great Leap Upward

The global population is forecast to reach 8 billion by 2025,[7] and estimates for 2050 see 10.6 billion souls living on the planet.[8] The swelling numbers are predominantly the result of high fertility rates in emerging and developing countries. (China is the exception because of the government's one-child policy; see the section *The Last Little Emperors?*) Births in these regions are in moderate decline, forecast to fall from 2.9 births per woman in 2005 to 2.0 per woman in 2050. But combined with increasing life expectancy, this is sufficiently high to sustain rapid population growth.

As a result, population numbers are booming in these parts of the world. In 2005, just seven countries accounted for half of the global population expansion. Six of them were from developing and emerging societies (Bangladesh, China, India, Indonesia, Nigeria, and Pakistan).[9] Between now and 2050, developing nations will account for 95 percent of global population growth.[10]

In contrast, populations in the developed world are stabilizing, with some even shrinking. Robust growth in life expectancy in the developed world is being offset by birth rates of just 1.6 births per woman across the world's industrialized nations.[11] According to the UN, Europe's population will fall by some 44 million between 2000 and 2050.[12]

## The Last Little Emperors?

China's "temporary" measure to control its swelling population has become possibly the world's most enduring and controversial exercise in social engineering. Still in place more than a quarter of a century after its introduction, the country's one-child policy has provoked fascination and outrage in equal measure.

The state's "family planning policy" is far from universal, applying mainly to ethnic Han Chinese in urban areas. Foreigners and ethnic minorities are exempt, as are rural residents, couples whose first child is female, and couples who are both only children. China's National Population and Family Planning Commission states that only 36 percent of people are affected.[13] Nonetheless, the restrictions have certainly had the intended effect.

When they were introduced by Premier Deng Xiaoping in 1979, China was experiencing runaway population growth. The number of people had mushroomed by 75 percent between 1949 and 1976.[14] Though estimates vary, experts now agree that the years of population control have succeeded in averting hundreds of millions of births.[15] Official estimates—disputed outside China[16]—put the total of prevented births at 400 million as of 2011.[17]

The policy has had undoubted social, economic, and psychological side effects, ranging from the undesirable to the outright shocking. Some pose a genuine threat to China's economic health.

The Chinese Academy of Social Sciences estimated in 2001 that 119 boys were being born for every 100 baby girls, which would consign more than 24 million Chinese men of marrying age to bachelorhood by 2020, since there will not be women available for them to marry.[18] (See the section *The Rarer Sex* for more on gender imbalance in Asia.) Also, from a socioeconomic perspective, the policy is depriving China's workforce of a vital chunk of female talent.

The policy has also been blamed for China's so-called 4-2-1 problem. Chinese tradition dictates that families take care of their older generations. As they become parents themselves, only children born under the one-child policy are therefore having to support two parents and four grandparents.[19]

Much has also been made of the psychological impact on the only children born since 1979—the "precious snowflake" generation,[20] lavished with love and attention by their parents and without siblings to share life with. Chinese society has to live with the "overweening sense of [their] own importance" that this is said to have imbued. Some employers now actually bar single children from applying for jobs.[21]

In 2013, a study suggested that this "little emperor" effect could hold serious implications for China's economic future. Australian academics ran socioeconomic experiments among around 400 Chinese people born before and after 1979. They found that those conceived under the one-child policy were significantly more pessimistic while far less conscientious, competitive, risk-averse, trusting, and trustworthy.[22] They were also more likely to display neurotic tendencies.[23] The researchers concluded that these people were "less likely to be in more risky occupations like self-employment" as a result, implying a "decline in entrepreneurial ability."[24]

Could China's giant social experiment prove an Achilles' heel to its growing economic dominance? Certainly, opinion is growing among the country's most influential academics, demographers, and policy advisers that it is time to put an end to the regulation.[25] And there have been discussions at the government level about potentially scrapping it altogether. As a visiting scholar at Fudan University in Shanghai told Britain's *Guardian* newspaper: "Policy change is inevitable .... It will come."[26]

## Survival of the Oldest

In 2002, the UN published a report portraying population aging in terms that constitute almost the very definition of a megatrend.[27] The UN described aging as "unprecedented," warning that the world's populace is maturing at rates "without parallel in human history," and that the twenty-first century will witness even *more* rapid aging. The study called the trend "pervasive—a global phenomenon affecting every man, woman and child."

In addition, population aging is "enduring," the UN said, asserting that "we will not return to the young populations that our ancestors knew." As a result, the trend has "profound implications for many facets of human life."

The report also highlighted that the older population is growing faster than the overall population in practically all regions of the world. In the latter half of the twentieth century, the number of over-60s had almost tripled, from 205 million globally in 1950 to 606 million in 2000.

The graying of the global population is a further consequence of the same trends driving its inexorable growth: falling birth rates, combined with extended life expectancy. Between 1950 and 2010, life expectancy globally increased by twenty years, to 68 years of age.[28] As a result, the global median age is set to rise from 28 years in 2005 to 38 in 2050.[29] By 2050, over-65s are predicted to represent more than a quarter of the industrialized world's population. While Japan is currently the only country where this group represents more than 30 percent of the populace, this will be so for some sixty-four nations by 2050.[30] By 2020, over-65s will outnumber children under age 5 globally for the first time ever.[31]

By that time, however, existing life expectancy forecasts may already be outdated, for the relentless rise in the human lifespan is making it immensely difficult to do accurate forecasting.[32] As recently as the 1980s, demographers were anticipating that the rise in life expectancy would slow to an eventual stop.[33]

The age to which people can hope to live is being pushed up across the world by progress in medical and nutritional science[34]—

advances that are set to make quantum leaps thanks to the technologies we shall explore in Chapter 6. And as Globalization 2.0 tips a greater proportion of the world's population into relative affluence (see Chapter 1), more people will gain access to improved healthcare, better quality food, healthier lifestyle options, and more active leisure pursuits.

## The Grayest Country on Earth

Home to the world's oldest population, Japan is, in the words of *The Economist*, "heading into a demographic vortex."[35] Indeed, Japan's demographics are deeply concerning. With the world's longest life expectancy, at 83 years,[36] Japan is aging faster than any other nation: By 2050, four in ten Japanese people will be 65 or older.

As a result, the country has been the first to experience population shrinkage due to natural causes.[37] In 2011, its population contracted by 204,000, the fastest rate since 1947. (Around 10 percent of this was the result of the catastrophic earthquake and tsunami in Tohoku in March of that year.[38]) Over the next forty years, the population is forecast to fall by 30 percent, or some 38 million people. At this rate, by the year 2050, the working-age population of Japan will be smaller than in 1950.[39]

And to up the ante, Japan's baby-boom generation is about to reach retirement age—a development that will "rock the foundations" of the country's creaking social security system, as one government demographer put it.[40]

Japan is facing the demographic abyss while mired in debt, the result of the economic collapse of the early 1990s and the protracted stagnation of the subsequent so-called lost decades. Already saddled with a 200 percent debt-to-GDP ratio[41] (one of the highest in the world[42]), the government will be required to spend almost 34 percent of the national income on welfare by 2025, according to official forecasts, in part due to its aging population.[43]

In 2000 the UN calculated that in order to maintain an adequate worker-to-retiree ratio, the Japanese government would need to either raise the retirement age to 77 or admit 10 million immigrants each year for half a century.[44] An almost completely homogeneous society, Japan currently has zero net immigration.[45]

## Golden Years?

The rapid expansion of the global population is clearly a cause for concern—not least where the environmental pressures covered in Chapter 2 are concerned. But is the steady rise of the world's median age necessarily a bad thing?

Eventually, yes. In a blog for the U.S. National Intelligence Council, American demographer Richard Cincotta explains that societies age over four structural phases. In the "youthful" phase, the median age is very low, under 25 years. The "intermediate" phase is marked by a median age of 25 to 35. As this stretches to 35 to 45, a society enters its "mature" phase. "Post-maturity" is reached as the median age drifts beyond 45.

According to Cincotta, nations perform best in socioeconomic terms during the "sweet spot" through the intermediate phase and the first of half of the mature phase. During this period, support ratios (working-age adults per dependent citizens) are at their highest, countries generally achieve sustained economic prosperity and political stability, and near-universal secondary education is usually attained.

In their post-mature phase, these benefits tail off, as a growing elderly population exits the workforce, draws on pensions and savings, and relies more heavily on the state, for healthcare in particular.[46]

As the experience of Japan illustrates (see the section *The Grayest Country on Earth*), the aging population exerts increasing pressure on a society's working-age population by eroding its support ratio. And as Cincotta signals, the decline in working-age adults per retiree in Europe and East Asia over the next twenty years will be "unprecedented." Over a fifth of Japanese people were over 65 in 2005.[47] In England, the number of over-65s is forecast to increase by more than half, and over-85s to double, by 2030.[48] And between 2005 and 2025, the number of people aged 15 to 64 is projected to fall by 7 percent in Germany and 9 percent in Italy.

This structural shift poses a severe threat to state welfare systems—a threat the *Financial Times* described as "bad enough to be frightening" in the case of some European states. The newspaper cited a "fiscal sustainability index" created by the Center for Strategic and

International Studies by analyzing demographics and welfare obligations. On this basis, Italy, Spain, France, and Holland were in worse financial shape than the "notorious demographic bust" that Japan is facing.[49]

Similarly, prior to the 2012 U.S. presidential election, *Forbes* described the U.S. Social Security system as "desperately broke," pointing to $20.5 trillion in unfunded obligations.[50] Combined, the employee pension funds of the fifty U.S. states were running a deficit of $1.26 trillion in 2009, up 26 percent from the previous financial year.[51]

As a result of such developments, governments are scrambling to extend the working lives of their populations. Retirement ages are being phased upward in the United States, Germany, France, and the UK, among other countries. Britain's pensions minister rang in 2013 by declaring that "the era of early retirement is over" in Britain, and warning that the government had no idea when younger workers could expect to retire.[52]

Richard Cincotta warns that the United States, Japan, and Germany are already in their post-mature phase. And no less than twenty-nine nations will be there by 2030 (twenty-six of them in Europe), with China only a couple of years away. In 2007, up to 75 percent of U.S. senior management were eligible for retirement by 2010, a rate that was only marginally better in Europe. Half of the top managers in America's largest 500 companies could retire in the next five years.[53]

## The Rarer Sex

In late 2012, an international furor began raging over the alleged rape and murder of a 23-year-old woman by five men on a bus in New Delhi. The incident provoked widespread condemnation, weeks of demonstrations in India, and a wave of soul-searching in the local and international media about the role and treatment of women in Indian society. The Australian newspaper *The Age* landed the blame for India's frightening prevalence of sexual assaults on women—twenty-two rapes per hour—squarely on its "masculinized" gender ratio.[54]

*(continued)*

According to leading academics, masculinization is the result of the "missing females" phenomenon, a consequence of gender bias in parts of Asia, North Africa, and Eastern Europe. Indian economist and Nobel Prize winner Amartya Sen estimated in 1990 that "a great deal more than 100 million women" were in effect missing from the population across Asia and North Africa. Sen attributed this to the relative neglect of women's healthcare and nutrition, compared to that afforded to men.[55]

Monica Das Gupta, a former World Bank demographer and authority on gender bias, analyzed data across three Asian societies from 1981 to 1992. She found 34 missing girls per 1,000 female births in South Korea, 45 in India, and up to 46 in China.[56] Das Gupta pointed to a consistent pattern of "manipulation of family composition by parents," which she described as "evidence of parental discrimination against daughters across East and South Asia."[57] Indeed, India's own 2011 census showed that more than 37 million girls up to age 6 were missing from the population.[58]

Das Gupta attributes the missing females phenomenon to a preference for sons, which is a culturally ingrained predilection that has survived "sweeping economic and social changes" to remain as deeply embedded in industrialized societies like South Korea as it has been in rural India and China.

Son preference drives discrimination in favor of male children at difference stages of the lifecycle: prior to conception, by ceasing to have children once a son is produced; during pregnancy, through sex-selective abortion; at birth, by sex-selective infanticide; and during early childhood, through neglect. This generates a disproportionate excess of boys over girls compared to societies without son preference.

The motives for son preference are deeply cultural. Patrilineal social orders in Asia confer unequal status on the genders. Bearing a son is considered more prestigious, lowering the importance of women. Woven into the social fabric, this bias has proved impervious to increased affluence, access to education, and urbanization.

Economic factors also play a role. In many rural societies, men are considered more suited to working in the fields. In India, they are also "cheaper" when it comes to marriage, given the need to provide dowries for daughters.[59]

Moral debates aside, there are evident pitfalls to gender bias, not least the correlation between crime and a male-dominated population, as *The*

*Age* suggested. As male-female ratios have climbed, crime rates have doubled in China, while rape has proved to be India's fastest growing offense, up a terrifying 792 percent since 1971.[60]

There is also a question mark over the demographic logic of gender bias in aging societies in which women are expected to tend to their elders' needs. If females decline in number as the aged increase, eventually men will need to take on some responsibility for eldercare—taking yet more people out of the workforce.

But whatever the rights and wrongs, and despite some early evidence that masculinization may be beginning to slow in China, India, and South Korea,[61] gender bias remains what Amartya Sen called "one of the more momentous, and neglected, problems facing the world today."[62]

## Peak Flow

During the twenty-five years prior to 2008, the number of people living outside their country of birth almost doubled.[63] The figure rose by 37 percent in the two decades before 2010, when the total reached 214 million. More than 60 percent of these people had migrated to developed countries, the largest number (70 million) settling in Europe.[64]

Given the economic and environmental developments highlighted in the first two chapters of this book, it is a reasonable assumption that the push and pull factors that drive migration will intensify in the coming decades. Environmental catastrophes had already created some 50 million migrants by 2010[65]—a trend we can expect to increase in frequency in the foreseeable future (see Chapter 2). And if the German Army's predictions are to be believed (also see Chapter 2), the impending exhaustion of oil supplies will bring about widespread economic slump, famine, political instability, civil unrest, and even armed conflict—a recipe for migration on an unimaginable scale.

Peak oil notwithstanding, Globalization 2.0 will generate opportunities to pursue greater wealth and a higher standard of living in a growing number of economies (see Chapter 1). This will prompt economic migrants to seek their place among the emerging middle classes in Asia, Latin America, and Africa. The successful early settlement of the first waves of such migrants will likely feed further flows, as those left behind will be encouraged to escape the constraints of their home countries.[66]

## IMPLICATIONS OF DEMOGRAPHIC CHANGE

As Japan's market for adult diapers demonstrates, demographic change is transforming companies' customer bases beyond recognition. It is changing the dynamics of a global marketplace that is growing, graying, increasing in age diversity, and undergoing unprecedented migratory movements.

Sophisticated business and management information will be required to sense the opportunities and threats that will emerge as a result. What glocalized market opportunities (see Chapter 1) will migratory trends generate? What exactly will aging mean for the healthcare, pharmaceutical, and medical equipment markets? What are the product design implications of a maturing population?

This latter question should challenge consumer industries in particular. How will they adapt products to the weakening eyesight, dexterity, and mental capacities of their customers? What will be the impact on consumer technology, which has thrived on exploiting Moore's Law,[67] packing more and more features into smaller and more complex devices?

### Star Wars

The demographic change megatrend also poses some serious internal challenges for organizations. Though humanity's numbers are multiplying, its relentless aging presents a troubling development for developed economies in particular: a shrinking working-age population.

For businesses, one consequence of a contracting workforce is an increasing scarcity of skilled labor, and therefore an intensifying war for talent. As the baby boomer generation reaches retirement age, organizations are facing a "leadership cliff." In 2007, a Hay Group report on the war for talent[68] highlighted the following:

■   Some 97 percent of organizations reported significant leadership gaps, according to the Corporate Leadership Council.

■   As many as 40 percent described this leadership shortfall as "acute."

■   The National College of School Leaders in the UK warned that the country is running out of head teachers (i.e., school principals).

■   The American Medical Association feared that 60 percent of CEOs in the healthcare sector would be eligible to retire within five years.

■   Up to 75 percent of senior management in the United States would be eligible for retirement by 2010, including 50 percent of CEOs.

What's more, population growth is being driven primarily in developing and emerging nations, where many people lack ready access to digital technology. This access is improving as economies become wealthier. But in the short term, we might expect to see a global shortage of the tech-savvy talent that is vital to the digital age.

Organizations will have to work harder to attract, integrate, and develop an adequate pool of potential star performers, which will include (as we shall see) international migrants, older workers, a higher proportion of women, and employees with eldercare as well as childcare responsibilities. This will mean finding new approaches to recruiting and identifying talent (see the case study *Growing Their Own*).

---

## CASE STUDY ▨ Growing Their Own

"Some of our people have done incredible things with their careers," claims Jan Schmidt-Dohna, managing director at Mubea. Mubea is a German automotive supplier, earning more than €1.5 billion ($1.8 billion) in annual revenues and with 8,000 employees at twenty locations worldwide. Its clients include just about every car manufacturer you might care to name. Yet despite its strength, the company has a talent challenge to contend with.

Mubea faces two key hurdles when it comes to recruiting talented engineers and technicians. The first problem is that as a behind-the-scenes supplier, the Mubea

*(continued)*

brand lacks the traction of a major OEM (original equipment manufacturer). The company's stock-in-trade is what Schmidt-Dohna calls "deeply technical, conventional engineering." The second problem is that the company's headquarters is located in a remote area, far from the major German cities that typically attract top engineering talent.

In response, Mubea has developed a homegrown approach to talent management to meet its specific recruitment and development needs. Mubea identifies high potentials early on—before they even begin their careers—and then works hard to develop them and provide opportunities they might not experience elsewhere.

Through links with German universities, Mubea forges connections with engineering students who show the potential to thrive in a complex, rapidly evolving global business. The company offers them internships, research projects, or placements that combine work with academic study.

A second strand of Mubea's talent strategy addresses its need for technicians. Like most German engineering firms, the company recruits these from the country's internationally respected apprenticeship program. But unusually, Mubea spends a great deal of effort on developing them for management roles, which are generally the preserve of engineering graduates. This provides rare career opportunities for employees without an academic background—openings that would not ordinarily be available to them at an OEM.

"Unusually, there is no glass ceiling here if you don't have an engineering degree," Schmidt-Dohna explains. "We give talented technicians the opportunity to take on international assignments, develop management skills, and progress to leadership roles."

According to Schmidt-Dohna, Mubea's approach to talent management produces the vast majority of its managers. "Internal development and promotion are a guiding principle for us—almost a mantra," he affirms.

To support its rapidly growing worldwide presence, Mubea is now rolling out its talent strategy globally. The company is founding an apprenticeship scheme similar to the German model in every country in which it operates, allowing local technicians to attain the German professional diploma.

---

The talent crisis will also oblige organizations to provide the lifelong learning and development opportunities necessary to building and maintaining the requisite talent pipeline.

## Brain Cycle

As talent becomes scarcer than ever before, the market for highly qualified individuals will become truly global. Companies will come to rely on international migration to identify and recruit the high potentials they need.

At one point, this practice caused a "brain drain" from emerging to industrialized economies, where pay and conditions are more beneficial. According to a study by Ohio State University, one in eight of the world's scientists most frequently cited between 1981 and 2003 were born in developing countries; 80 percent of them moved to the developed world.[69]

However, a "brain cycle" is now emerging, as domestic competitors begin to dominate in emerging markets and offer more competitive packages. Experienced, onetime migrants will look to return to their home countries, taking with them the knowledge and competencies they learned in the West—a development with the potential to further accelerate local development.

In 2000, 100 percent of Indian business school graduates said they preferred to work for a Western multinational rather than a local organization. By 2010, this figure had been cut in half. Among their Chinese counterparts, the proportion plummeted from 55 percent to just 18 percent in three years between 2007 and 2010.[70]

A shrinking workforce will also pitch national policies against each other in the global competition for talent, particularly where nationally significant sectors such as science and healthcare are concerned. China's "One Thousand Talents Scheme" aims to recruit the world's best researchers from abroad and persuade Chinese academics to return, in a bid to boost innovation. Meanwhile, the European Union offers incentives to work within its European Research Area scientific program.[71]

Negotiating these is likely to prove strained and contentious,[72] potentially giving rise to geopolitical tensions.

## Age Concern

Organizations will also need to learn to cope with the changing nature and needs of an aging workforce. In the face of widening age diversity, companies will need to design and implement effective, bidirectional knowledge transfer programs, to address the growing intergenerational divide highlighted in Chapter 3.

Age-appropriate employment models will become commonplace. For instance, working relationships with more senior employees may become more fluid. As they reach retirement age, some older workers will find their knowledge and experience increasingly scarce, especially in specialized fields (such as science and engineering) where technical skills are already at a premium. They may consider semi-retirement or take on consultant roles in order to take advantage of this demand and continue to help their former employers.

Family-friendly approaches will be required to attract the widest possible pool of talent, young and old. This will mean implementing HR processes that support staff needs at both ends of the age spectrum, for example, those needing to look after older relatives as well as those with children.

In 2010, the University of Pittsburgh analyzed more than 17,000 U.S. employees of an American multinational, finding that 12 percent had care responsibilities for an older person. These workers reported poorer health than their non-caregiver colleagues. They were significantly more prone to depression, diabetes, hypertension, and pulmonary disease, regardless of age, gender, or job. They were costing their employer 8 percent more in healthcare as a result, equivalent to $13.4 billion per year, extrapolating from all U.S. companies.[73]

Companies and governments are beginning to recognize this increasing pressure on workers to help look after elderly relatives. Help with eldercare now features in the benefits packages of U.S. corporations such as IBM and HP.[74] In addition, the German and Swedish governments have introduced legislation to grant employees the right to periods of "care leave," during which employers must continue to pay 75 to 80 percent of their salary.[75]

## Breaking Glass

Aging and migration will not be the only factors driving increasing diversity in the workforce. Demographic change may also help to crack the glass ceiling that women face in the workplace. Businesses will no longer be able to marginalize female candidates when it comes to filling senior positions—adding to the political pressures already on them in this regard, especially in Europe. The global talent scarcity will compel companies to open up their boardrooms more readily to women.

Yet companies will still face a significant challenge to coax female (and some male) talent into leadership positions. Family considerations may take greater priority in the highly individualized employment market outlined in Chapter 3, while board roles and culture may simply not appeal to some women (and some men). Gender-blind employment conditions and HR procedures will be needed to strike the desired balance between family and career, especially among the upper levels of organizations.

## Duty of Care

According to a recent book, *Winning the War for Talent in Emerging Markets: Why Women Are the Solution*, emerging markets have at their disposal a potent weapon in the global war for talent: their educated and ambitious women.[76] These women definitely exist. As coauthor Sylvia Ann Hewlett told *Forbes* magazine, 65 percent of university graduates in China are women, and in Brazil the proportion is 60 percent.[77] India boasts a similar rate.[78]

What's more, according to Hewlett, more than 80 percent of women in India and 70 percent in China and Brazil claim to aspire to senior management roles. (Just 36 percent of American women have such high-powered intentions.[79])

And these are not futile ambitions on the part of Chinese and Brazilian women. Hewlett points out that in India in 2009, 11 percent of CEOs were women.[80] According to the World Economic Forum, Brazil achieved the same proportion in 2010.[81] These rates put the 3 percent of women in America's Fortune 500 and the UK's FTSE 100[82] to shame. Fully 91 percent of Chinese businesses have women in senior leadership positions.[83]

Look below the surface, however, and there are considerable social constraints on women in emerging economies that create barriers for female

*(continued)*

talent. Childcare, perhaps surprisingly, is not the main issue. Emerging societies tend to value extended family, and nurseries and domestic help come relatively cheap. But significantly, in the context of demographic change, a woman's duty to take care of her parents and in-laws is often the greater constraint.[84] A staggering 70 percent of highly educated women in BRIC countries have substantial eldercare responsibilities.[85]

And despite the inroads made into boardrooms, gender bias also works against women. Unequal treatment has prompted around half of female workers in India, China, and Brazil to consider resigning. Grueling 60- to 70-hour weeks are a disincentive, as are basic safety fears for commuting females.

In their book Hewlett and her coauthor, Ripa Rashid, set out four key strategies for companies to help women to overcome these hurdles. These are (1) stretch assignments and international postings to maintain women's ambitions; (2) an infrastructure for female leadership, to help combat gender bias; (3) providing safe transportation; and (4) flexible work arrangements to accommodate family obligations.[86] The authors argue that by executing such strategies, employers can be catalysts not only for change in the workplace but for a more fundamental social and cultural evolution in emerging economies.[87]

## Diverse Challenges

Unprecedented workforce diversity will dramatically redefine the roles of senior leaders. Widening age diversity in the workforce will require sensitive handling. Leaders will be charged with bringing out the best in the different generations within their teams. More customized, age-appropriate working practices (e.g., less rigid hours) and task distribution will be essential. It will also be the job of leaders to steer the most effective course between the greater expertise and experience of older staff and the more adventurous attitudes and risk-inclined behaviors of younger team members.

All of this will require that leaders have a thorough knowledge of each of the individuals under their management, in order to make decisions and allocate tasks that play to their strengths.

Increased migration will create more internationalized teams. Fostering intercultural (as well as intergenerational) teamwork and collaboration will therefore be a key objective for leaders, as will gaining the commitment of men and women of varying ages, cultures, and values. This will demand strong intercultural understanding and carefully adapted team-building strategies from the leaders responsible for integrating and engaging their people.

Leaders will need to find ways to encourage more women and cultural minorities to take on senior positions, for example, by creating less conventional leadership profiles that take account of individuals' family considerations. Mentoring programs may be necessary to strengthen retention among ethnic minorities and women.

In addition, establishing lifelong loyalty will be crucial. As more senior workers' skills and experience become scarcer and more valuable, extended loyalty programs will be needed to encourage "wise old heads" to continue to contribute informally to their organizations. Leaders will not be able to afford to burn bridges.

## THE DEMANDS OF DEMOGRAPHIC CHANGE

Here is a summary of the key challenges leaders face from demographic change.

1.   *Enabling new levels of diversity.* Loyalty and commitment—not to mention performance—will depend on an organization's ability to let each team member thrive, whatever his or her nationality, cultural background, gender, age, personality, approach to work, experience, skills, or abilities. Organizations will need to provide the structures, policies, and environment to harness such considerable diversity.

2.   *Connecting generations and cultures.* By fostering understanding, collaboration, and knowledge exchange, leaders will play a pivotal role in overcoming divisions between generations and cultures, and ensuring that they all work productively together.

3.   *Managing and motivating diverse teams.* A challenge for leaders will be to understand what is and what is not negotiable from each individual's cultural and personal perspective. Considerable listening skills and empathy will be required to identify what motivates each team member. A single rallying cry to the whole team will no longer suffice. Leaders will have to learn to live with ambiguity and base decisions on conflicting trends and demands.

# 6 Great Expectations?: Technological Convergence

*"Anything invented before your 15th birthday is the order of nature. That's how it should be. Anything invented between your 15th and 35th birthday is new and exciting, and you might get a career there. Anything invented after that day, however, is against nature and should be prohibited."*
—**Douglas Adams,** novelist

## AT A GLANCE ▪ TECHNOLOGICAL CONVERGENCE

**Five Essential Points**

1. *Technological progress is likely to transform many aspects of our lives.* Advanced scientific disciplines—nanotechnology, biotechnology, IT, cognitive science, and robotics—will drive major innovations in important areas such as healthcare, logistics, and nutrition.

2. *Convergence will drive the greatest innovations.* The coming together of these scientific fields will make possible the greatest leaps forward, transforming some industries, threatening others, and creating a myriad of new product markets.

3. *R&D will take center stage.* Research and development will become an interdisciplinary function, requiring an even higher skill base. Making sure that R&D has the right mix of skills will be a key leadership responsibility.

4. *Convergence will necessitate new levels and forms of collaboration.* Diverse scientific disciplines, businesses, academia, and even competing companies will need to work together on pioneering research programs. Meanwhile, companies will need to do away with conventional organizational boundaries to enable unprecedented levels of collaboration and knowledge sharing.

5. *Societies will debate the ethical boundaries of technological advancement.* Societies will need to question the rights and wrongs of some areas of innovation—for example, the potential to slow aging and enhance human cognition—and set a framework for acceptable progress. Businesses will need to respect this debate.

### Five Questions Business Leaders Should Ask

1. How do we ensure that our leaders have the skills and systems to keep abreast of scientific innovations?

2. What are the implications of innovations in NBIC (nanotechnology, biotechnology, information technology, and cognitive science) and GNR (genetics, nanotechnology, and robotics) for our markets and employees?

3. What additional skills does our R&D function require in this new era of technological convergence? How do we acquire these?

4. Will our organizations allow intensive internal and external collaboration? Do our leaders have the necessary collaborative skills?

5. How do we ensure that our leaders are attuned to society's ethical concerns and expectations when it comes to technological advancement?

---

Back in the 1940s, tough-talking American comic strip detective Dick Tracy captivated readers by speaking into a high-tech gadget that seemed unthinkable at the time. Tracy communicated via a two-way radio that he wore on his wrist. This futuristic vision has become reality with Samsung launching "smartwatches."[1]

Try googling "real-life Star Trek inventions." You'll find that there are hundreds of sites expounding the once unimaginable technologies featured in the science-fiction TV series that have since become part of everyday life. Examples include the PC and tablet, automatic doors, videoconferencing, MRI scanning, painless injections, voice and bio-metric recognition, PDAs, cell phones, and wireless earpieces.[2]

The technological future has always looked dazzling when viewed from the present. As renowned futurologist, inventor, and sci-fi author Arthur C. Clarke remarked: "Any sufficiently advanced technology is indistinguishable from magic."

The world we live in today would have been inconceivable to our parents—and it was ever thus. As noted earlier, in 1907 the journal of the U.S. National Association of Teachers declared that "pen and ink will never replace the pencil."[3] Almost ninety years later, a teacher on a district committee proclaimed, every bit as emphatically, that "teachers will never use emails."

Only a few decades ago, the notion of withdrawing money from a machine in the wall, or listening to a device in the car that tells us where to go, would have seemed the stuff of sci-fi. So would the idea that just about all of the knowledge most of us could ever need would be available anytime, anywhere, *on a phone.*

It is important to retain this perspective as we consider the technologies set to transform many aspects of life in the twenty-first century.

## THE MEGATREND: TECHNOLOGICAL CONVERGENCE

The technological fields in question are variously grouped as NBIC (nanotechnology, biotechnology, IT, and cognitive science) and GNR (genetics, nanotechnology, and robotics). Before exploring the poten-tial of NBIC and GNR technologies, it is worth pausing to define what is meant by each of the fields they refer to.

- *Nanotechnology:* The manipulation of matter at the atomic and molecular level. It is so named because it is generally concerned with materials and devices measuring up to 100 nanometers (a nanometer is one-billionth of a meter). Nanotechnology makes possible the creation of new chemical syntheses, materials, and fine particles, with applications as diverse as medicine, nutrition, car manufacturing, food production, computing, and sports equipment.

- *Biotechnology:* The creation or modification of products and processes using living organisms or biological systems. Strictly speaking, biotechnology is as old as humanity itself. Activities as basic as the cultivation of crops, domestication of animals, and fermentation of alcohol come under this definition. In modern parlance, however, the term includes scientific disciplines such as genetics, embryology, cellular and molecular biology, biochemistry, and chemical and bioprocess engineering.

- *Information technology:* The application and networking of computer systems (in the form of hardware and software) in order to store, transmit, and manipulate data. IT is, of course, a more familiar concept to most of us, as users of PCs, laptops, cell phones, and social media. It is the technology driving the digital age examined in Chapter 4.

- *Cognitive science:* The interdisciplinary study of the mind, mental processes, intelligence, and intelligent behavior. The brain is a phenomenally complex organ, and cognitive science recognizes that the mind cannot be fully understood by any one discipline. As such, the field comprises neuroscience, psychology, linguistics, artificial intelligence, sociology, anthropology, and philosophy.

- *Genetics:* The study of genes, hereditary transmission, and variation in living organisms.

- *Robotics:* The design and development, construction, operation, and application of software-controlled mechanical systems capable of complex tasks usually undertaken by humans.

Many of the applications of NBIC/GNR—actual and potential— would have sounded like sci-fi imaginings relatively recently: genetically modified food, artificial intelligence, neuro-implants and pharmaceuticals, nanodrugs that target specific cells in the human body, and even a molecular assembler[4] that could, theoretically at least, manufacture anything, "at a cost no greater than wood."[5]

Yet fantastical though some of these concepts seem, we should remember that advanced NBIC/GNR technology already surrounds us:

- At the turn of the millennium, more than a third of all soybeans and a third of the corn produced globally contained genes combined with those of other species.[6]

- Nanoparticle silver, prized for its antibacterial and odor-eliminating properties, is used in bandages, washing machines, and even socks.[7]

- In medicine, tissue engineering enables the fabrication of artificial skin, bladders, pancreases, cartilage, bones, bone marrow, and more. The global market for tissue-engineered products is expected to total $27 billion by 2018.[8]

- The first edition of the iPhone featured 500 times more computing power than the guidance systems that took Apollo 11 to the moon.[9]

- The highly intuitive touchscreen interfaces used to operate smartphones and tablets were made possible by our advanced understanding of human cognitive processes.

## We Ain't Seen Nothin' Yet

As an example of everyday NBIC technology, touchscreens are particularly appropriate as they are the result of the combined application of IT and cognitive science. For as we shall see, an immensely powerful convergence within the various NBIC and GNR disciplines is set to drive human invention to new levels and in new directions.

In a famous article on GNR, Sun Microsystems cofounder Bill Joy referred to the "almost magical inventions" that these technologies would unleash in the near future.[10] It should be noted that Joy was expressing deep concern over the direction in which GNR could take us (see the section *Honey, I Shrunk the Future*). But whatever the rights and wrongs, commentators herald the potential for the convergence of NBIC and GNR technologies to transform our everyday lives, creating new materials and driving giant leaps forward in fields such as IT, medicine, and nutrition.

For example, scientists at Harvard University and the MITRE Corporation have developed the world's first nanoprocessor, a breakthrough they describe as a step toward "a new class of much smaller, lighter-weight electronic sensors and consumer electronics."[11] The tiny circuit uses minimal power and can be programmed to carry out arithmetic and logical tasks (basic ones, at this time).

The ability to manipulate molecules is also allowing engineers to build new high-performing materials with improved heat resistance, absorption, flexibility, antibacterial qualities, and shape-forming possibilities. One such substance, graphene, could be a game changer all by itself. The thinnest and strongest substance known to man,[12] it is effectively two-dimensional. Its anticipated applications are astonishing (see the case study *Slim Hopes*).

---

## CASE STUDY ■ Slim Hopes

Just as the world of cinema is going three-dimensional, the world of materials science, it seems, is heading in the opposite direction. Graphene is a new, essentially two-dimensional material just one carbon atom thick. A pile of 3 million sheets of graphene would measure only .04 inches (1 millimeter) thick.[13] Yet tests have proven it to be the strongest material ever produced, around 200 times more robust than structural steel. The scientists who demonstrated this announced that "it would take an elephant, balanced on a pencil, to break through a sheet of graphene the thickness of Saran Wrap."[14]

Graphene also conducts heat and electricity more effectively than any other material. It is immensely flexible and highly impermeable, even to gases. This potent combination of properties gives the substance a spectacular array of possible applications. Purely as a composite material, it has many potential uses.[15] In addition, being impermeable, it could be used to help detect gas leaks.[16] In electronics, it is expected to form the basis for more powerful and much slimmer devices. It could also be used to digitize almost anything, from clothes to food packaging.[17]

Graphene's flexibility is already being exploited to develop unbreakable, bendable consumer technology. In 2010, a scientist working with graphene declared that we would soon be able to roll up our cell phones and place them behind our ears "like a pencil."[18]

The 2010 Nobel Prize for Physics was awarded to the scientists who pioneered the development of graphene, in recognition of their remarkable breakthrough. Three years later, the European Commission's Future and Emerging Technologies program awarded a grant of some €1 billion to the Graphene Flagship Consortium, to help further develop and commercialize the material.[19] (The Consortium is made up of European universities, the European Science Foundation, Nokia, and the German nanotechnology R&D company AMO.) Little wonder, then, that the BBC called graphene a "miracle material."[20]

---

In medicine, nanotechnology could usher in a new generation of intelligent, sensor-rich surgical tools and imaging devices, which could mechanize diagnosis and surgery and significantly reduce reliance on human judgment and techniques.[21] A robotic system has already been developed for automated eye surgery, making operations both more precise and simpler to perform.

Meanwhile, nanobots—tiny robots that are injected into the bloodstream—are being developed to detect and eliminate illness.[22] According to some commentators, a technique known as RNA interference has the potential to disable the genes responsible for certain diseases and aging.[23] Futurologist Ray Kurzweil told the *New York Times*, "by 2030, we'll ... basically wipe out disease."[24] A computer scientist, Kurzweil is renowned for his zealous views on the potential of NBIC and GNR technology—views that others dispute. But clearly, the impact of nanotechnology will be powerful.

Nano-innovations also have the capacity to transform food production and nutrition. Antibacterial nanomaterials could detect and eliminate harmful bacteria during manufacture and be inserted into packaging to make food last longer. And nanosensors in so-called interactive foods would allow consumers to choose flavors and colors and could even detect vitamin deficiencies in the human body, releasing controlled amounts of nutrients in response.

For agricultural purposes, similar devices could sense when crops need water and then trigger dispensers. And pesticides delivered by nanoparticles would be released only once they were eaten by insects, avoiding the contamination of crops.[25] Bioscientists are also working on pesticides that are based on scorpion and spider venom. Delivered via specific bacteria and viruses, these substances would kill only disease-carrying insects, leaving humans and the environment unharmed.[26]

## The Sweet Spot

Ray Kurzweil wrote in 2007 that "with the completion of the human genome project in 2003 and the advent of techniques such as RNA interference … medicine has transformed itself into an information technology."[27] Radical though it may be, his observation neatly captures the phenomenon behind some of the more dizzying developments: scientific and technological convergence. It is the coming together of the NBIC and GNR disciplines that is bringing about the most staggering possibilities.

Nanotechnology and IT are joining forces to develop spray-on Wi-Fi transmitters, roll-up cell phones, and tiny computer processors. And as we shall see, neuroscientists and cognitive scientists are collaborating to improve our mental capacity, while experts in robotics and biotech are attempting to merge human and robotic intelligence.

Knowledge from the fields of IT, biotechnology, and cognitive science is being combined to help us optimize our sleep patterns. Consumer devices can now monitor sleep, measure breathing, movement, and brain activity, and detect shallow sleep phases to wake users at the optimum time.[28]

A further example of the power of technological convergence is the use of DNA for data storage. As humanity generates ever greater volumes of information in the digital era, attention has turned to DNA as a durable storage facility, with infinitely greater capacity than computer disks or magnetic tape. The European Bioinformatics Institute has designed a way of coding and accurately retrieving 2.2 petabytes of digital information onto a gram of synthesized DNA. A petabyte is $10^{15}$ bytes, the equivalent of the data contained on around 468,000 DVDs. At that level of storage density, scientists claim that their system could comfortably hold the 3 zettabytes ($3 \times 10^{21}$ bytes) of electronic data estimated to have been generated by humankind to date.[29]

## Sky's the Limit

At the outset of 2013, *Wired* presented an overview of what the magazine considered some the most forward-looking ideas in progress and innovations in development at the time.[30] Among these "massive ideas" were:

- An electrically powered, two-seater microlight that achieves double the mileage of a conventionally fueled equivalent aircraft. The plane is already on the market, and the Slovenian company responsible has also developed a solar-powered trailer that can charge it—emission-free—in just five hours.[31]

- Harvesting desert sunlight to create near-infinite sources of energy. The surfaces of the world's deserts absorb more energy in a day than is consumed annually across the entire globe.

- Spray-on nanotransmitters that create a Wi-Fi network anywhere.

- Augmented reality technology in glasses (currently being developed by Google) and even in contact lenses.

- The mass production of diamond to make its highly useful chemical properties—hardness, heat conduction, and low friction—affordable for industrial use. Potential applications include everything from foundations and girders in buildings to replacement bones.

# Homo-Improvements

The comic British sci-fi novel *Better Than Life* (based on the popular *Red Dwarf* TV series) tells of a future in which athletes are genetically designed and grown in laboratories: 20-foot-tall basketball players, swimmers with fins and gills, and so on. For the 2224 soccer World Cup, the Scottish team develops a goalkeeper who is nothing more than an 8-foot by 16-foot rectangle of human skin, completely filling the goal. They still fail to qualify for the second round.[32] Even though they were exaggerating for effect, the authors could probably never have envisioned the potential for humans to enhance themselves, physically and mentally, that NBIC and GNR technologies might unleash.

Of course, when the book was published in 1991, the use of pharmaceuticals to enhance athletic performance was already widespread and well documented. Anabolic steroids and human growth hormone have long been used to help build muscle; injections of EPO (erythrpoietin) enhance red blood cell production and boost the flow of oxygen to the muscles (so-called blood doping); while beta-blockers are taken to calm nerves, not only by athletes but also by artistic performers and public speakers.

But the convergence of NBIC and GNR could take human enhancement to new levels. As previously noted, biological techniques to eliminate diseases and slow the aging process are already being researched (a development with complex implications for the aging global population, examined in Chapter 5), while developments in nanorobotics have the potential to boost health and improve nutrition.

The prospect of cognitive enhancement also looms. A UK study in 2012 found that 16 percent of American and 10 percent of British students admitted to using prescription drugs for performance-enhancing purposes—for example, to heighten awareness and boost memory function during exams. Similarly, a poll by *Nature* found that a fifth of people across sixty countries confessed to taking psychiatric medications to boost mental performance.

The British study found academics to be just as prone to using artificial cognitive improvement as students. The head of one university laboratory in the United States told researchers that all of his staff regularly take modafinil, a drug prescribed to treat narcolepsy that also improves decision making.[33]

The potential to enhance the mind may go further still. With access to the majority of human knowledge available at the touch of a button, NBIC/GNR technology could prompt humankind to seek new forms of intelligence. William Sims Bainbridge, director of Human-Centered Computing at the U.S. National Science Foundation, pointed to the "technologically augmented cognition, perception, and communication" that might be made possible via "personal sensory device interfaces" (which heighten the human senses), "enhanced creativity tools," and the "humanization of computers, robots and information systems."[34]

## Project Cyborg

This humanization of robots—and vice versa—has been the lifework of Kevin Warwick, a controversial cybernetics professor at the University of Reading in the UK. Warwick's experiments involve controlling robots via artificial cells grown from rat brain cultures.[35] Prior to this, he had a chip implanted into his forearm, allowing him to activate simple computer-controlled devices, such as electronic doors, lights, and heaters, simply by walking past them.

Warwick also had electrodes connected to nerve fibers in his arm, with no significant side effects or signs of rejection.[36] This enabled him to control much more complex machines, such as an electric wheelchair and a robotic hand. What's more, his wife was able to stimulate artificial sensations in his arm via a similar apparatus in hers.[37] This first electronic communication between the nervous systems of two human beings was hailed by Warwick as a "first step towards thought communication."[38]

### Honey, I Shrunk the Future

"We are on the cusp of the further perfection of extreme evil... [of] a surprising and terrible empowerment of extreme individuals." Strong words indeed from Bill Joy, the cofounder of Sun Microsystems, who presents a terrifying vision of where GNR might take humanity. According to Joy, radical groups or individuals will no longer need extensive facilities and hard-to-obtain materials to commit atrocities—only knowledge and expertise. The risk of such "knowledge-enabled mass destruction" will be intensified by the uncontrolled self-replication of which these technologies are capable. [39]

Joy is not alone in expressing deep reservations about the dangers inherent in NBIC and GNR convergence. The Central Intelligence Agency observed in 2003 that the effects of biologically engineered agents "could be worse than any disease known to man" and that the know-how to develop such weapons was already in existence.[40]

Even K. Eric Drexler, a passionate exponent of the power of nanotechnology, urged a degree of caution. Drexler was the first to envisage the molecular assembler, a machine that could manipulate atoms and molecules

*(continued)*

to produce almost anything, but he warned that such nanodevices could also be "engines of destruction." Drexler was also the first to warn of the hypothetical "gray goo" catastrophe, where infinitely self-replicating nanobots consume the entire earth. In his book *Engines of Creation*, Drexler wrote: "We cannot afford certain kinds of accidents with replicating assemblers." [41]

So the nanotechnology doomsday scenario is just that: *the destruction of all life on earth.* This begs a question, posed inevitably by Joy: "If our own extinction is a likely, or even possible, outcome ... shouldn't we proceed with great caution?"

Or maybe we should desist altogether. As author and philosopher Henry David Thoreau wrote more than 160 years ago, "a man is rich in proportion to the number of things which he can afford to let alone."[42]

Apocalyptic scenarios aside, there are some credible and troubling health concerns surrounding nanotechnology. Nanoparticles are potentially small enough to be inhaled (like asbestos) or absorbed through the skin and into the bloodstream. This would expose the whole body to them, the health effects of which are not yet known.[43] Yet nanoproducts are already on the market.

But whatever the arguments for and against, abstention from progress is a highly improbable outcome, for two main reasons. First, there is the human thirst for knowledge, or what Joy called the "rapture of discovery and innovation ... that is the nature of science's quest." Worryingly, amid this rapture, less than 2 percent of investment in nanotechnology research is being spent on risk analysis.[44] Second, in a global capitalist system, the staggering commercial opportunities offered are not likely to be put to one side.

Nevertheless, such concerns have led to calls for a careful and diligent approach to NBIC/GNR technologies, not to mention government regulation. Nanotechnology is being singled out for particular attention. But regulating such new, rapidly developing, highly specialized, and phenomenally complex fields will surely be fraught with difficulty—all the more so as they converge to drive increased complexity and a level of technological sophistication that few will understand. And as the banking crisis illustrates, trying to make rules to control an industry whose intricacies are not fully understood can prove wholly ineffective.

# IMPLICATIONS OF TECHNOLOGICAL CONVERGENCE

Nobody knows what the future will look like. It is impossible to predict which of the developments examined in this chapter will ultimately reach technical or commercial viability, and what their marketable applications might be—and it is beyond the purpose of this book to attempt to do so.

What we can be certain about is that people will grasp with both hands the opportunity to significantly enhance their knowledge and capability. After all, it is human nature to try to drive technological advancement as far as possible, or at least, as far as is deemed socially and ethically acceptable (more on this below).

More than the actual innovations that emerge, it is this innate desire to take GNR/NBIC–based progress to its limits that will have profound implications for industries, organizations, and societies.

## Mixed Fortunes

What is also certain, however, is that as technological convergence progresses, it has the potential to create new industries, transform existing sectors, and threaten the very existence of some business models. By 2014, an estimated 15 percent of all manufactured products may rely on nanotechnology.[45] In addition, analysts expect the global market for nanotechnology to be valued at $2.6 trillion by 2014—roughly equivalent to the size of the current IT and telecommunications industries combined.[46]

On the downside, a report speculated in 2012 that car insurance would one day become obsolete, envisioning a time when there will be "almost no accidents."[47] Now, it may be premature to herald the demise of a sector with global revenues estimated at almost $660 billion in 2011.[48] A senior insurance executive, however, told us that the industry *is* giving serious thought to the impact of future technologies on liability, and therefore its business model.

There is little doubt that insurance premiums will progressively decline as innovations in computing and materials technology make cars safer. And so, it is worth recalling that scientists have recently created graphene, the hardest and possibly the most versatile substance known to man. Plus, if successful, Google's driverless cars project[49] would require a whole new actuarial model: Insurers would effectively be covering the hardware and software rather than the drivers.

Elsewhere, 3D printing poses a threat to the whole concept of large-scale industrial manufacturing (see the case study *A New Dimension*). And if production were to become localized, what would be the impact on the global shipping, distribution, and logistics sectors? Similarly, what might become of the millions of unskilled workers whose jobs could potentially be performed by unpaid robots? How would this affect the dynamics of globalization explored in Chapter 1?

In healthcare, meanwhile, robotic surgery could move responsibility from highly qualified physicians to lower-paid technicians, potentially creating "a financially sustainable way to meet the aging population's growing need for more healthcare."[50] And healthcare is set for even more remarkable advancements in light of recent breakthroughs. The much-vaunted prospect of nanobots targeting diseased cells moved a step nearer to reality in 2012. Researchers at Harvard University used DNA to construct a robotic device capable of targeting precise cells with specific "molecular instructions"—to switch off, for example.[51]

Meanwhile, advances in gene sequencing have reduced the time to decode a newborn baby's genome from several months to just fifty hours—a potentially lifesaving improvement for a critically ill infant.[52] Also, gene editing took a major stride forward in 2013 with the development of techniques to isolate and alter any given gene, potentially disabling currently incurable illnesses.[53]

Tissue engineering also took a stride forward. A study published in *Nature Medicine* reported that a rat's kidney had been "rebuilt" in a laboratory and transplanted into a live specimen, where it produced urine. The kidney is one of the most complex organs to have been regenerated in this way. The ability to regrow organs would present two major breakthroughs. First, it would overcome the need for patients to wait for donors. Second, the tissue grown would be compatible with the patient, doing away with the need for a lifetime of taking immunosuppressive drugs.[54] And hopes of repairing organs and tissues were raised further still in 2013, when scientists managed to create embryonic stem cells from human skin.[55]

---

## CASE STUDY ■ A New Dimension

When *The Economist* describes a technology as part of a "third industrial revolution," something extremely significant is clearly on the horizon. The words apply well to 3D printing, which has been described as "remarkable," "amazing," "the reinvention of manufacturing," and "potentially life-changing."[56]

3D printing is not actually printing at all. It is an additive manufacturing process that layers plastic resin, shaping it into three-dimensional objects based on digital designs. 3D printing is technological convergence in action. The technique combines the capabilities of software engineering, robotics, digital tools, and materials science. And its potential applications are, says *The Economist*, "mind-boggling."[57] It is already commonly used to create customized components in industries as diverse as architecture, construction, and engineering, and in automotive, aerospace, and medical equipment. And as the technology advances, printing in biomaterials and metal is also becoming possible.[58]

The hype is in part due to the fact that 3D printing is now going mainstream. The industry stands on the cusp of the sort of revolution that computing went through in the 1970s and 1980s. As costs plummet and 3D printing machines become more readily available, its use is spreading from industry specialists to early adopters and hobbyists. Consumer interest is ballooning as printers become available for as little as $400.[59]

But the main cause of the commotion is the potential of 3D printing to turn some aspects of industrial production on its head. Small and affordable, 3D printers can sit pretty much anywhere, meaning that items can be made where needed—studios, homes, garages, remote mountain villages—rather than having to be shipped from a factory. The devices are also highly customizable: Program in a small tweak to the de-

*(continued)*

sign, and the machine adapts the product to suit. This will prove a highly attractive proposition in the era of individualization and mass customization highlighted in Chapter 3.

3D printing can also be expanded or upgraded on demand. For example, any 3D printer can make a replica of itself, so no heavy up-front investment is needed. Start with one machine and print more as you go.

The implications are far-reaching. 3D printing could eventually mean a drastic reduction in the need for production-line manufacturing, component production, and global distribution and logistics. Imagine, for example, if you could make replacement parts in the comfort of your own home when your car or household appliances break down. No need to order, to wait for the repairperson—or even to pay. Just download the design you need and hit "print."[60]

In addition, 3D printing undermines mass production's key economic advantage: It does away with economies of scale. Its cost efficiencies result from its *lack* of scale, as well as its up-front affordability, customizability, and proximity of manufacture. One aptly named supplier, Desktop Factory, told the *Wall Street Journal* that 35 percent of its orders were from small businesses.[61]

As *The Economist* explained: "The 3D printer can run unattended, and make many things too complex for a traditional factory to handle. In time, these amazing machines may be able to make almost anything, anywhere .... Legions of entrepreneurs and tinkerers [will] swap designs online, turn them into products at home and market them globally from a garage."[62]

There are barriers to mass adoption of 3D printing, however. These include the digital infrastructure required to support the technology; questions over the intellectual property of designs that are downloaded, shared, and adapted; the ability—currently, at least—to print only in resin, which lacks strength and flexibility; and calls for regulation to prevent homemade gun production.[63] This last concern was placed in the spotlight in May 2013, when an American law student announced that he had fashioned a working gun from a 3D printer bought on eBay, then promptly published the design online. The blueprint was downloaded more than 100,000 times in less than a week, causing the U.S. government to demand its removal.[64]

Whatever the challenges and concerns, however, this disruptive innovation is on the rise—and probably coming soon to a garage near you.

## Place Your Bets

The hype curve surrounding NBIC/GNR technologies is steep, but the reality is that the many innovations they have unleashed remain at wildly different stages of development. And as noted, it is impossible to know which will and will not come to fruition.

This unpredictability will force organizations to gamble considerable resources on cutting-edge R&D programs, with little or no advance indication as to which ideas will succeed or fail. Organizations will be obliged to pursue innovations simply to stay in the game and avoid being behind when breakthroughs occur.

Take, for example, attempts to develop pesticides from spider and scorpion venom. Should this prove possible, the commercial potential for a multinational agribusiness could prove enormous. Missing out would not be an option. In addition, as we shall see, this R&D imperative will also place huge demands on companies in terms of their efforts to collaborate with other organizations.

## Research Engines

R&D operations may therefore need to be diversified, and teams will need to develop the necessary skills to meet the challenges of vanguard research projects. Whether to build or buy R&D capability may increasingly become a business-critical decision.

Companies will need to consider creating platforms to enable a common understanding between specialists from the different NBIC/GNR fields within their R&D teams—something we are already starting to see happen in adjacent technological fields such as IT, telecommunications, and mobile. Over the past few years, a rash of innovation centers has been established by giants such as Microsoft, Intel, Samsung, Vodafone, Verizon, and AT&T. These facilities bring together developers, partners, and even competitors to push the boundaries of new technologies and codevelop new products. Verizon's outfit hosts some eighty organizations, all focused on exploiting 4G wireless connectivity by "thinking of something that's not currently connected, but should be."[65]

Experts from different disciplines must be willing and able to co-operate and compromise. In addition, business leaders may find themselves being called on to manage vast knowledge pools and co-ordinate the skills of these experts to maximum advantage. Generalist managers may be needed to facilitate R&D teams, acting as "translators" between the various specialists.

## Big Collaboration

Innovating, developing, and commercializing applications from a fusion of scientific fields will demand new levels of collaboration, both within and between organizations. The era of technological convergence will require that divisions and companies, and even *entire disciplines*, work together in new ways. This applies to disciplines that are not only highly complicated, specialized, and advanced but also extremely diverse. Nanoengineers will need to collaborate with bio-chemists, IT programmers with geneticists, psychologists with neuroscientists, and so on. Pioneering research will sometimes demand the combined knowledge of all of the above and more. And to raise the stakes further, vanguard projects will frequently take these people into new, virgin territory.

This "big" collaboration will require more than good organization. The various specialists will need to decide how to maximize their very different expertise to achieve the desired end as effectively and efficiently as possible. And they will need to find a common language in order to pool and understand each other's know-how.

## Beyond Boundaries

Scientific convergence and big collaboration may create a new kind of "organizational convergence." If corporations are to exploit the explosive commercial power of new technologies and defend against market threats, they will need to move beyond traditional organizational boundaries and configurations. This will mean going much further than the usual efforts to break down silos and create collaborative platforms.

More open ways of working will be needed to enable new levels of cooperation. Scientists will need to find ways to bring together the tried and tested—but very different—procedures of, say, IT project management and drug development. Success will depend on the ability of senior technical experts from different fields to cooperate and compromise.

The complexity of technological convergence will also make knowledge exchange between companies—even between competitors—vital. For leaders, this will mean unleashing and directing initiatives that they may not fully understand from a technical point of view (a similar challenge to that posed by the digital era). Leaders will be obliged to manage vast and diverse pools of technical knowledge and professional skills, coordinating and mediating among collaborating organizations and scientific fields—all while keeping projects focused on the ultimate objective.

The need for more intensive collaboration is not lost on senior business leaders. According to IBM's 2012 Global CEO Study, the ability to collaborate is the most important trait that chief executives are seeking in employees. Three-quarters describe it as a "critical" attribute. In addition, the study found, the majority of CEOs are "partnering extensively" in order to drive innovation.[66]

Moreover, Hay Group research suggests that the world's top twenty companies for leadership are more likely to take remedial action if senior managers are not collaborating, even if the individuals concerned are generating strong business results. These companies are also better prepared for the challenges presented by big collaboration, as they are quicker to reorganize how their people work together when the need arises.[67]

Fortunately, the technological innovation that demands organizational convergence will also help to enable it. Social communication platforms are becoming increasingly sophisticated, promising virtual collaboration spaces and tools for cross-organizational and interdisciplinary collaboration.[68]

## Debating Societies

As noted, humanity will look to drive progress as far as it can, and technological advancement will pose new dangers along the way—from concerns over the production of guns in garages and the health effects of nanoparticles to the ethical pros and cons of cognitive enhancement and a hypothetical gray goo Armageddon (see the section *Honey, I Shrunk the Future*).

These ethical and philosophical questions lie beyond the scope of this book, but they will need to be considered at a societal level. Individual societies will be required to debate what they consider the limits of acceptable progress. How far should the bounds of human capability be pushed? Which innovations should and should not be pursued? When do the pitfalls of progress outweigh the benefits? And what are the downsides to *not* pursuing a potential advance?

Governments and businesses will need to be sensitive to this debate as they make regulatory and investment decisions. They will need to tread cautiously as they navigate societal expectations surrounding technological advancement and reflect carefully on the ethical boundaries as they consider regulation and product innovation.

## Influencing Innovation

Of course, not all progress will present ethical dilemmas. Bendable cell phones that can be rolled up and rechargeable aircraft, for example, are not likely to provoke existential fears or moral outrage. The fate of ethically neutral innovations such as these will be determined not by society but by the market. Businesses will decide which ethically neutral innovations to invest in and which to leave on the drawing board.

Commercial considerations will therefore have a significant influence on the direction of technological progress. And corporations, as well as deciding which inventions are commercially viable, will be in a position to demand application-oriented innovation. Knowing that a certain outcome is technically possible and potentially lucrative, corporations will be the catalysts for much NBIC and GNR research.

As a result, application-oriented ventures will become common. Companies will consider strategic alliances, joint ventures, mergers, and acquisitions to strengthen their innovative capacity. Witness Nestlé's acquisition of the medical nutrition division of the pharmaceutical company Novartis in 2007. The deal not only gave Nestlé a dominant position in the health-enhanced foods market, but it was also touted as boosting the company's R&D capability.[69]

## THE DEMANDS OF TECHNOLOGICAL CONVERGENCE

In summary, leaders will need to:

1. *Learn to live with uncertainty.* The outcomes, implications, and applications of technological convergence are highly unpredictable. Leaders will need to be comfortable with uncertainty and ambiguity, and they will have to keep constantly abreast of progress and its consequences for their customers and staff.

2. *Foster new forms of collaboration.* Intensive cooperation within the company, with other companies, and with academic institutions will be essential. To enable this to occur, organizations will need to dismantle the boundaries between disciplines and departments. Leaders will need to promote and manage knowledge exchange internally and with partner organizations, including competitors.

3. *Innovate ethically.* Products that overstep the boundaries of acceptable progress will not be tolerated. Businesses and their leaders will be expected to act with integrity and respect the societal debate on technological advancement.

# 7 Reinforcers, Dilemmas, and the Perfect Storm

*"Two paradoxes are better than one; they may even suggest a solution."*
—**Edward Teller,** nuclear physicist

## AT A GLANCE ▪ A PERFECT STORM OF MEGATRENDS

Each individual megatrend will create tough challenges and enormous complexity for organizations and leaders. However, the megatrends do not develop in isolation. They develop together, and as such, they will greatly intensify the difficulties for business leaders.

The megatrends combined will result in a set of five key *reinforcers* (consequences driven and strengthened by several megatrends at once) and four significant *dilemmas*.

**The five reinforcers are:**

1. *Stakeholder proliferation.* Leaders must be sensitive to the expectations of a rapidly expanding network of stakeholders, which will increase complexity just at the point where leaders are looking to create simplicity.

2. *Power shift.* Leaders' power will shift to their various stakeholders, reducing the authority of leaders to lead organizations through the challenges presented by the megatrends.

3. *New working practices.* A new "social practice" of work will emerge as work and the workplace go mobile, the boundaries between personal and professional life break down, and a resistance to formal authority takes hold among younger generations.

4.  *Cost explosion.* The costs of businesses will explode as a result of a scarcity of talent and natural resources; the research into, development of, and use of advanced technology; and the demands of globalization.

5.  *Ethicization of business.* Concerns over the environment and NBIC technology, combined with the transparency of the digital era, will demand the highest ethical standards of organizations and their leaders.

**The four dilemmas relate to:**

1.  *Mobility.* While globalization will drive a greater need and desire to travel, environmental concerns will demand that travel is seriously reduced.

2.  *Resources.* Scarcity of natural resources will coincide with spiraling demand for them.

3.  *Hierarchies.* Complexity tends to generate more intricate structures, yet growing individualism will call for flatter organizations.

4.  *Horizons.* The immediacy of the digital era is at odds with the need for long-term solutions to climate change.

---

A *perfect storm* has been a much used metaphor since the release of a hit disaster movie of that title in 2000. The meaning of the term captures the combined effect of the megatrends on the business environment—well—perfectly. A perfect storm is an improbable confluence of circumstances that dramatically exacerbates the effects of a given situation—for example, the six megatrends as they develop in parallel, each feeding and intensifying the others.

Globalization 2.0, for example, will create new wealth, resulting in more demand for products and services, which will place greater pressure on the environment. Rising wealth will also drive greater individualism, which will inflate the demand for technology, Internet access, digital devices, and social networks—in turn reinforcing digitization. Technological convergence will create many new product markets, with yet further implications for climate change and globalization. And so on: The crossovers are many and complex, resulting in a tempest of challenges, questions, and complexities for organizations to grapple with. For leaders, life under the perfect storm thrown up by the megatrends will be complex, chaotic, and overwhelming.

# THE MEGATREND STORM

This chapter looks at the consequences of all six megatrends in combination. Each megatrend has multiple consequences, some of them contradictory, while others are mutually strengthening and supporting.

Combined, the megatrends will result in five *reinforcers* and four *dilemmas*, each of which will prove immensely difficult for organizations and their leaders to address.

By *reinforcers*, we mean powerful consequences that result from—and are thus reinforced by—two or more of the megatrends in tandem. The nature of reinforcers is such that they are intimately linked and therefore overlap to a degree. It is these reinforcers that will have the greater impact on the future of business leadership.

At the same time, a series of tensions, contradictions, and inconsistencies between the megatrends will make the lives of leaders especially difficult, as they present a series of quandaries with no clear solutions: *dilemmas*.

# REINFORCERS

The five reinforcers are shown below:

---

### The Megatrend Storm: The Five Reinforcers

---

1.  Stakeholder Proliferation. A multiplication of the vested interests that leaders must take into consideration

---

2.  Power Shift. Away from leaders and toward stakeholders

---

3.  New Working Practices. The emergence of a new "social practice" of work

---

4.  Cost Explosion. Due to scarcity of talent and natural resources and the use of advanced technology

---

5.  Ethicization of Business. A demand for the highest ethical standards from organizations and their leaders

---

Let's look at each reinforcer in detail.

## Reinforcer 1. Stakeholder Proliferation

In simpler times, leaders effectively had one principal group of stakeholders to concern themselves with: shareholders.[1] Of course, investors remain of paramount importance today and will continue to do so. But as we have seen over the last couple of decades, leaders increasingly need to address the demands of a complex array of other stakeholders. This is because one consequence of the megatrends is a greater proliferation of stakeholders that organizations must appease if they are to succeed.

Indeed, the megatrends redefine the very concept of a stakeholder. Stakeholders are no longer limited to groups of people. Abstract entities such as society and the planet itself have become crucial considerations. Leaders must increasingly consider the impact of their decisions within this new stakeholder landscape, which could include the constituents discussed below.

### Consumers / Customers

Globalization 2.0 will demand that leaders simultaneously take a global and local perspective. They will no longer be able to think simply in terms of their market, consumers, or customers. The glocalization effect will oblige them to consider the distinct needs of their German, Spanish, American, Russian, Chinese, Indian, Mexican, Argentinian, and South African customers, and so on. In a globalized world, there is no longer "the market" but a plethora of markets, each with different attitudes, desires, preferences, and buying habits.[2]

Individualism will exacerbate this fragmentation of markets. Not only will each local market have its unique properties, but increasingly, the preferences of each individual customer will diversify as societies become wealthier. This will mean opportunities to customize products and even co-create them with customers (made possible by the advancements of the digital era). But it will present a serious threat to organizations that are slow to respond.

### Local Managers

Glocalization will also demand a more localized approach to decision making. The opportunities and threats that emerge in each market will be influenced by its unique expectations, customs, traditions, and ways of doing business. As a result, decisions in each locality may be very different.

Leaders will need to strengthen regional and local management if their organizations are to respond to glocalized market dynamics and diversified customer needs, meaning an expanded—and more diverse—group of managers to lead.

### The Global Workforce

Another new stakeholder group will be the global workforce. Unethical treatment of outsourced workers in emerging markets will not be tolerated—not by employees themselves (as demonstrated by the riots that erupted at Foxconn in China in 2012[3]) nor ultimately by the market (as discussed below). A workforce in revolt and customers voting with their feet are no way to placate shareholders.

In addition, the individualization megatrend will drastically intensify the demands of the workforce. Employees will expect to be treated not just ethically and fairly but as individuals, and they will insist that leaders respect their personal needs and ambitions. They will make demands of their organizations—regarding working hours, work-life balance, family commitments, and the like—that would have been unthinkable a decade ago.

A global workforce of thousands of people, all demanding to be regarded as individuals, will make for a phenomenally complex stakeholder.

### Environment and Society

The environmental crisis will create yet more stakeholders. As customers increasingly demand that organizations create sustainable products and operations, the planet itself will become a stakeholder. Greenwashing will not pass muster: Only a genuine contribution to the survival of the planet will be satisfactory.

As the consequences of climate change become more grave, this desire for sustainability will be a societal issue. People are more likely to demand that companies (and governments) act to safeguard living conditions for future generations. As such, society will join leaders' ever expanding list of interests to satisfy.

### Competitors

Technological convergence will further complicate the stakeholder landscape. The need for "big" collaboration will force companies to cooperate closely with other organizations, including competitors, in order to move complex technical innovations forward. The sort of "coopetition" that is common in the automotive industry—where rival manufacturers frequently work together to develop new engines—will likely become routine in many industries.

Coopetition will prove particularly demanding for leaders on an emotional and cognitive level. They will need to maintain a difficult dual perspective and approach as they work with competing companies, viewing them simultaneously as vital partners and market threats. This will mean continually having to make careful judgments on how much to give, how much to take, and how much to hold back, striking a balance between establishing a productive working relationship and keeping a professional distance.

### The Complexity Paradox of Stakeholder Proliferation

As we have seen in the preceding chapters, each megatrend will vastly complicate the environment in which organizations operate. This puts the onus on leaders to reduce complexity wherever possible.

Yet combined, the megatrends will create even more complexity by multiplying and fragmenting stakeholders—*at the very point when leaders need to attempt to simplify matters.*

Cutting through complexity requires clarity. Yet how can leaders deliver a clear, consistent message to an increasingly disparate set of audiences with very different demands?

In addition, what will stakeholder proliferation mean for the brands of multinational organizations? Should companies look to reduce complexity by operating as a unified global brand, instantly recognizable wherever they trade? Or should they obey the laws of glocalization, adapting their identity to each local market?

| Stakeholder Proliferation | |
|---|---|
| **Stakeholders** | **Megatrends** |
| Diverse workforce<br>Diverse customers<br>Local managers | Globalization 2.0 |
| Workforce<br>Customers | Individualization |
| Planet<br>Society | Environmental crisis |
| Competitors | Technological convergence |

## Reinforcer 2. Power Shift

The *New Oxford Dictionary of English* defines *power* as the "ability to direct or influence the behavior of others."[4] Conventionally (and as we will see in more detail in the next chapter), this is how leadership works. Leaders hold influence over others, which is what enables them to execute their strategies and implement their decisions.

However, the megatrends will erode this authority, shifting the power of leaders to an array of groups, individuals, and entities—inevitable in a climate of stakeholder proliferation.

### Global to Local

As noted, to cope with Globalization 2.0, decision-making processes will need to include local levels. Senior leaders will need to vest regional and local managers with the right amount of power to make and implement the right decisions to cope with glocalization.

### Talent

In addition, leaders will find themselves with progressively less influence over their workforces. Demographic change—in particular, the aging of the population—will result in a growing scarcity of highly educated, qualified, and experienced staff. As a result, talented employees will have the power to choose and shape their roles and careers to suit themselves (much like our programmer friend, Arvi, in Chapter 3), as organizations battle for their services.

Meanwhile, individualism will give talent, both young and old, the confidence to flex its new-found muscle in the workplace. The notion of a war for talent tends to conjure up perceptions of businesses competing to recruit the latest crop of "bright young things." But skilled workers of all ages will reap the benefits of demographic change. As the baby boom generation hits retirement, older, experienced heads with rare skill sets will be as valuable as promising and ambitious new graduates. And as we saw in Chapter 5, these older workers will be in a position to carve careers that are compatible with their later stage in life.

### Digital Natives

By contrast, the digital era will give a distinct power advantage to younger generations.[5] Digital natives will inevitably benefit from superior knowledge of the information technology on which organizations will come to depend.

And they will be instinctively more comfortable with the blurring of traditional boundaries between our public and private lives. Living their lives in a virtual goldfish bowl will come more naturally to them. But more important, corporate behavior will be laid bare by the transparency of the digital realm. Organizations' reputations will not solely be in the hands of their leaders but of a generation of employees who will think nothing of airing their grievances anonymously on public platforms.

### Customers

The openness of the digital era will also shift power from organizations to their customers, who can easily vent their frustrations with a company's product or service on online feedback and review forums. And in a more individualistic world, these customers will be all the more willing to express dissatisfaction.

In addition, customers will readily take issue with the ethics of organizations that do not shape up in the sustainability stakes. Meanwhile, under Globalization 2.0, leaders will need to pay deference to the individual demands of customers in different localities.

### Environment and Society

Finally, leaders' power might be squeezed by rising environmental consciousness, a growing societal consensus on climate change and sustainability, and government responses in the form of legislation.

### The Power Paradox of the Power Shift

Much like the proliferation of stakeholders, this power shift away from leaders will present them with a paradox. Leaders will need greater power to be able to make and execute the big decisions needed to address the challenges, complexities, and threats of the megatrend storm. Yet the megatrends themselves will do quite the opposite. They will act to erode leaders' power, transferring it to the very stakeholders that leaders are tasked with leading through the challenges of the megatrends.

To cope with the consequences of the megatrends, leaders will need to act from a position of authority. How can they do this if they *lose* influence due to precisely these forces?

| Power Shift | |
| --- | --- |
| **Leader's power shifts to** | **Megatrends** |
| Local managers | Globalization 2.0 |
| Workforce | Demographic change<br>Individualization |
| Younger generations | Digital era |
| Customers | Digital era<br>Individualization<br>Environmental crisis<br>Globalization 2.0 |

## Reinforcer 3. New Working Practices

In previous chapters, we examined how each individual megatrend is having a deep-seated effect on how, when, and where people work. Taken together, however, it is clear that the megatrends are bringing about dramatic social, emotional, physical, and procedural changes in work and the workplace. For many people, they are transforming traditional attitudes toward work, life, and how the two interact.

This is resulting in what we call a *new social practice of work*. It is a fundamental overhaul of deeply embedded working processes, routines, and behaviors, and of long-established expectations of the workplace and work-life balance.[6]

This new model of working consists of several elements, which will combine to make work look very different for many people in 2030.

### The Mobile Workplace

As noted in Chapter 4, a consequence of the digital era will be an evolution toward the fully mobile workplace. However, digitization is not the only force driving this change. Technological convergence will also produce innovations that redefine the workplace—and not only for office-based functions. As we saw in Chapter 6, much is being made of the potential for 3D printing to localize manufacturing—an unthinkable prospect just a decade ago. And individualism will bolster the expectation that employees use digital technology to work whenever and wherever they see fit.

This fragmentation of the workplace will skew the traditional leader-follower relationship between managers and employees. It will be difficult for leaders to maintain control over geographically dispersed teams that they rarely meet. Leaders will need to find new ways to command respect and authority.

### Virtual Work

In addition to the workplace, work itself will become increasingly virtualized in the digital era. Increasingly, virtual tools and platforms will enable work to be done remotely, an opportunity that the digital native generation will grasp with both hands.

But again, digitization will not be the only cause. Virtual working (and workplaces) will be necessary as organizations operate in an increasingly globalized environment (at least until NBIC advances allow us to be in two places at once!).

Virtual working will not just save executives from grueling travel schedules. Reducing the need to travel will also play a significant part in organizations' sustainability strategies, to the approval of an increasingly eco-conscious society. What's more, it will be a major cost-saver (welcome in an era of rising costs, as discussed below), as global travel becomes extremely expensive in the face of accelerating climate change.

## Blurred Boundaries

The blurring of private, public, and working life also represents a drastic change in social practice. As explained in Chapter 4, life in the digital era will be "always on." It will also be always in public, as we play out our lives on Facebook and Twitter. Meanwhile, social networks will bring work relationships into our personal space.

Leaders need to accept that conventional distinctions will collapse between work and personal time, professional and social relationships, and, crucially, leader and follower status. They will also need to be sensitive to the perils of the always-on culture. While younger generations may be happy glued to their smartphones and tablets, this comes with a risk. If "always on" means being always at work, this will take a toll on employees' physical and emotional well-being—and with it their performance. Even in a constantly connected world, people need time away from the job.

Digitization may give younger workers an advantage in the workplace. But fluid work schedules and lack of close supervision will demand considerable discipline and self-control—not qualities readily attributed to Generation Y—in order to ensure that deadlines are met and tasks performed to standard.

## Individualized Attitudes

A further consequence of the combined megatrends will be a growing anticollectivism and antiauthoritarianism among the workforce. Individualism, by definition, runs counter to collective working.

Leaders will be tasked with somehow fostering cooperation between teams with increasingly diverse values and attitudes. To make matters worse, the younger generation has a tendency to reject formal authority and insist on operating virtually. How will leaders create a sense of unity and belonging in such a diverse, highly individualized climate?

### The Leadership Paradox in New Working Practices

Again, the new social practice of work will result in a paradox for leaders to come to grips with. How are they to lead employees they never see? These employees are dispersed in different places, given to working anywhere, anytime. And in some cases, they do not consider their organization's leaders to be *their* leaders at all.

| New Working Practices | |
|---|---|
| **Practice** | **Megatrends** |
| The mobile workplace | Digitization |
| | Technological convergence |
| | Individualization |
| Virtual work | Digitization |
| | Globalization 2.0 |
| | Environmental crisis |
| Blurring of boundaries | Digitization |
| Anticollectivism and antiauthoritarianism | Digitization |
| | Individualization |

## Reinforcer 4. Cost Explosion

Rising costs are a common lament among business leaders and consumers alike. But under the megatrend storm, costs are set to explode across the board, as a result of a range of factors.

### Environmental Crisis

Enormous cost pressures will result from the environmental crisis. Chapter 2 explored how decreasing oil supplies, the need to exploit more problematic unconventional oil sources, and a scarcity of rare earth minerals will push up the cost of many products and services. That chapter also examined the economic Armageddon scenario that this could unleash.

Yet oil and rare earths are not the only resources threatened with scarcity. Global warming and increasing pollution will threaten water supplies, further pushing up the price of just about everything we produce. Hotter temperatures and dwindling water would also hit food production, making the basics of life far more expensive.

### Demographic Change and Individualism

The talent shortage resulting from demographic change will drive up employee costs. This will be intensified by workers' increasing demands in an era of individualism. Responding to the diverse needs and expectations of employees will likely require even more resources.

### Globalization 2.0

The complexity required to succeed in fragmented local markets will be costly. So will the processes to enable the customization and co-creation necessary to engage an increasingly individualized customer base.

### Technological Convergence

In the highly competitive race for innovation described in Chapter 6, researching, developing, and commercializing NBIC advancements will be expensive. Organizations will need to pay a premium for world-leading specialists to conduct R&D programs in vanguard technologies. And the demands of big collaboration will mean managing multiple partnerships, which are notoriously resource-intensive to make work.

In addition, the products and materials that stem from NBIC breakthroughs will be based on state-of-the-art technology—and therefore very costly. And the laws of supply and demand may push prices up further still. With so many potential applications in so many industries, will a substance such as graphene be produced in adequate quantities to satisfy global demand?

The implications of the cost explosion are potentially game changing. Societies worldwide may need to accept a new reality, in which their disposable incomes and quality of life are squeezed. In this context, leaders may need to communicate a "new normal" to customers, preparing them for an era of potentially significant price hikes.

At the same time, however, companies will still need to ensure that their products remain affordable to a critical mass of customers and that their employees can continue to make a living. Faced with soaring costs, we may need to find different ways of living, working, and doing business.

| Cost Explosion | |
|---|---|
| **Cost Drivers** | **Megatrends** |
| Natural resources<br>Power<br>Fuel<br>Precursors<br>Food<br>Diseases caused by pollution | Environmental crisis (scarcity of resources and climate change) |
| Talent shortage<br>Late career work environments<br>Work migration | Demographic change |
| Demands and expectations of individualized workforce | Individualization and value pluralism |
| Complex organization structures<br>Individualized customer base | Globalization 2.0 |
| Race for innovation<br>Rare specialists<br>Technologies | Technological convergence |

## Reinforcer 5. Ethicization of Business

It is probably fair to say that in recent years, the business world has not displayed the highest moral standards. Global organizations in several industries have come under the media spotlight for unsavory practices. The behavior of the banking sector, for example, is well documented, and not only for its role in the global financial crisis. Fines have been imposed for fixing interest rates, money laundering, and widespread misselling of products to businesses and consumers.

Yet as we've seen several times in this chapter, the megatrends—climate change in particular—will demand impeccable ethics from organizations and their leaders. Consumers will expect that companies contribute to a fairer society and establish trusting relationships with customers. This calls for high levels of integrity, authenticity, and transparency. Business needs to raise the bar.

This ethicization will derive from several megatrends, discussed below.

### Environmental Crisis

As noted, concerns over climate change will oblige companies to implement sustainable business models to help alleviate environmental damage. It is a pressure that will build on organizations from all angles: customers, shareholders, employees, governments, and society at large.

### The Digital Era

The blurring of the public and the private, the transparency that this engenders, and widening access to information will all require leaders to act with the utmost integrity to protect the reputation of their organizations. Sincerity and credibility—of values, acts, and words—will be essential attributes.

Leaders will not get away with false promises or putting on an act for very long. As noted, customers and employees—particularly those of the digital generation—will be only too quick to post their disapproval on their blogs, Twitter feeds, and Facebook pages. Word will spread and momentum will gather rapidly. Reputations will be built or destroyed in a matter of hours.

## Technological Convergence

As we saw in Chapter 6, NBIC technologies will break new ground, forcing societies to debate the implications of progress and set the ethical framework for scientists and corporations. Organizations will need to be sensitive to this debate, and they will be expected to behave ethically by respecting the limits of what is deemed acceptable innovation.

## The Morality Paradox in the Ethicization of Business

Intriguingly, the ethical demands on leaders present yet another paradox, in the context of three other reinforcers: the erosion of their authority, its transfer to an increasingly complex stakeholder community, and the cost explosion.

How are leaders to maintain ethics that are beyond reproach when rising costs are putting severe pressure on profits, and when their power is diminishing over the multiplicity of stakeholders they need to bring with them?

| Ethicization of Business | |
| --- | --- |
| **Ethical Move** | **Megatrends** |
| Sustainable business models | Environmental crisis |
| Values-based reputation management | Digitization Individualization |
| Ethical framework for scientists and corporations | Technological convergence |

# DILEMMAS

The four dilemmas caused by the megatrends are shown below:

| The Megatrend Storm: The Four Dilemmas |
| --- |
| 1.   Mobility. The desire for more, the need for less |
| 2.   Resources. Growing scarcity of and demand for raw materials |
| 3.   Hierarchies. Flatter or more complex structures? |
| 4.   Horizons. The immediacy of the digital era versus the long view of climate change |

## Dilemma 1. Mobility

Globalization 2.0 will mean more business done across borders, necessitating more travel. It will also open up the option to travel—a long-standing symbol of wealth and privilege—to millions more people. In addition, growing individualism will drive the demand for travel as a leisure pursuit. Meanwhile, leaders will need to spend time with greater numbers of stakeholders, and in more places, to keep abreast of local market dynamics.

However, mobility poses a dilemma. Addressing climate change will require a drastic reduction in carbon-emitting travel and transportation of products.

One argument in response to the environmental crisis is that industry, a primary cause of global warming, will ultimately provide the solution. Products will come along and new energy sources will be found that reduce and potentially eliminate the ecological impact of human activity. As we saw in Chapter 6, 3D printing could localize production, reducing the need to transport goods, while harvesting desert sunlight could unleash untold quantities of clean energy.

However, this seems to be an optimistic scenario. Chapter 6 also highlighted the unpredictability of technological progress. Hoping for some sort of salutary black swan (in this context, an unforeseeable, disruptive technology) is simply not realistic.

It also seems highly unlikely that technology will deliver a solution that eliminates the need for travel, yet meets the basic human need for real-world contact. Of course, digital innovation has already given us virtual platforms over which to communicate and transact, and these will no doubt become more sophisticated in time. And it is possible that digital natives will feel less need for human contact to maintain relationships.

But social networks, for all their power and popularity, mostly connect people who already know each other. Several studies[7]—not to mention our many conversations with digital natives—suggest that few digital natives actually build and maintain purely digital relationships. The people they trust most are those they know in the real world.

This is because humans are essentially social beings. However digitized life becomes, there remains an essential part of us that feels chemistry, creates bonds, and establishes trust more readily when face to face. As people, we value an intimacy that will surely never be realized in a virtual realm.

Leaders will therefore have to make tough decisions about travel. How can they function without actually meeting the people they manage, particularly in a time when growing numbers of increasingly diverse stakeholders all expect to be treated as individuals?

## Dilemma 2. Resources

Growing consumer demand as a result of Globalization 2.0 will require more intensive use of natural resources that are, as we saw in Chapter 2, in scarce supply. Demand for technology in particular will soar. Digitization and individualization will drive sales of laptops, tablets, smartphones, MP3 players, gaming consoles, and so on. Globalization will generate new automotive markets. NBIC innovation will create new machines with powerful applications in healthcare, agriculture, food production, and other important fields.

All of this adds up to runaway demand for rare earth metals. But as explained in Chapter 2, viable sources of these elements are already in short supply, are typically found in remote locations, and are currently produced in only one country, China. As a result, prices have already rocketed over the last decade, and demand is forecast to outstrip supply globally in just a few years' time.

And of course, producing more technology will require more energy and therefore more oil—the global supply of which has possibly already peaked.

So how will industry continue to satisfy spiraling demand for technology in the face of a dwindling supply of essential raw inputs? Again, one possible scenario is that innovations will emerge that offer solutions. Will more common materials—or entirely new substances like graphene—be used instead? Could the efficiency with which rare earths are recycled and reused be improved? Might humankind even go searching for minerals on other planets?

Short of such advances, the reality could be an end to the ever cheaper technology that Western consumers have come to expect. Very likely, we will simply have to get used to relying on a smaller number of significantly more expensive devices.

That may be straightforward enough in the consumer sphere, where individuals can make rational decisions about how much of their disposable income to spend on gadgets. But such choices may prove more emotive in other fields. Could life-saving medical innovations be shelved because of a lack of necessary raw materials? Might poorer countries be denied more reliable methods of agricultural production because the equipment is too expensive or because it is deemed commercially unviable by manufacturers? These are potentially controversial dilemmas that may prompt the involvement of governments and pressure groups as well as corporations.

## Dilemma 3. Hierarchies

On the one hand, a future shaped by the megatrends would imply the need for flatter management structures: Employees exert their individualism, want more responsibility, display less respect for formal authority, and insist on working remotely. On the other hand, increasingly large, diverse, and global corporations will require ever increasing levels of coordination to execute operations, share ideas, deliver products to market, improve processes, drive innovation, and cope with the increased complexity described above.

So how thin can hierarchies become while still exerting the necessary control? A flatter structure can potentially speed decision making, or slow it down by compensating with an intricate matrix structure that relies on informal as much as formal control. Creating lean structures that retain adequate control will prove a tricky balance.

Effective control stems from clarity: clarity of *purpose* and clarity of *accountability*. When people understand their organization's purpose, *and* their own role in achieving it, they are more likely to align their behavior to reaching organizational goals. However, organizations typically struggle to provide this clarity, and creating it will be an acute challenge with more stakeholders and more complexity to manage.

So how will global organizations provide younger employees with the freedom they demand? This will call for "bounded autonomy"— that is, autonomy with a clear direction and plainly defined boundaries (there will be more details on bounded autonomy in Chapter 8).

Paradoxically, it may be possible to cater to the needs of younger generations by actually creating more layers of management. As we saw in Chapter 3, Generation Y is, in its own way, ambitious. Members of Generation Y may not want conventional leadership roles, but they expect their concerns to be listened to and their abilities to be recognized, and they demand rapid career progression. Perhaps a multilayered hierarchy offering frequent promotions is the solution after all.

## Dilemma 4. Horizons

The environmental crisis caused by 250 years of human activity is probably the most intractable problem facing the world today. It will require complex solutions designed and implemented over long periods of time, possibly many decades.

Yet younger generations have short attention spans. As noted in Chapter 4, credible research suggests that extensive use of digital tools affects how the brain operates. Digital natives are natural multitaskers, able to efficiently scan large downloads of information and rapidly draw conclusions. However, they have a higher inclination toward short attention spans. Long-term thinking, painstaking analysis of detail, and thoughtful consideration are not typically among their strengths. Patience is not one of their virtues.

But these will be essential qualities in a world that requires complex solutions to complex problems, the environment being uppermost among them. Where, when, and how will organizations find time for people to think through these issues and consider solutions? How can they find the right people and build the right roles to enable this?

Deep reflection will be needed to navigate an increasingly complex world, characterized not only by climate change but by the new globalization, unprecedented technological innovation, and a changing workforce.

## QUESTIONS, QUESTIONS

So what can leaders do about the perfect storm caused by the megatrends? How will they cope with the multitude of challenges, complexities, and dilemmas coming their way? How do they find the right answers to the many questions posed in this chapter? How are they to lead their organizations through the maelstrom?

To begin to answer these questions, we need to understand the nature of leadership, now and in a future transformed by the megatrends. We examine this in the remaining chapter.

# 8 Footnotes, Not Headlines: The Altrocentric Leader

*"If men define situations as real, they are real in their consequences."*
—**William Isaac Thomas** and **Dorothy Swaine Thomas,** sociologists

## AT A GLANCE ▪ THE ALTROCENTRIC LEADER

### Five Essential Points

1.  *The era of alpha-male leadership is over.* Leaders who place themselves center stage and lead predominantly by coercing and pacesetting have a misguided understanding of the nature of leadership. They will not cope with the mega-trend storm.

2.  *Leadership is a social practice.* Leadership is not a set of fixed attributes possessed by certain people. It is a relationship, the nature of which depends on its context. It is a shared activity that results in shared knowledge, understanding, and meaning. Being a leader or a follower is not a dichotomy but is subject to constant flux: An individual can be a leader in one context and a follower in another.

3.  *The leader of the future is altrocentric.* Altrocentric leadership is required in the light of the megatrends. Altrocentric leaders have a different self-image from that

of alpha-male leaders. They do not seek the spotlight. They understand that leadership is a relationship and that the difference between leaders and followers is contextual.

4. *Altrocentric leaders are characterized by values and inner strength.* They possess empathy, ego-maturity, and intellectual curiosity, and they are open on an emotional level. They have a strong ethical perspective and a genuine concern for diversity.

5. *Altrocentric leaders are adept at engaging stakeholders and at complex strategic thinking and execution.* They understand the changing context in which their organizations exist, and they recognize the complex stakeholder community they serve. They engage in cross-boundary partnering and work with their organizations to co-create a powerful narrative. They provide bounded autonomy and develop effective senior leadership teams.

---

Former German Premier Gerhard Schröder earned various nicknames during his time in office. One such moniker was the "Basta Chancellor," a reference to his habit of abruptly ending discussions or emphasizing his point by simply declaring *basta* (Italian for "enough"). Schröder's predecessor, Helmut Kohl, used to refer to an upcoming minister in his cabinet as *mein Mädchen* (German for "my girl"). Kohl's "girl" became quite famous in her own right. She was Angela Merkel.

Jürgen Schrempp headed the automotive company Daimler-Chrysler for ten years until 2005. There is a story about Schrempp's apparent reaction to management guru Tom Peters' assertion that managers will be no more than "footnotes" in the history of their companies. Schrempp is said to have banged his fist on the table and shouted, "I will be a *headline!*"[1]

These anecdotes paint a picture of strong, alpha-male leaders, dominating the pack with their coercive, tough-minded, and egocentric personalities. Schröder and Kohl were responsible for some widely acclaimed achievements during their time as leaders. (Schrempp was less effective. A champion of shareholder value, he managed to reduce DaimlerChrysler's share price by two-thirds over the course of his regime.[2]) But it is hard to escape the feeling that there is something of the past about this paternalistic, tub-thumping style of leadership, for two principal reasons. First, the superhero, alpha-male (and some-times, alpha-female[3]) approach is based on a distorted view of lead-ership. Second, it will prove woefully inadequate in the megatrend era.

As noted, the six megatrends, and the reinforcers and dilemmas that derive from them, will create a complex, unpredictable, and par-adoxical environment for leaders. One-dimensional, egocentric, head-line-seeking, *basta* leadership will no longer cut it.

## WHAT IS LEADERSHIP?

To comprehend why alpha-male leadership has had its day, we first need to understand the nature of leadership and what constitutes being a leader. This is not as simple as it sounds, which may be why two-thirds of the many thousands of leadership books and papers published neglect to even define the term.[4] There is little or no con-sensus in the literature on what leadership actually is, beyond the fact that it entails influencing others. In which case, why not just call it *influencing?*

In the absence of a properly defined concept, we tend to rely on an intuitive notion of leadership, a broadly accepted view that sees leadership and leaders as a given. An individual either is a leader—with certain specific qualities that define him as such—or is not. Each of us falls into one category or the other.

We would challenge this notion. It is far too simplistic a definition, and so it does not withstand a deeper analysis.

Some might say that I am the leader of a company if I have been appointed managing director. But *manager* and *leader* are different concepts. Being managing director gives me formal decision-making authority and responsibility for achieving certain objectives—which makes me a *manager*. If leadership were merely formal authority, then the concept of leadership would be redundant, as it would fail to add anything meaningful to the concept of management. In effect, we would need only the latter.

It is only when we begin to analyze the relationship between lead-ers and followers that leadership takes on a more defined identity. To illustrate this, let's consider two distinct roles from the world of music: that of a pianist and that of the conductor of an orchestra.

Imagine an individual who is both (which is fairly common). Let's place her alone on a desert island, with only her piano for company. (OK, that's a bit more unusual, but bear with us.) Here, she can still be a pianist. She can play her piano to her heart's content; she requires no audience to do this. But she cannot be a conductor—*conductor* literally meaning "leader"—without an orchestra to conduct.

*Conductor*—and by the same logic, *leader*—are relational terms, whereas pianist is not. For leaders to exist, they require other entities—*followers*—to also exist. They are nothing in isolation.

And the leader-follower relationship is more complex still. Leaders and followers are not distinct entities but different relationships in different circumstances.

Contrary to the generally accepted view of leadership, there is not one set of leaders and one set of followers in life. In fact, many people are both. One might be a leader (captain, coach) of his soccer team but a follower in his hiking club. He might be a department leader and a follower in a cross-functional project team at work. In our working lives, most of us have staff below us *and* leaders above us.

So leadership is not only relational; it is also contextual. It is not a set of fixed attributes possessed by certain individuals. It is a relationship, the nature of which depends on its context. Being a leader or a follower is not a dichotomy but is subject to constant flux.

This might explain why there are very few job titles that include the word *leader*. Senior representatives of organizations are directors, managers, executives, vice presidents, or chairs. But they are rarely *leaders*. One common (more junior) exception is team leader, a title that actually describes the role both relationally and contextually, by defining whom the individual leads, and who follows.

The intuitive understanding of leadership, and of leaders and followers, is what the alpha-male approach is based on. De facto, I am the leader, you are the followers. *Basta.*

But it misconstrues the nature of the beast. The truth is that leadership is a social interaction, a context-dependent relation between individuals. It is, in effect, a social practice, which for our purposes is defined as a shared activity that results in shared knowledge, understanding, and meaning.[5]

## DON'T THROW THE BABY OUT WITH THE BATHWATER

So if leadership is a shared practice and if leaders and followers are not set roles but are interchangeable depending on the context, then we might reasonably conclude that there can be no prescribed leadership competencies or behaviors, no general "recipe for success"—despite what thousands of management books would have us believe.

Some leadership commentators certainly seem to think there is not one set of competencies for leaders. For them, effective leadership demands a radically different perspective from traditional, competency-oriented leadership frameworks.[6] There may be some merit in this logic in an environment vastly complicated by the megatrends. This is especially so when traditional notions of leadership, which focus on the individual and her specific traits, are misguided.

But there is no reason to throw the baby out with the bathwater entirely. If we decide that there are no suitable leadership qualities for the megatrend storm, then we might as well give up on the idea of leadership altogether. Instead, it might be more helpful to ask: What is a leader's *role* in the social practice of leadership? And what attributes and competencies will help individuals to effectively perform this role?

## LEAVE YOUR EGO AT THE DOOR

As noted, it is generally accepted that an important aspect of leadership is influencing others. Broadly speaking, there are six ways a leader can influence people: (1) by giving commands, (2) by setting the pace, (3) by sharing the vision, (4) by coaching, (5) by creating harmony, and (6) by including others in the decision-making process.[7] (See the chart below). Each of these approaches has its strengths, and its effectiveness depends on the context, the situation at hand, and the individuals a leader needs to influence.

| The Six Most Effective Styles of Leadership | |
|---|---|
| **Style** | **Primary Concern** |
| Directive | Gaining immediate compliance from team members |
| Pacesetting | Accomplishing tasks to high standards |
| Visionary | Providing long-term vision |
| Affiliative | Creating group harmony |
| Participative | Achieving group consensus and generating new ideas |
| Coaching | Developing team members |

Source: © 2006 Hay Group. All Rights Reserved.

Alpha-male leaders tend to resort largely to the first two styles, taking a directive and pacesetting approach.[8] This might seem natural enough to individuals who discern a clear dichotomy between leaders and followers (rather than seeing leadership as a relational and collective experience). To them, leadership is unilateral. I lead, you follow. *Basta.*

But life under the megatrends will demand a different understanding of leadership. Let's be clear: We are not suggesting that future leaders need to be beta-males and females, unremarkable types who avoid risk and confrontation. Leadership in 2030 will call for individuals who choose *not* to see themselves as heroes, as headlines, or as patrons (*mein Mädchen*), and who do not put their egos first. The leaders of the future will not be egocentric. They will be *altrocentric.*

*Altrocentric* is a neologism meaning the opposite of *egocentric* (*alter* meaning "the other" in Latin). The defining characteristic of altrocentric leaders is a primary focus on and concern for others rather than themselves.

It is important to note that being altrocentric does not mean having no ego. Altrocentric leaders are confident individuals with strong personalities. But they take their ego out of the picture, and they know how to keep it in check. They see themselves as just one integral part of the whole. Altrocentric leadership is based on a firm grasp of the relational, contextual, and shared nature of leadership. It is an approach sometimes described as post-heroic leadership.[9]

## THE ENDANGERED ALPHA MALE

Alpha-male leadership may be outmoded and based on a mistaken understanding of a leader's role, but this kind of leader still remains widespread. So they must be having some success, or they would have already died out—unless leading that way is simply human nature (see the section *Born to Lead?*).

### Born to Lead?

When former U.S. Secretary of State Henry Kissinger called power "the ultimate aphrodisiac,"[10] he may have been on to something, at least according to Irish neuropsychologist Ian Robertson. Robertson's view is that power stimulates the same part of the brain as sex and cocaine, and that success increases the production of dopamine and testosterone in both men and women. According to his 2012 book *The Winner Effect*, there is a clear link between power and the production of these hormones.[11]

But it would be a mistake to conclude that individuals with higher testosterone levels are natural born leaders, because hormone levels vary with people's roles. Robertson contends that if people are promoted to higher levels of an organization, their dopamine levels increase, and vice versa. As a result, too much power can actually distort the personality. A little like leadership itself, then, hormonal activity in the brain is contextual and role-dependent.

So would this mean that there is no "leadership gene," no predisposition to leadership in the makeup of certain individuals? Yes and no.

British behavioral scientist Jan-Emmanuel De Neve and his colleagues analyzed genetic samples of around 4,000 identical twins, along with information about their jobs and leadership roles.[12] He discovered a definite correlation between a genotype called rs4950 and the likelihood of becoming a leader.

*(continued)*

De Neve rated the heritability of leadership role occupancy at an estimated 24 percent. In other words, less than a quarter of the difference between people who do and do not occupy formal leadership roles can be accounted for by genetic factors. This leaves plenty of scope for people to "learn" leadership and for social influences to be the dominant factor in shaping whether or not an individual becomes a leader.

So how is it that a faulty approach to leadership can continue to thrive? It is because of what is known as the Thomas theorem: the idea that "if people define situations as real, they are real in their consequences."

American sociologists William I. Thomas and Dorothy Swaine Thomas put forth the theory that the interpretation of a situation is enough to prompt action, whether or not that interpretation is correct. In other words, people's perception of what is correct is enough for that view to *become* reality.

For example, if a young male is perceived and labeled as deviant (because of his appearance, accent, or demeanor), there is a high probability that he will become deviant. If German gossip columns expect Brad Pitt and Angelina Jolie to attend a certain party in Berlin, and they bill the event as a hot ticket, then local celebrities will probably turn up—and the party will become a hot ticket.

In the same way, if alpha-males resort to banging their fists and shouting *basta*, and the people who work for them accept this, then by default, this *becomes* the reality of leadership—however restricted an approach it may be.

And this approach may actually get results (and in fairness, it can be particularly effective, in the short term, during a crisis). But the approach ignores the relational, contextual, and collective nature of leadership, and so it will typically fall short of what *could* be achieved. It will fail to fully leverage the motivation and abilities of the team.

This is what Hay Group's research has proved over many decades about the impact on performance of the different leadership styles.[13] And under the pressures of the megatrends, the reductionist, alpha-male interpretation of leadership will prove more limited than ever, for several reasons.

First, the shortcomings of this approach will be a significant performance risk amid the overwhelming pressures of the megatrends.
Egotistical "I-am-the-headline" attitudes will fail to grasp the complexity of the situation and the challenges at hand. The more a leader
wants to be a headline, the faster he will become a footnote.

Second, as noted, alpha-male leadership is a misguided approach.
It is a case of one side of the equation trying to define a two-way relationship. And it will become more and more irrelevant in an era
marked by growing individualism and a power shift away from leaders
to employees. If people have the power, they are less inclined to tolerate coercive leaders.

Third, alpha-male leadership is not compatible with the new
working practices discussed in Chapter 7. How do you command and
control highly mobile teams that work remotely and operate virtually?
How powerful can fist-banging really be in a Skype meeting?

In addition, the ethicization of business runs counter to the logic
of individualistic leadership. Leaders will need to be transparent and
open, willing to engage in a dialogue with others, and ready to listen
to opposing views. Also, value pluralism will encourage people to demand greater respect from their leaders and greater symmetry between leaders and followers, leaving less scope for the *basta* approach.

And finally, the dilemmas spelled out in Chapter 7 will create a
landscape that is too complex, ambiguous, and changeable for one-
dimensional, alpha-male leadership, or for any one "superhero" to
deal with.

So if the alpha male is ill-equipped for leadership in 2030, why will
the altrocentric leader fare any better? It is because of a fundamental
difference between the two: their self-image and their motives.

## Self-Image

Self-image (or self-understanding), as the term suggests, refers to how
one sees oneself. (For our purposes, we include "social role" in this
definition, even if it can be distinguished from self-image.) In the context of leadership, it is the degree to which a leader might view herself
as a decision maker, team motivator, expert, coach, teacher, change

agent, and so on. This may sound simple enough. But the right self-image will be critical to effective leadership under the megatrend storm.

## Self-Image Matters: "Feminine" Leaders, "Masculine" Leaders

A study of the different leadership styles men and women tend to use sheds a fascinating light on the power of self-image.[14] In 2004, Ruth Malloy of Hay Group analyzed forty-five highly successful female executives in senior leadership positions, mostly at Fortune 500 companies, and compared them to forty-four successful male counterparts and thirty-four less successful executive women.

The results are revealing. Malloy found that outstanding women were twice as likely as men to use leadership styles typically considered "feminine" (coaching, participative, and affiliative). At the same time, however, these same women also made frequent use of styles often labeled as "masculine" (directive, pacesetting, and visionary). The upshot: Using a broader range of styles led to more motivating working climates, resulting in higher performing teams and business units.

Meanwhile, the less successful women executives relied predominantly on the more "masculine" leadership styles—and created the weakest climates of all three groups.

What does this tell us about self-image? The effective women leaders avoided being influenced by the gender expectations that come with leadership roles. They were able to overcome the traditional gender and role stereotypes that are learned and reinforced by our social education. This enabled them to use a broader range of leadership styles and behaviors to motivate their teams and get the best from the people they led.

This made them better performers than women whose self-image, and their perception of their role as a woman leader, encouraged them be more "masculine" in their approach. This led to less success. Even successful male leaders would create higher performing climates by moving beyond a narrow, typically "masculine" self-image.

Only with the right self-image can an individual comprehend that leadership is a relationship, that the difference between leaders and followers is contextual, and that he will ultimately be a footnote, not a headline. When Frank Appel, CEO of Deutsche Post, describes himself as the chief enabling officer and the chief energy officer,[15] he seems to be on the right lines.

So what do we mean by the "right" self-image? What does this look like in terms of competencies and behaviors?

There are many personal characteristics that influence what we do and how we behave, which exist at different levels of consciousness. We might think of them as being levels of an iceberg.[16] (See Figure 8-1.) Conscious characteristics are visible above the water. These include our skills and knowledge. Nonconscious characteristics—our traits and motives—lie below the water. They are less visible.

**Figure 8-1** ▪ Conscious, Semiconscious, and Nonconscious Characteristics

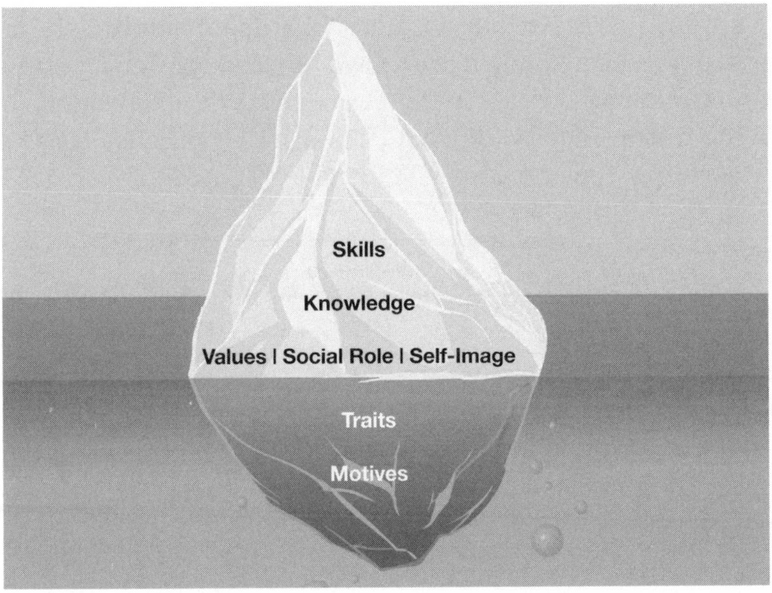

Skills

Knowledge

Values | Social Role | Self-Image

Traits

Motives

Self-image, social role, and our values (for example, the degree of priority we give to career or family, or both) lie close to the waterline: They could be described as semiconscious. They are formed and reinforced by our upbringing and education. Once shaped, they tend to remain fairly stable in most people. But as they are learned characteristics, they can be relearned. They can be developed and changed over time.

## Motives

Deep underwater, we find what renowned psychologist David McClelland calls our *social motives*, the inner drivers that prompt us to behave or act in a certain manner. The least conscious characteristics, these are extremely important, as they influence almost everything we do.

Much more than self-image and values, motives are developed in early childhood, and they remain reasonably constant during one's lifetime.

McClelland identified three key social motives: achievement, affiliation, and power (see below). The achievement motive is the need to meet or exceed a standard of excellence and to continually improve one's performance. Affiliation is the need to create and maintain harmonious relationships with others. The power motive is the drive to make an impact on and have an influence over others.

| Social Motives | |
|---|---|
| **Motive** | **Driver** |
| Achievment | Excellence |
| Affiliation | Harmony |
| Power | Influence |

All three motives exist in all of us to a greater or lesser degree. But what differs greatly between individuals is their "motive profile," the relative strengths of each of the three motives.

Imagine a professor who spends hours alone in her study, buried in research, churning out academic papers that hardly anybody reads. She would have little contact with or influence on others, so she would probably display low affiliation and power motives. But her prolific output might suggest a very strong achievement motive.

In business organizations, some technical specialists (engineers and scientists, for example) show little appetite for managerial roles, preferring to continue developing their expertise in their chosen field. Again, this indicates a high achievement motive. Politicians, on the other hand, are often driven by a very strong power motive: They desire the influence to effect change.

Typically, the motive profile of senior managers in a turnaround situation goes as follows: low on affiliation, moderately high on achievement, markedly high on power. Importantly, however, there are different kinds of power motive, and altrocentric leaders display very different power motive profiles compared to alpha-males.

## POWER DRIVERS

McClelland (and subsequently others) identified four stages of power through which we all progress during our lifetimes. But crucially, some people progress further than others (see Figure 8-2).

During the first stage, we derive power from other people. This is *dependent power.* It is typically seen in children arguing that "my daddy is bigger than your daddy."

As we mature and enter the second stage, we begin to realize that we are a source of power and strength in ourselves and that we can exploit this to our advantage. This *independent power* is typical of adolescence: for example, the rebellious teenager who tells his parents in a fit of pique, "I don't need you. I can take care of myself."

**Figure 8-2** ▧ The Four Stages of Power

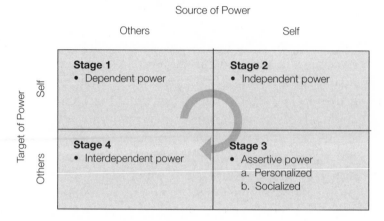

Source: © 2000 Hay Group. All Rights Reserved.

More relevant to leadership are the third and fourth stages. At the third stage, we realize that we can assert our power to make others feel stronger or weaker. This *assertive power* stage itself evolves over two phases. As a rule, people initially exert personalized power, influencing others for their own self-aggrandizement in order to feel and be perceived as strong, capable, or influential. *Personalized power* is a common characteristic of alpha-male leaders, who exercise their power in ways that further their own interests, reputation, career, or material standing. Many alpha-male leaders get stuck in this phase, never developing beyond it.

In the second phase of assertive power, *socialized power*, individuals use their strengths to make others feel stronger and more capable—the very opposite of personalized power.

In the fourth and final stage, people see themselves as just one part of a greater whole. They are aware that power stems not just from themselves but also from others. This *interdependent power* allows them to help others feel strong and capable and to strive to pass on to others what has benefited them.

People with a strong interdependent power motive tend to take a longer-term perspective. They recognize the complexity and ambiguity of leadership, and they have realistic aspirations for what can be achieved. They avoid cynicism and stereotyping, making the effort to understand individuals and empathize with their needs. And they realize that not everybody will be driven by the same goals as they are.

## ALTROCENTRIC POWER

The altrocentric leaders needed to cope with leadership in 2030 will be driven by socialized and, ideally, interdependent power. Why so? Because of the consequences of the megatrends that we have examined. The proliferation of stakeholders and new working practices will erode leaders' positional power and authority. In this context, directive, pacesetting, command-and-control styles will not be accepted as default leadership behavior. Good leaders—great leaders—will understand that the key source of their power is other people. And they will use this to empower those around them.

## COMPETENCIES OF THE ALTROCENTRIC LEADER

As mentioned, motives are difficult to observe directly as they are deeply rooted in the personality.[17] However, behavior can be observed, and patterns of behavior indicate a person's underlying concerns and motives (as well as his or her traits, values, etc.). We call these *behavioral competencies*. So it is possible to outline the competencies that the altrocentric leaders of the future will need, in terms of the behaviors they will need to display.

To do this, we analyzed the consequences of each megatrend as spelled out in Chapters 1 to 6—from a behavioral competency perspective. The result is the competency map shown in Figure 8-3.[18] We would not claim that the map is exhaustive or expect an altrocentric leader to possess every competency. That would require some sort of superhuman. Rather, the competency map of the altrocentric leader is a hypothetical model (an "ideal type," as Max Weber would have described it[19]) that enables us to outline the actual behaviors that will help leaders to cope with the megatrends.

**Figure 8-3** 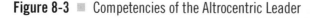 Competencies of the Altrocentric Leader

Let us examine each competency group and each of the competencies themselves in turn.

## 1. Inner Strengths

Altrocentric leaders are characterized by what we call *inner strength*. This means that they are emotionally stable, intellectually open, self-aware, and willing to pause and reflect on matters. They possess what influential American psychologist Daniel Goleman called EI (emotional intelligence). EI is the capacity to recognize our own feelings and those of others, to motivate ourselves and effectively manage our emotions.[20]

These inner strengths are fundamental qualities for an altrocentric leader. Without them, an individual is highly unlikely to possess or be able to develop the essential competencies set out below. As a result, such a person will struggle to generate the loyalty of a highly diverse workforce and to act with the integrity and sincerity required in an ethicized business environment.

**Ego-Maturity**

This is a defining characteristic for altrocentric leaders. Ego-mature leaders accept that they cannot and should not know everything, and so they are comfortable with uncertainty and ambiguity. The megatrend storm will hold no fears for them.

Ego-maturity is the ability to subjugate one's own emotions, motives, and interests to the greater good of the group (e.g., the company, community, industry, or environment), even at personal cost. Ego-maturity implies a reflective and critical awareness of one's own limits, behaviors, ambitions, and values, as well as effective emotional self-control.

Ego-mature individuals do not panic or indulge in mood swings and sudden outbursts; they do not crack under pressure. They are steady, reliable, and composed. They work well with people and treat them fairly, irrespective of personal chemistry. And they understand that they themselves are not of primary importance within the group but are as interchangeable as any other team member.

**Intellectual Curiosity and Emotional Openness**

Altrocentric leaders have a desire to know more. They go beyond asking routine questions and settling for obvious answers, constantly challenging conventional wisdom and traditional approaches. They rarely satisfy themselves with the first solution that presents itself.

They are also open on an emotional level. They actively seek to broaden their horizons and listen attentively to others. They gravitate to people with different backgrounds and outlooks from their own, so as to learn from exposure to different perspectives. And they are not threatened by the ambiguity that results from multiple points of view. The broad perspective that this instills will be essential to cope with the complexity of the megatrends.

**Empathy**

Empathy is a precondition for altrocentric leaders if they are to attract, retain, and understand the needs of an increasingly diverse and individualized workforce.

Altrocentric leaders have the ability and willingness to hear, understand, and respond to the unspoken thoughts, feelings, and concerns of others. They grasp others' perspectives and know how best to approach them. And they are able to actively elicit the views and concerns of others, test their understanding of these views and concerns, and reflect back their interest in others' views and feelings.

## 2. Values

The values that leaders hold and portray to the outside world will be scrutinized in an ethicized and individualized environment. By presenting an acceptable standard of ethics and integrity, companies will be able to woo and hold on to customers and employees.

The very best companies understand this. Hay Group's annual *Best Companies for Leadership* study identifies the world's most effective companies at developing leaders. In 2011, the study found that 45 percent of respondents at these companies value ethics in their leaders, compared to only 19 percent of companies overall.[21]

### Ethical Standards

As noted in Chapter 7, behaving ethically and "doing the right thing" will no longer be just a moral obligation. It will be a critical success factor in an ethicized, transparent climate, in which power is transferred from leaders to their many stakeholders. This will require leaders whose professional and personal behavior meets the highest standards.

Altrocentric leaders integrate ethical values, social responsibility, and concerns for health, safety, and the environment into their decision making. They continually seek innovative ways to improve business performance while contributing to the greater good.

### Concern for Diversity

The business case for a diverse workforce is clear in light of the megatrends. It will be critical to an organization's ability to respond to Globalization 2.0, innovate new technologies, and respond to demographic changes in labor and customer markets.

Altrocentric leaders recognize this. They not only value difference, treating all team members with equal respect, but they also promote values that actively forge and sustain diversity in their teams. They adapt their leadership practices to foster diversity and generate a collaborative climate among the most diverse groups of people. And they ensure that processes such as recruitment and development do the same, for example, by encouraging minority groups and helping to prepare minority candidates for executive roles.

## 3. Strategic Business Thinking

It is a given that strategy should be part of a business leader's job. Over time, therefore, strategic thinking has come to be viewed as a baseline competency for senior executives—but not necessarily one that distinguishes the best from the rest.

Under the megatrends, however, this will change. Strategy will be placed center stage. Complex strategic thinking will be critical to steering organizations through the complexities, ambiguities, and uncertainties of Globalization 2.0, climate change, scarcity of resources, and the NBIC revolution.

Encouragingly, the organizations studied in Hay Group's *Best Companies for Leadership* value strategic thinking in their leaders more than any other ability. In fact, for the first time in many years, this competency topped the list.[22] Leading organizations have realized that without complex strategic thinking, they will not survive the megatrend storm.

### Contextual Awareness

Altrocentric leaders understand the context in which their organizations sit: the global market, localized trends, external forces (such as megatrends), and the many implications of these. They grasp the dynamics that drive their business's relationships with its workforce, competitors, partners, and regulatory authorities. And they keep abreast of the broader societal, regulatory, technological, and environmental issues that affect the company. This enables them to sense the current and future impact of global business trends on the company and clarify how the business will take advantage of opportunities and defend against threats.

**Stakeholder Recognition**

Intuitively recognizing the diverse and complex interests that their company must serve, altrocentric leaders will not miss a trick when it comes to stakeholder proliferation. This is an important quality, as it will provide future leaders with an accurate view of precisely whom the organization serves. Altrocentric leaders are not in the habit of assisting only the needs of financial investors or focusing purely on shareholder value. They take into account the interests of all stakeholders with the potential to impact the company's ability to achieve its objectives.

These might be internal audiences, such as leadership teams and the company's global workforce (with its diverse cultural perspectives). They may be external stakeholders, including customers, suppliers, and partners. And they may even be wider influences with no direct relationship to the organization, but to whom the business still has a core responsibility in the eyes of the altrocentric leader—for example, local communities, social and environmental interests, and the general public.

## 4. Stakeholder Interaction

It would be all too easy to understand stakeholder interaction purely in terms of collaboration. And of course, this is vitally important to effective stakeholder interaction. But altrocentric leaders will take a much wider perspective.

Their ego-maturity, emotional intelligence, ethical standards, and strategic abilities will enable them to engage in a process of mutual *meaning-making* with the people they lead, and to come to grips with the challenges of cross-boundary partnering (see below).

### Meaning-Making

Meaning-making is a highly sophisticated form of interaction that will be a key distinguishing feature of altrocentric leaders. As such, we elaborate on this critical competency in a little more detail.

As a social interaction, leadership always creates shared meaning. Even alpha-male leaders create meaning for their followers, however simplistic ("Just *do* it!") or unpalatable ("or else ... " ) that meaning might be—and however unsatisfactory the effect.[23]

What's important here is the emphasis on *making*—not just providing—meaning. As we've seen, altrocentric leaders understand the relational and contextual nature of leadership, and thus they take into account the perspectives of all involved. This enables them to construct meaning jointly with their internal stakeholders, rather than simply handing it down from on high. To the altrocentric leader, meaning-making is not a unilateral task; it is a two-way affair. Meaning is co-created, which promotes a shared understanding of "why we are here": the purpose, direction, and goals of the organization.

The first stage in the meaning-making process may sometimes need to be a disruptive or even destructive act, an urgent wake-up call like that contained in Nokia CEO Stephen Elop's famous "burning platform" memo.[24] The memo marked the beginning of Elop's strategy to create a shared understanding of the world in which Nokia found itself, and to include as many people as possible in the meaning-making exercise (see the case study *Meaning-Making—Nokia's Leap of Faith*).

The megatrends drive the need for strong organizational narratives to focus people on new ways of working and operating. This in turn will demand new ways to engage an increasingly remote, virtual, diverse, individualized, demanding, and powerful workforce.

In this context, the art of altrocentric leadership will be to give people as much freedom to act as possible within certain necessary limits. This is what we call "bounded autonomy" later in this chapter. A key means of creating bounded autonomy is meaning-making (see the case study *Partaking in Bounded Autonomy and Altrocentric Leadership*).

In an article in the *McKinsey Quarterly*, Susie Cranston and Scott Keller pointed out that business leaders typically tell their workforces one of two stories.[25] They tell either the turnaround story ("we are performing terribly and must change dramatically to survive") or the good-to-great story ("we are doing great, but we have the potential to become the global market leader"). The problem is that both stories focus purely on the company. So Cranston and Keller recommend that leaders should tell four more stories: a societal story, a customer story, a team story, and an individual story.

These might run something like: "We are reducing our carbon footprint to protect the environment" (the societal story). "We produce the highest quality components so that our clients' products are reliable" (the client story). "We provide the infrastructure for our teams to work together effectively and efficiently" (the team story). "We value difference and create career opportunities for all" (the individual story).

This broader perspective is commendable. But the suggested approach misses an important point: Storytelling is a unilateral exercise. What the leaders of the future must do is engage people in a mutual meaning-making process, creating a single, shared story that takes multiple perspectives into account.

---

**CASE STUDY** ▪ Meaning-Making—Nokia's Leap of Faith

"The Nokia Leadership Team is very proud of the culture and engagement we've achieved," says Juha Äkräs, executive vice president for HR at Nokia and a member of the Nokia Leadership Team. "What's more, the business has clearly picked up."

In September 2013—a few months after we spoke to Äkräs—Microsoft saw fit to pay €5.4 billion ($7.2 billion) for Nokia's cell phone division. Yet just two years earlier, the onetime global market leader did not even have a high-end smartphone available. The situation facing Nokia at that time was stark. The mobile phone manufacturer had experienced a dizzying fall from grace, drastically losing market share in every market segment (see Chapter 1). There was no coping strategy to speak of. Commentators wrote Nokia off as a serious competitor.

That's when former Microsoft divisional president Stephen Elop became CEO. His appointment came as a surprise to many and somewhat of a shock to many Finns: The Canadian was the first foreigner to head up the pride of Finnish industry in almost 150 years. It was a clear signal that radical change was needed.

So what did Elop do about Nokia's dire fortunes? In the first instance, he communicated. He immediately began to proactively communicate with as many employees as possible, face-to-face, over email, and on blogs and internal social media. He asked their views on what should change, what should not change, and what should be addressed most urgently.

His outreach found an enthusiastic audience: Elop received some 2,000 replies. What he discovered confirmed his worst fears. Nokia was dogged by arrogance, complacency, sluggishness, bureaucracy, confusion, and disengagement. There was a chronic lack of strategy, direction, leadership, accountability, and ownership. As a result, the company had missed the smartphone boat and (to switch metaphors) was burying its head in the sand.

Elop quickly realized the nub of the problem: *There was no shared story at Nokia. There was no one Nokia narrative.* He knew that to get the company back on track, he would need to create such a narrative. He would need to engage people in a meaning-making process.

This would require a radical, urgent, and disruptive intervention. Elop needed to challenge long-held perceptions and confront people with the reality of their situation. He needed to be blunt (and, therefore, very un-Finnish). He needed to yell: *Red alert. We need to reinvent ourselves. Or we will die.*

So he gave his famous "burning platform" speech.[26] To Nokia's entire workforce, he compared the company with a burning oil rig in the North Sea. A man standing on the platform has two choices: Stay where he is and be engulfed by the flames, or plunge into the freezing waters 30 meters (100 feet) below. Elop pulled no punches as he spelled out his company's circumstances: "Nokia, our platform is burning."[27] The speech was subsequently distributed as an internal memo, which was instantly and widely leaked.

What had Elop done? He had gone out of his way to challenge Nokia's sense of identity. He had questioned what people thought the company meant. *He had destroyed the existing meaning.* And in doing so, he had deliberately generated disruption, frustration, and uncertainty.

Yet the speech was well received, even warmly welcomed by many Nokia employees, despite the anxieties it undoubtedly raised. "There was a sense of relief that the new CEO had identified the problems we faced and was prepared to air them and take them on," Äkräs recalls.

However, Elop's work had barely begun. He gathered a team around him, renaming the Group Executive Board simply the Nokia Leadership Team (NLT)—placing an explicit emphasis on *leadership*. Many other boards, committees, and layers of bureaucracy were dismantled.

Working closely with the NLT, he then formulated his turnaround strategy. He gave each member greater autonomy and pushed decision-making authority further down the hierarchy and to more local levels. The NLT had agreed on an entirely new

*(continued)*

direction for the company just eleven weeks after Elop arrived. "The top team now meets weekly and is fully aligned with the strategy," says Äkräs.

The NLT was charged with establishing the plan for the next phase of the turn-around: the alignment and engagement of the rest of the company. Äkräs explains: "We developed a structured approach to improving engagement and put in place cru-cial communications loops."

A crucial part of this process was to embed three core behaviors into the Nokia culture: accountability, urgency, and empathy. "We needed to address the lack of ac-countability and of any sense of urgency that had allowed us to fall so badly behind," says Äkräs. "But we needed to do this while *listening*: to customers, to employees, and to suppliers."

The next stage was to cascade the new vision of Nokia, its purpose, and its val-ues throughout the organization. This meant empowering every leader—and eventu-ally every employee—to be able to tell *their* "Nokia" story, and to be able express why *they* work for Nokia, why *they* believe in the company, how *they* feel it is making a dif-ference, and why the world is a better place because of Nokia's existence.

To achieve this, the NLT engaged the next 200 executives, plus a group of front-line managers, to help cascade the new culture, vision, and direction down through the company. The role of these "new Nokia builders" was to create transparency, foster involvement, establish a permanent dialogue with the workforce in order to boost engagement and provide feedback to the NLT.

Though a challenging time (thousands were laid off and dozens of sites were closed), it was also a time of meaning-making at Nokia, as the company began to develop a new identity. The company's last seven quarterly engagement surveys have shown a consistent upward trend over the two years since 2011.

"The fighting spirit is back," says Äkräs." Cynicism is no longer the default attitude. People see Nokia as their home once again, as the values-driven organization it had always been. While creating a new Nokia, we have worked hard to retain the spirit and heritage of our 150-year history, from the days when the firm made rubber prod-ucts through to our present business making mobile handsets and services."

Nokia involved hundreds of its people in a transparent, shared meaning-making process. The company's experience demonstrates just why meaning-making cannot be achieved by alpha-male leaders telling a dramatic story, then giving people orders from on high.

"We needed to go through a shared and very public hand-wringing process, just to get back into a challenger position," Äkräs says.

It is a sobering thought: Nokia, once the dominant global player, having to fight to achieve challenger status. And at the time of writing, it remains to be seen what the future will hold following the takeover deal.

But for the time being, Elop's meaning-making process has clearly been having the desired effect. Certainly, many commentators seem impressed by his leadership and by the turnaround he has effected at Nokia. Indeed, the Microsoft deal instantly triggered strong speculation that Elop would succeed Steve Ballmer, who had announced his retirement as CEO of the software giant just a couple of weeks earlier.

---

### Cross-Boundary Partnering

Faced with the complex world of the megatrends, altrocentric leaders have the inner strength to accept that they will not have the answer to everything and cannot make every decision alone. They are also mature enough to appreciate that others might be better suited than they are to tackle some challenges or make some decisions.

They are aware of the need for collaborative ventures to seize opportunities that can only be exploited collectively. They understand the necessity for and the rigors of coopetition, and they respect their competitors as partners.

Given this awareness, altrocentric leaders act to promote extensive collaboration across multiple boundaries: across borders, disciplines, organizations, functions, and departments. They pull together individuals from different parts of the organization to create the right teams for short-term projects and for long-term, cross-boundary collaboration. They work collaboratively with internal colleagues and external partners, without relying heavily on their positional power.

## 5. Execution

Execution of strategy is a primary responsibility for any business leader. But altrocentric leaders go about execution in a different way. First, they create engaged, high-performing decision-making teams, in which they are careful to position themselves as first among equals—with the emphasis on *equals*. Then, rather than simply holding people to account, they empower them, giving them autonomy within a clear framework of basic rules and considerations.

### Bounded Autonomy

Altrocentric leaders empower those they lead by providing them with as much autonomy as possible, combined with clear boundaries to create stability and direction and set the necessary limits.

These leaders are willing and able to delegate authority, creating the conditions for others to act with purpose and meaning while still being held accountable. And they take the time to coach and give feedback along the way (and proactively ask for feedback as well). This is interdependent power in action. It is how altrocentric leaders make their organizations stronger, more independent, and more responsive to changing conditions.

Fostering these conditions may call on altrocentric leaders to show their harsher side now and then. As mature individuals with a socialized power motive, altrocentric leaders do not feel the need to resort to the fist-banging ways of the alpha-male. But they are quite capable of handling the hard side of leadership if necessary. They know when to be directive and will not hesitate to deal with underperformance or misconduct or to remove people if the occasion demands.

---

**CASE STUDY** ■ Partaking in Bounded Autonomy and Altrocentric Leadership

Juergen Erbeldinger's partake AG might be described as an innovation consultancy. A boutique firm of around seventy consultants, it helps some of Germany's biggest businesses to find solutions to their innovation challenges. This demands creativity, which can be stifled by process, rules, and bureaucracy. So partake did away with as much of this as possible.

At partake, there is little structure to speak of—at least, not on the operational side of the business. (There are, of course, support functions such as finance and HR.) There is no director of consulting, no operations manager, and so on. There are no set teams, no project leaders, no job titles or descriptions. The office layout is flexible: Desks and partition walls are movable, allowing people to configure the space around them as projects come and go.

"The philosophy is simple," says owner and CEO Juergen Erbeldinger. "Work on projects you're interested in, work with people you like to work with, and work in a space that suits you."

The company may be an extreme case, the ultimate in autonomy. And of course, "structurelessness" of this kind is far easier to make work with a team of seventy or so than with several thousand employees. Plus, the partake system is more suited to a creative business than to many other sectors.

However, what's interesting about partake is that it is not a start-up or the brainchild of a young whiz kid with alternative ideas about how to operate a business. Erbeldinger is a forty-something entrepreneur. He has a twenty-year track record of running a traditional consultancy with a conventional organizational structure. But he decided it was time to do things differently.

For instance, a partake consultant might come up with an idea that becomes a live project if it gains the support of one other colleague. A team then forms around the project, based on who is interested and feel they can contribute. The team develops the idea and takes it to market, pitching to the appropriate clients. Each consultant sets her own billing rate on the project, negotiating this with the other team members.

All of this begs the question: Where are the boundaries? The company imposes just two. First, projects pass through what Erbeldinger calls an *innovation funnel.* This consists of several stages—research, concept, analysis, prototyping—each of which aims to test the viability of the idea as it moves toward launch.

Second, the consultancy embeds creative time into its working practice. A fifth of each consultant's time is dedicated to developing existing concepts, a further 10 percent to coming up with brand-new ideas.

There is a third boundary, but it is not imposed by the firm. According to Erbeldinger, partake's system is in effect self-governing. "With autonomy comes responsibility," he says. "Team members control themselves. They know what we need them to deliver. We trust them to do their job well, use common sense, and take responsibility when their personal strengths are needed, whatever the context or project. That creates a culture of performance, self-management, and 'doing the right thing.'"

Take, for example, the practice of consultants setting their own billing rates. This results in a self-regulating internal market, in which individuals must "sell" themselves. As a result, they cannot overcharge: Their rates must be seen by the team as offering value to the client.

*(continued)*

As noted earlier in this chapter, the ability to create bounded autonomy is an essential competency of the altrocentric leader. In partake's case, however, enabling such an autonomous structure also called for some of the other capabilities set out in our competency map (e.g., ego maturity). First, despite the lack of formal hierarchy, the right approach to leadership remains crucial. As Erbeldinger points out, even for him as the owner, leadership is contextual. "Sometimes we lead, sometimes we assist. That applies to everyone."

Also, creating such a culture in the first place demanded ego-maturity and an interdependent power motive. "I had to learn to let go," Erbeldinger recalls. "I had to realize that in the past, employees supported my ideas because I was the boss, not necessarily because my ideas were any good. I had to learn to trust others to a degree I had not thought possible: a painful process for an entrepreneur of my generation."

In addition, creating the new structure presented a meaning-making challenge. As the firm evolved, therefore, there was an inevitable amount of staff turnover. Interestingly, this was particularly notable among those who had been line managers under the old, more conventional hierarchy. Erbeldinger explains: "The new, flat structure was designed to remove personal power, so a few chose not to stay. We were moving toward a results-oriented environment, based on team spirit, not individual power. That's not for everyone."

But most were engaged by the new vision, he contends. And it seems to particularly resonate with Generation Y. "Younger generations choose to work for us because we do things differently. They have an entrepreneurial attitude, a will to generate fresh ideas, which suits our culture."

---

## Senior Team Leadership

Altrocentric leaders have a strong team ethic. They realize that the megatrends will provide too huge a challenge for any one individual to deal with and that a highly effective leadership team will be needed to steer their organizations through the storm. And they understand that other team members may be better suited to make some decisions than they are. This is why they see themselves as first among equals.

So they go about systematically building an exceptional team, with genuine decision-making authority, and creating the conditions to allow it to perform.[28] They do this by first selecting a group of highly collaborative individuals with diverse and complementary profiles. This may seem an obvious step, but it is surprising how many leaders fail to get this fundamental task right.

Once the right team is in place, altrocentric leaders engage in a meaning-making process with them to co-create a compelling sense of common purpose. They then put this purpose into action by identifying tasks for the team to achieve together.

Finally, they encourage their team to think differently about the company's business and operating models, strategic direction and execution, and the opportunities and threats it faces in the light of the megatrends.

In this chapter, we have developed a concept of leadership that is more future-fit, more appropriate to cope with all of the challenges deriving from the megatrend storm. We have also defined the competencies that would enable an altrocentric leader to manage her business successfully in the future. As stated, this altrocentric leader is an ideal type, a construct, but also a vision of what the future of leadership could look like.

But how do we become altrocentric leaders? There is no simple recipe.

It's a journey. Let's start with exploring some questions.

# Conclusion: The Journey to Altrocentric Leadership

*"They always say that time changes things, but you actually have to change them yourself."*
—**Andy Warhol,** pop artist

Altrocentric leadership is necessary in order to cope with the megatrend storm. But there is no algorithm, no single test or training program for the development of an altrocentric leader. Altrocentric leadership is not a template or form that can be filled in.

This is because each altrocentric leader is different, even if each shares common features and some of the competencies described above. Each has a different self-image and self-understanding based on his unique characteristics.

So it would be misleading to recommend a set of specific tips, steps, or points of advice to follow in order to become an altrocentric leader. Altrocentric leadership is a journey with no clear destination—a journey full of ambiguities, uncertainties, open-ended questions, and (for that matter) a few potential dead ends along the way.

But we can provide help along the way. Individuals can be supported, guided, and coached on the journey. And a good place to start is by posing a series of questions to help you reflect on where you are currently.

## Question 1: What Is Your Self-Image?

Knowing your self-image is fundamental. As we've seen, the way people see themselves and understand their role is what shapes their behavior. Some female leaders adopt "masculine" leadership styles, because they *understand* (mistakenly) that this is how a woman should lead. Some male leaders avoid "feminine" styles because these do not fit their "male" self-image.

How do you see yourself? Do you consider yourself a leader? What do you value? Are you able to overcome gender (and cultural and age) stereotypes? Can you transcend clichés and traditional perceptions of roles? Are you ready to question your own preconceptions and prejudices?

## Question 2: What Drives You?

What motivates you to go to work every day? Are you driven by managing and excelling at difficult tasks or by the atmosphere in the office and the fact that you work with people you like? Do you derive your energy from shaping tasks, having an impact, and getting things done through others? Are you motivated by positional power and personal reputation? Do you try to develop others' strengths?

Understanding your underlying motivation is essential because socialized power is a precondition of altrocentric leadership. Since our motives are nonconscious, they are difficult to address, but there are specific tests to help you to gain a better understanding.

## Question 3: How Well Do You Know Yourself and Your Limitations?

Do you reflect critically on your performance and on your strengths and weaknesses? Are you aware of your limits? Are you in control of your emotions?

Self-awareness, self-control, and self-management are crucial emotional competencies for an altrocentric leader. Try using an emotional intelligence inventory to understand yours and psychometric tests to give you further insight into important psychological traits.

## Question 4: Are You Open?

Are you a curious person? Do you enjoy learning and broadening your horizons? Do you listen carefully to others, without feeling uncomfortable with the ambiguity that might arise from hearing different views? Do you actively seek out people who are different from you? Do you engage and empathize with others and understand their thoughts, feelings, and concerns?

Social awareness, empathy, and listening are all important emotional competencies for altrocentric leaders. Emotional and social intelligence inventories, training, and guides can support you in understanding and developing them.

## Question 5: What Leadership Styles Do You Use?

Do you take a command-and-control approach to leading? Do you set the pace, running on ahead and demanding that others follow? Are you careful to provide clarity to people and share the big picture with them? Do you take a long-term perspective on people's development and invest your own time in coaching, mentoring, and sponsoring them? Do you include your team in the decision-making process? Do you create an environment where people feel safe and emotionally supported?

Altrocentric leaders use a wide range of leadership styles, knowing which to employ in which situation and with which individuals. There are diagnostic tools to give you a clear understanding of how you lead and the impact this has on your teams.

## Question 6: How Broad Is Your Perspective?

Do you regularly scan the market environment and analyze current developments and future trends? Do you make the effort to incorporate all relevant stakeholders into your business perspective—internally, externally, locally, and globally? Do you ensure that consequences are fully understood and appropriate concepts created? Have you introduced the systems and processes to enable this?

Altrocentric leaders know that strategic thinking is a key competency to cope with the megatrend storm. Engage yourself and your team in an exercise aimed at understanding the full range of stakeholders that your organization serves, and the impact that each has on your strategy. Develop scenarios to model the effects on your organization of the megatrends, increased competition, regulatory changes, societal demands, and so on.

## Question 7: Do You Personally Create Loyalty and Manage Reputation?

Are you passionate about and value diversity and pluralism? Do you understand that digital natives, Generation Y, and late career workers all have different needs and motivations? Do you value people as individuals?

Do you have a strong sense of your business's ethical philosophy? Do you possess interpersonal and intercultural understanding? Do you understand the implications of a blurred public/private divide on your organization's reputation?

Altrocentric leaders personally create loyalty and proactively manage their own and their company's reputations. They behave ethically, authentically, and with integrity. They truly respect people's individuality and take their needs into account.

Place a strong personal emphasis on diversity and on intergenerational, cross-country management. Make people accountable for doing the same and for putting in place processes and systems to achieve this. Values questionnaires can help clarify what you value most in your job.

## Question 8: Do You Engage Colleagues in a Meaning-Making Process?

What defines your organization's identity? What is your company's purpose (beyond making money, which is the sole objective of very few organizations)? Do you know?

Are you aware of what creates meaning for your coworkers? What is your organizational narrative? Is it relevant to the realities of the outside world?

Have you engaged colleagues in a meaning-making process? Are your managers developing a narrative that incorporates the five crucial perspectives?

Meaning-making is a crucial leadership competency that comes naturally to altrocentric leaders. Without a convincing organizational narrative, it is highly unlikely that a company will cope with the complexities of the megatrends.

Review whether your organization's narrative is appropriate. Engage your top team in a meaning-making exercise. Make use of the visionary leadership style.

Consider using value questionnaires, the "five stories," a strategy decode (interventions focused on clarifying the strategic intent of the business and building consensus within the team on specific objectives and priorities), and culture and climate diagnostics to understand where you stand and where you need to go.

Recruit your management tiers below the top-team level to help gain traction and engagement for your narrative throughout the company. Focus on internal communications. Put the right communications loops in place.

Employee engagement surveys will help you to understand and monitor the alignment, engagement, and enablement of your workforce as you go through the meaning-making process.

## Question 9: Do You Truly Collaborate and Partner with Others?

Do you take teamwork and collaboration seriously, or do you merely pay lip service to them? Do you have an understanding of collaboration in its widest sense, and do you give proper consideration to joint ventures with external organizations and even competitors? Do you understand and practice coopetition?

Do you pull together individuals from different parts of the organization to create the right teams for short-term projects and long-term collaboration? Do you work in close cooperation with colleagues and partners, without having to fall back on your own authority?

Technological convergence, glocalization, climate change, and scarcity of resources will demand new levels of cooperation. This will prove a significant stretch for many leaders, from both a psychological and organizational point of view.

Reflect on your self-understanding and your motives: Are you willing and able to share power? Work with people you see as collaboration "stars." Co-create systematic processes to foster and strengthen cross-boundary collaboration (including matrix collaboration).

## Question 10: Do You Personally Take Ownership of the People Agenda in Your Organization?

Do you take ownership of human resources in your organization? In particular, do you own the core people agenda, that is, the attraction, motivation, and retention of people in mission-critical jobs?

Do you know which colleagues you absolutely need to develop, motivate, and retain? Do you personally coach, mentor, and sponsor your high potentials? Do you personally work with your top team on talent and succession management?

Altrocentric leaders maintain an unwavering focus on people. They see human resources as a strategic business issue and their chief human resources officer as a strategic business partner. They establish a strong HR practice and are personally aware of and involved in the most important people issues in their organization.

Establish HR as a strategic business partner. Ensure that you and the top team personally engage in the assessment and development of people in mission-critical roles. Arm yourself with technology to help keep track of the most important people issues. There are dedicated smartphone apps that perform this function.

## Question 11: Do You Provide Bounded Autonomy?

Do you personally give direction and empower your coworkers to take ownership and accountability? Do you give as much autonomy to divisions, units, and individuals as possible, while ensuring that the basic principles, rules, and guidelines are clear and reinforced? Do you work with your top team to create the framework within which autonomy is provided?

Do you take corrective action when people step outside the limit and when they fail to provide autonomy?

Bounded autonomy is key to coping with the complexity of the megatrends. Delegation and—more to the point—*freedom* to act with as little bureaucracy as necessary will create the flexibility that organizations need to respond to a fast-changing world.

Ensure that employees know that they can take whatever steps are necessary to get the job done and achieve their objectives. Clearly set limits that reflect the purpose, strategy, values, and goals of the organization.

## Question 12: Have You Created a Decision-Making Top Team?

Have you selected the right people for your leadership team? By *right*, we mean not necessarily the best managers and technical experts but those who are willing and able to truly collaborate and to co-create the direction and strategy, and who ideally have diverse and complementary profiles.

Have you agreed on the direction your organization needs to take? Have you agreed on common tasks for which the whole team is responsible? Have you created a structure to enable them to be effective?

Does the team have the right support? Do team members and more importantly, the team as a whole receive developmental feedback and coaching?

Altrocentric leaders are team players at heart. They are keen to develop a genuine decision-making team because they know that without this, they will be unable to manage the challenges ahead.

Understand what competencies your top team needs to have. Establish a thorough development process for this, which ideally would be co-created. Work with coaches to help the team reach its full potential. Do not tolerate members undermining the team agenda.

So we have dared to look into the future.

We have looked forward to a future shaped by a perfect storm made up of six global megatrends: Globalization 2.0, the environmental crisis, individualization and value pluralism, the digital era, demographic change, and technological convergence. And we have described the leaders they will need to steer them through it.

But as we made clear in the Introduction, it is impossible to predict these things with absolute certainty. We are not in position to lay out a blueprint for the future of the business environment and business organizations.

Doing so would be to make the same mistake as the nineteenth-century urban planners who were unable to see that their world wouldn't be engulfed in horse manure after all, or the chroniclers of that age who could not imagine a world in which Britain did not have an empire on which the sun would never set.

Instead, we have attempted to guide, to suggest, and to question; to point readers in the right direction; and to prompt thoughts and ideas about how to cope with a future that will be very different from the present and unimaginably more challenging.

From here, the future is in your hands. As we've made clear, the solutions will be different for every organization. It is left to each business, and each leader, to fathom which solutions are right for them.

Developing altrocentric leaders will require considerable time, energy, and investment. Leaders need to start thinking very differently *now* about how they will operate. They will need to think outside the box, the building, the organization, and the sector. They will need to think out of the ordinary if they are to stay afloat amid the megatrend storm.

Abraham Lincoln said that the best way to predict the future is to create it.

Let's embark on this journey!

# Endnotes

## Introduction

1. Nobody knows for sure who first said this. It is generally attributed to Mark Twain, but also on occasion to the renowned Danish physicist Neils Bohr. But then, attribution is very difficult, especially about the past.

2. This phrase was coined by Stephen Davies in "The Great Horse Manure Crisis of 1894," *The Freeman*, September 2004. Other sources consulted on this topic include "The Great Horse Manure Crisis of 1894," *Bytes*, July 16, 2011, bytesdaily.blogspot.com/2011/07/great-horse-manure-crisis-of-1894.html (a blog discussion based on Davies's article) and Eric Morris, "From Horse Power to Horsepower," *Access*, Spring 2007.

3. Denise Roland, "Chinese Firm Geely Saves London Taxi Cab Maker Manganese Bronze," *Daily Telegraph*, February 1, 2013.

4. "Geely Buys London Black Cab Manufacturer for US$17m," *Want China Times*, February 2, 2013.

5. Rolf Kreibich, "Zukunftsforschung" [Future Research], *Arbeitsbericht* no. 23, 2006, Institute for Future Studies and Technology Assessment, Berlin. Kreibich was the first president of the Free University of Berlin and has been director of the Berlin Institute for Future Studies and Technology Assessment for thirty years. The view on social sciences advocated here is sometimes called postempiricist. See Georg Vielmetter, *Die Unbestimmtheit des Sozialen. Zur Philosophie der Sozialwissenschaften* [The Indeterminacy of the Social: On the Philosophy of Social Science], eds. Axel Honneth, Hans Joas, and Claus Offe (Campus Press, 1998), and "Postempiristische Philosophie der Sozialwissenschaften—eine Positionsbestimmung" [Postempiricist Philosophy of Social Science—A Positioning], A. Reckwitz and H. Sievert, eds., *Interpretation, Konstruktion, Kultur, Opladen: Westdeutscher* [Interpretation, Construction, Culture], (Westdeutscher Verlag, 1999).

6. John Naisbitt, *Megatrends: Ten New Directions Transforming Our Lives* (Warner Books, 1982).

7. Z_punkt Gmbh, *Die zwanzig wichtigsten Megatrends* [The Twenty Most Important Megatrends] (Köln Karlsruhe, 2008).

8. Nassim Nicholas Taleb, *Fooled by Randomness: The Hidden Role of Chance in Life and in the Markets* (Random House, 2001); and Taleb, *The Black Swan: The Impact of the Highly Improbable* (Random House, 2007).

9. The concept of the *Lebenswelt* ("life-world," or everyday life) has been elaborated by various philosophers from different traditions, including the hermeneutical, phenomenological, and Wittgensteinian schools. See Alfred Schütz and Thomas Luckmann, *Structures of the Life-World*, Vol. 1, *Studies in Phenomenology and Existential Philosophy* (Northwestern University Press, 1973); Peter L. Berger and Thomas Luckmann, T*he Social Construction of Reality: A Treatise in the Sociology of Knowledge* (Anchor Books, 1966); Peter Winch, *The Idea of a Social Science and Its Relation to Philosophy* (Routledge & Kegan Paul, 1958); Charles Taylor, *Erklärung und Interpretation in den Wissenschaften vom Menschen* [Explanation and Interpretation in Human Sciences] (Suhrkamp, 1975); and Georg Vielmetter, *Die Unbestimmtheit des Sozialen.*

10. It is unclear whether this is a genuine historic quote. See quoteinvestiga tor.com/2012/04/21/students-bark and "Probable Quotes from History," *The MATYC* [*Mathematics Association of Two-Year Colleges*] Journal 12, no. 3, Fall 1978, p. 189.

11. You can find brief summaries of the six megatrends in the following papers and articles: Yvonne Sell and Georg Vielmetter, "Report on Best Global Practice: Leadership," *Benefits & Compensation International,* January/February 2012; Vielmetter, "Business Shift Calls for 'Post-Heroic' Leadership," *Wall Street Journal,* January 17, 2012; and Vielmetter, "Adapt to Survive—A Picture of Leadership in 2030," *European Business Review,* November/December 2011.

## Chapter 1

1. Various commentators have defined different phases of globalization as versions 1.0, 2.0, etc., most famously Thomas L. Friedman in *The World Is Flat* (2005). As this chapter explains, our book draws a different distinction between the globalization of the twenty-first century and that which went before.

2. IMF, *Globalization: Threat or Opportunity?* International Monetary Fund, April 12, 2000.

3.  William Scheuerman, "Globalization," *Stanford Encyclopedia of Philosophy*, Summer 2010 edition.

4.  Karl Marx and Friedrich Engels, *Manifest der Kommunistischen Partei* [The Manifesto of the Communist Party] (1848); and Scheuerman, "Globalization."

5.  Martin Heidegger, *Poetry, Language, Thought* (1971).

6.  IMF, *Globalization*.

7.  Leo Lewis, "Fears Can't Be Wiped Away with a Jubilee Tea Towel," *The Times*, June 5, 2012.

8.  Jim O'Neill, Dominic Wilson, Roopa Purushothaman, and Anna Stupnytska, *How Solid Are the BRICs?* Goldman Sachs, Global Economic Paper no. 134, December 1, 2005.

9.  Wayne M. Morrison, *China's Economic Conditions*, Congressional Research Service, June 26, 2012.

10. IMF, *World Economic Outlook*, International Monetary Fund, April 2011.

11. John Hawksworth and Anmol Tiwari, *The World in 2050*, PwC, January 2011.

12. Aileen Wang and Nick Edwards, "China to Keep Investing in Euro Zone Debt," *Reuters*, February 15, 2012.

13. Andrew Clark and Kathryn Hopkins, "Stop Wasting Our Time, China's Top Investor Tells Europe," *The Times*, May 23, 2012.

14. Claus Hecking, "Capital Study: Chinese Investment in Europe Hits Record High," *Spiegel Online International*, April 16, 2013.

15. Germany Trade & Invest, *Markets Germany Newsletter*, March 2012.

16. "Geely Earns Net Profit of 1.54b Yuan in 2011," *China Automotive Information Net*, March 26, 2012.

17. Pedro Nueno and Liu Shengju, "Geely-Volvo: Road to a Cross-Country Marriage," *China Connecting Conversations*, September 23-24, 2011.

18. Peter Wonacott, "CIC Targets a Capital Shift," *Wall Street Journal*, May 10, 2012.

19. John Paul Rathbone, "China Is Now Region's Biggest Partner," *Financial Times*, April 26, 2011.

20. Economist Intelligence Unit, *Country Report: Brazil*, August 2011.

21. Dambisa Moyo, "Beijing, A Boon for Africa," *New York Times*, June 27, 2012.

22. Jim O'Neill, *Building Better Global Economic BRICs*, Goldman Sachs, Global Economic Paper no. 66, November 30, 2001.

23. Georg Blume, "Brasilien, Indien, China: Was wollen die neuen Großmächte?" [Brazil, India, China: What Do the New Major Powers Want?], *Die Zeit*, March 29, 2012.

24. Ibid.

25. Ding Ying, "FTA Driving Asian Growth," Beijing Review, January 27, 2011; and Embassy of Switzerland in Beijing, China, *Biannual Economic Report*, June 2012.

26. The nations are Brunei, Cambodia, China, Indonesia, Laos, Malaysia, Myanmar, the Philippines, Singapore, Thailand, and Vietnam.

27. HSBC Global Research, *The World in 2050: Quantifying the Shift in the Global Economy*, January 2011.

28. Dominic Wilson and Raluca Dragusanu, *The Expanding Middle: The Exploding World Middle Class and Falling Global Inequality*, Goldman Sachs, Global Economic Paper no. 170, July 2008. It should be noted that since the global financial collapse of 2008, numbers and earnings for the global middle class are also being impacted in developed societies, particularly in Europe. This has led to falling middle incomes, especially in countries more acutely affected by the subsequent Eurozone crisis. According to some commentators, there is also a longer term trend toward financial inequality within some developed economies, for example, Germany. However, this is not inconsistent with overall growth in the middle class globally, and it is an issue that is beyond the subject matter of this book.

29. Yuval Atsmon, Peter Child, Richard Dobbs, and Laxman Narasimhan, "Winning the $30 Trillion Decathlon: Going for Gold in Emerging Markets," *McKinsey Quarterly*, August 2012.

30. Homi Karas, *Working Paper 285—The Emerging Middle Class in Developing Countries*, OECD Development Centre, January 2010.

31. Yuval Atsmon, Vinay Dixit, and Cathy Wu, "Tapping China's Luxury-Goods Market," *McKinsey Quarterly*, April 2011.

32. Clementine Fletcher, "Diageo Takes on Chivas, Cognac with Johnnie Walker in Shanghai," *Bloomberg*, May 18, 2011.

33. "China's Premium Car Market Set for Huge Growth," *IHS Automotive*, April 17, 2012.

34. "Global Market Share of Nokia Smartphones from 1st Quarter 2007 to 2nd Quarter 2012," *Statista*, 2012.

35. Alexander Spektor, "Samsung Overtakes Nokia to Become World's Largest Handset Vendor in Q1 2012," *Strategy Analytics*, April 27, 2012.

36. Emil Protalinski, "HTC Passes Nokia in Market Cap," *Techspot*, April 7, 2011.

37. Sophie Crocoll, "Zeit der Lotusblüte" [The Era of the Lotus Blossom], *Süddeutsche Zeitung*, June 30, 2012.

38. Anne C. Lee, "Most Innovative Companies, #5 Huawei," *Fast Company*, July 12, 2012.

39. Peter Burrows, "Samsung Faces Chinese Challenger Huawei with Cheaper Smartphones," *Financial Post*, July 19, 2012; and Hayley Tsukayama, "Apple's iPhone 5: What Does It Cost to Make?" *Washington Post*, September 20, 2012.

40. Paula Dwyer, "Congressional Report on Huawei Smacks of Protectionism," *Bloomberg*, October 8, 2012; and Dan Ikenson, "Huawei, ZTE and the Slippery Slope of Excusing Protectionism on National Security Grounds," *Forbes*, October 9, 2012.

41. Yu Hongyan, "Haier Leads in Global Refrigerator Sales," *China Daily*, January 19, 2009.

42. Office Suisse d'Expansion Commerciale, *South Korea Information and Communication Industry*, August 2011.

43. Business Monitor International, *Philippines Food & Drink Report*, January 2012.

44. "Face Value: A Busy Bee in the Hamburger Hive," *The Economist*, February 28, 2002.

45. "Jollibee Posts 16% Revenue Growth in 2010," *Balita*, February 21, 2011; and Jeannette Yutan, *Jollibee Foods Corporation—2Q12 Results Driven by Robust Domestic Operations*, J.P. Morgan Asia Pacific Equity Research, August 14, 2012.

46. Yutan, *Jollibee Foods Corporation*.

47. Business Monitor International, *Philippines Food & Drink*; and Jollibee Foods Corporation, USA Store Finder, January 2013.

48. Business Monitor International, *Philippines Food & Drink*.

49. Carlos H. Conde, "Jollibee Stings McDonald's in Philippines," *New York Times*, May 31, 2005.

50. "Face Value: A Busy Bee."

51. Conde, "Jollibee Stings McDonald's."

52. "Face Value: A Busy Bee."

53. Karen Cho, "China's Recipe for Success," *European Business Review*, November 2012.

54.  Ibid.

55.  Ibid.

56.  Warren Liu, *KFC in China: Secret Recipe for Success* (John Wiley & Sons, 2008).

57.  Cho, "China's Recipe for Success"; and Helen H. Wang, "Yum! China: From Rebranding to Reinventing," *Forbes*, September 3, 2012.

58.  Andrew Hill, "Inside Nokia: Rebuilt from Within," *Financial Times*, April 13, 2011.

59.  Chikodi Chima, "Tianji Kickstarts Professional Social Networking in China," *Venture Beat*, October 31, 2011.

60.  "Viadeo Closes $32 Million Round: One of the Largest European Internet Investments in the Last 12 Months," Viadeo press release, April 12, 2012.

61.  Mark Lee, "LinkedIn Has 2 Million Users for English-Language Service," *Bloomberg*, April 24, 2012.

62.  C. Custer, "Tianji, China's Biggest Professional Social Network, Is Growing Fast," *Tech in Asia*, November 3, 2011.

63.  Marcel Grzanna, "Facebook? Tianji!" *Süddeutsche Zeitung*, February 15, 2012; and Custer, "Tianji, China's Biggest."

64.  Jeremy Brand Yuan, "Tianji's Infographic on Professional Social Networking in China," *Tech Orange*, October 31, 2011.

65.  Chima, "Tianji Kickstarts."

66.  Virginie Mangin, "Playing the Long Game," *CNBC Business*, January/February 2012.

## Chapter 2

1.  Fiona Harvey, "World Headed for Irreversible Climate Change in Five Years, IEA Warns," *The Guardian*, November 9, 2011.

2.  IEA, *World Energy Outlook 2011*, International Energy Agency, November 9, 2011.

3.  Harvey, "World Headed for Irreversible."

4.  U.S. National Climate Assessment and Development Advisory Committee, *Federal Advisory Committee Draft Climate Assessment Report*, January 2013.

5.  Bill McKibben, "The Climate Change Deniers: Influence Out of All Proportion to Science," *The Guardian*, June 4, 2012; and Anita Blasberg and Kerstin Kohlenberg, "Die Klimakrieger" [The Climate Warrior], *Die Zeit*, November 22, 2012.

6.  Committee on America's Climate Choices and the National Research Council, *America's Climate Choices* (National Academies Press, 2011).

7.  Naomi Oreskes, "Beyond the Ivory Tower, the Scientific Consensus on Climate Change," *Science*, December 3, 2004.

8.  "A Brief History of Climate Change," *BBC News*, October 5, 2009.

9.  IPCC, *Fourth Assessment Report: Climate Change 2007*, Intergovernmental Panel on Climate Change, 2007.

10. Fiona Harvey, "Scientists Attribute Extreme Weather to Man-made Climate Change," *The Guardian*, July 10, 2012.

11. U.S. National Climate Assessment and Development Advisory Committee, *Federal Advisory Committee Draft*, 2013.

12. The states were Indiana, Illinois, Iowa, Missouri, Kansas, Nebraska, Oklahoma, and Colorado.

13. Jim Suhr, "Drought Worsens in Key Farm States," *USA Today*, August 10, 2012.

14. Jason Samenow, "U.S. Has Hottest Month on Record in July 2012, NOAA Says," *Washington Post*, August 8, 2012.

15. "Hitzerekord: 2012 war heißestes Jahr in der US-Geschichte" [Record Heat: 2012 Was the Hottest Year in U.S. History], *Spiegel Online*, January 8, 2013.

16. Brian K. Sullivan, "U.S. Hit by 12 Weather Disasters Costing $1 Billion Each in '11, Most Ever," *Bloomberg*, December 7, 2011.

17. Stefan Rahmstorf, "Will This Summer of Extremes Be a Wake-up Call?" *The Guardian*, August 16, 2010.

18. Michael Hanlon, "Extreme Weather Has Just Begun," *Sunday Times*, December 30, 2012; Mark Kinver, "2012 Was UK's Second Wettest Year on Record," *BBC News*, January 3, 2013; and Andrew Johnson, "Downpours Make 2012 England's Wettest Year on Record," *The Independent*, December 27, 2012.

19. David Porter, "Hurricane Sandy Was Second-Costliest in U.S. History, Report Shows," *Huffington Post*, February 12, 2013.

20. Ilya Gridneff, Tom Arup, and Jacob Saulwick, "City Sizzles in Record Heat," *Sydney Morning Herald*, January 19, 2013.

21. Justin Gillis, "Study Indicates a Greater Threat of Extreme Weather," *New York Times*, April 26, 2012.

22. Harvey, "Scientists Attribute Extreme Weather."

23. Jeremy Rifkin, *The Hydrogen Economy: The Creation of the Worldwide Energy Web and the Redistribution of Power on Earth* (Tarcher, 2003).

24. U.S. Environmental Protection Agency, *Global Greenhouse Gas Emissions Data, Trends in Global Emissions*, www.epa.gov/climatechange/ghgemissions/global.html#three.

25. United Nations Energy Programme, *The Emissions Gap Report*, November 2010.

26. World Bank, *Turn Down the Heat: Why a 4°C Warmer World Must be Avoided*, November 2012.

27. IPCC, *Fourth Assessment Report.*

28. IEA, *World Energy Outlook 2008*, International Energy Agency, 2008.

29. "Reaching 2009 International Climate Change Goals Will Require Aggressive Measures," *Science Daily*, December 2, 2012.

30. Markus Becker, "Interview mit Dennis Meadows: 'Für eine globale Mobil-machung ist es zu spät' " ["Interview with Dennis Meadows: 'Too Late for a Global Mobilization' "], *Spiegel Online*, December 4, 2012; and Jorgen Randers, *2052: A Global Forecast for the Next Forty Years* (Chelsea Green, 2012).

31. Bill Pennington, "The Burden and Boon of Lost Golf Balls," *New York Times Golf Blog*, May 2, 2010.

32. Gazelle Emami, "9 Shocking Things Made from Oil," *Huffington Post*, May 25, 2011.

33. Zentrum für Transformation der Bundeswehr, Dezernat Zukunftsanalyse [Federal Defense Force Transformation Center, Future Analysis Branch], *Streitkräfte, Fähigkeiten und Technologien im 21. Jahrhundert— Umweltdimensionen von Sicherheit—Teilstudie 1: Peak oil, Sicherheitspolitische Implikationen knapper Resourcen* [Armed Forces, Capabilities and Technologies in the 21st Century, Environmental Dimensions of Security, Sub-Study 1, Peak Oil, Security Policy Implications of Scarce Resources], November 2010.

34. IEA, *World Energy Outlook 2010*, International Energy Agency, November 2010.

35. The exact timing of peak oil remains the subject of much debate. As the German Federal Defense Force report (see Note 33) states, it can be determined with certainty only in retrospect.

36. Rob Fisher and Sharad Apte, *Peak Oil: Does it Matter?* Bain & Company, December 15, 2010.

37. Zentrum für Transformation der Bundeswehr, *Streitkräfte*.

38. IEA, *World Energy Outlook 2010*.

39. Roland Berger Strategy Consultants, *Trend Compendium 2030*, 2011.

40.  Kristie M. Engemann and Michael T. Owyang, *Unconventional Oil: Stuck in a Rock and a Hard Place*, Federal Reserve Bank of St. Louis, October 2007.

41.  Pernille Seljom, *Technology Brief PS02, Unconventional Oil Production*, IEA Energy Technology Systems Analysis Programme, May 2010.

42.  Ibid.

43.  Ibid.

44.  Engemann and Owyang, *Unconventional Oil*.

45.  Christian Tenbrock and Fritz Varenholz, "Amerika im Gasrausch" [America on a Gas High], *Die Zeit*, February 7, 2013. In 2012, the U.S. Energy Information Administration revised its estimate of U.S. gas reserves down 42 percent (though they are still considerable).

46.  UNICEF and the World Health Organization, *Progress on Drinking Water and Sanitation*, 2012 Update.

47.  United Nations, *Water: A Shared Responsibility: United Nations World Water Development Report 2*, 2006.

48.  United Nations, *Managing Water Under Uncertainty and Risk: United Nations World Water Development Report 4*, 2012.

49.  United Nations, *Water in a Changing World: United Nations World Water Development Report 3*, 2009.

50.  Thomas Schlick and Dirk Kohlen, *Automotive Insights: The Rare Earth Challenge*, Roland Berger Strategy Consultants, December 2011.

51.  "China Warns its Rare Earth Reserves Are Declining," *BBC News*, June 20, 2012.

52.  Suranjana Roy Bhattacharya, "China's Rare Earths Production Is Becoming a Contentious Issue," *Gulf News*, August 9, 2010.

53.  Steve Gorman, "As Hybrid Cars Gobble Rare Metals, Shortage Looms," *Reuters*, August 31, 2009.

54.  Schlick and Kohlen, *Automotive Insights*.

55.  The seventeen rare earth elements are cerium, dysprosium, erbium, europium, gadolinium, holmium, lanthanum, lutetium, neodymium, praseodymium, promethium, samarium, scandium, terbium, thulium, ytterbium, and yttrium.

56.  Paul Toscano, "How Are Rare Earth Elements Used?" *CNBC.com*, November 5, 2010.

57.  Ralf Kalmbach, Wolfgang Bernhart, Philipp Grosse Kleinman, and Marcus Hoffman, *Automotive Landscape 2025: Opportunities and Challenges Ahead*, Roland Berger Strategy Consultants, 2011.

58.  Roland Berger Strategy Consultants, *Trend Compendium 2030*, 2011.

59.  Rifkin, *The Hydrogen Economy*.

60.  Zentrum für Tranformation der Bundeswehr, *Streitkräfte*.

61.  Reed Livergood, *Current Issues No. 22—Rare Earth Elements: A Wrench in the Supply Chain?* Center for Strategic and International Studies, 2010.

62.  Michael Martina, "China Halts Rare Earth Production at Three Mines," *Reuters*, September 6, 2011; *BBC News*, www.bbc.co.uk/news; and Keith Bradsher, "After China's Rare Earth Embargo, a New Calculus," *New York Times*, October 29, 2010. http://www.nytimes.com/2010/10/30/business/global/30rare.html?pagewanted=all

63.  GRAIN, *Seized: The 2008 Land Grab for Food and Financial Security*, October 24, 2008.

64.  World Bank, *Awakening Africa's Sleeping Giant: Prospects for Commercial Agriculture in the Guinea Savannah Zone and Beyond*, 2009.

65.  Zentrum für Transformation der Bundeswehr, *Streitkräfte*.

66.  Peter Bunyard, *Climate Chaos: Threat to Life on Earth* (Educar Editores, 2010).

67.  Kira Matus et al., *Health Damages from Air Pollution in China*, Massachusetts Institute of Technology, Joint Program on the Science and Policy of Global Change, March 2011.

68.  John Vidal, "2010 Could Be Among Warmest Years Recorded by Man," *The Guardian*, June 2, 2010.

69.  Nathan van der Klippe, "Northwest Passage Gets Political Name Change," *Edmonton Journal*, April 9, 2006.

70.  Tom Mitchell and Richard Milne, "Chinese Cargo Ship Sets Sail for Arctic Short Cut," *Financial Times*, August 11, 2013.

71.  Gail Whiteman, Chris Hope, and Peter Wadhams, "Climate Science: Vast Costs of Arctic Change," *Nature*, July 25, 2013; John Vidal, "Rapid Arctic Thawing Could Be Economic Timebomb, Scientists Say," *The Guardian*, July 25, 2013.

72.  KPMG, *Corporate Sustainability: A Progress Report*, 2011. Large corporations are defined in the report as having annual revenues of more than $5 billion.

73.  Ron Pernick, Clint Wilder, and Trevor Winnie, *Clean Energy Trends 2012*, Clean Edge, March 2012.

74.  James Melik, "China Leads World in Green Energy Investment," *BBC News*, September 16, 2011.

75.  Ken Shulman, "Think Green," *Metropolis*, August/September 2001.

76. Ibid.

77. Florence Williams, "Prophet of Bloom," *Wired*, October 2002.

78. "Business Week/Architectural Record Awards," *Architectural Record*, 2004.

79. Mary-Anne Toy, "China's First Eco-Village Proves a Hard Sell," *The Age*, August 26, 2006.

80. Rod Newing, "Credibility and Integrity Are Vital Elements," *Financial Times*, June 7, 2010.

81. Bertelsmann Foundation, *Bürger wollen kein Wachstum um jeden Preis* [Citizens Don't Want Growth at Any Price], August 2011.

82. National Geographic and GlobeScan, *Greendex 2012: Consumer Choice and the Environment, Highlights Report*, July 2012.

83. KPMG, *Corporate Sustainability*.

84. Guy Chazan, "Total Warns Against Oil Drilling in Arctic," *Financial Times*, September 25, 2012.

85. Peter Senge et al., *The Necessary Revolution: How Individuals and Organizations Are Working Together to Create a Sustainable World* (Doubleday, 2008).

## Chapter 3

1. Pkw-Markt, "Modellvielfalt wächst weiter" [Number of Car Models Grows Again], *Auto-Presse*, February 1, 2006.

2. "China's Higher Education Students Exceed 30 Million," *People's Daily Online*, March 11, 2011.

3. "Mehr Väter in Elternzeit" [More Fathers on Paternity Leave], *Frankfurter Allgemeine Zeitung*, December 3, 2010.

4. "Jeder fünfte Vater bezieht Elterngeld" [One in Five Fathers Receive Paternity Pay], *Der Spiegel*, August 3, 2010.

5. Allegra Stratton, "Training Scheme Sees 900% Rise in Apprenticeships for Over-60s," *The Guardian*, November 14, 2011.

6. Abraham Maslow, "A Theory of Human Motivation," *Psychological Review*, 1943.

7. Ronald Inglehart, *The Silent Revolution: Changing Values and Political Styles Among Western Publics* (Princeton University Press, 1977).

8. "Bollywood's Expanding Reach," *BBC News*, May 3, 2012; and Anita N. Wadhwani, "'Bollywood Mania' Rising in United States," America.gov, August 9, 2006.

9.   "Nigeria Surpasses Hollywood as World's Second Largest Film Producer—UN," United Nations News Centre, May 5, 2009; and Dialika Krahe, "Nollywood's Film Industry Second Only to Bollywood in Scale," *Spiegel Online International*, April 23, 2010.

10.   Jip de Lange, Alessandro Longoni, and Adriana Screpnic, "Online Payments 2012: Moving Beyond the Web," *Ecommerce Europe*, 2012.

11.   "Internet World Stats," www.internetworldstats.com.

12.   Lim Yung-Hui, "1 Billion Facebook Users on Earth: Are We There Yet?" *Forbes*, September 2012.

13.   Ibid.

14.   Dave Lee, "Facebook Surpasses One Billion Users as It Tempts New Markets," *BBC News*, October 5, 2012.

15.   Ingrid Lunden, "Twitter Passed 500M Users in June 2012, 140M of Them in US; Jakarta 'Biggest Tweeting' City," *TechCrunch*, July 2012.

16.   Michael Rundle, "China is Twitter's Most Active Country (Despite It Being Banned There)," *Huffington Post*, September 26, 2012.

17.   Juri Allik and Anu Realo, "Individualism-Collectivism and Social Capital," *Journal of Cross-Cultural Psychology*, January 2004.

18.   Geert Hofstede, *Culture's Consequences: Comparing Values, Behaviors, Institutions, and Organizations Across Nations* (Sage Publications, 2001).

19.   Ibid.

20.   Carl Bialik, "Starbucks Stays Mum on Drink Math," *WSJ Blogs*, April 2, 2008.

21.   Andrew Trotman, "A Latte? That's Now a 'Really, Really Milky Coffee' in Debenhams," *Daily Telegraph*, November 2, 2012; and Rachel Tepper, "Debenhams, British Department Store, to Drop 'Confusing' Coffee Terms," *Huffington Post*, October 31, 2012.

22.   Barry Schwartz, *The Paradox of Choice: Why More Is Less* (HarperCollins, 2005).

23.   Henry Ford, *My Life and Work* (Ford & Crowther, 1922). The Ford Model T was initially available in several colors but was later manufactured only in black.

24.   Frank T. Piller, *Observations on the Present and Future of Mass Customization* (Springer Science+Business Media, 2008).

25.   Chris Anderson, "The Long Tail," *Wired*, October 2004.

26.   Ibid.

27.   Piller, *Observations on the Present*.

28.   Chris Anderson, *The Long Tail: Why the Future of Business Is Selling Less of More* (Hyperion Press, 2006).

29. Geoffrey A. Fowler, "Facebook: One Billion and Counting," *Wall Street Journal*, October 5, 2012.

30. Lim, "1 Billion Facebook Users."

31. Lunden, "Twitter Passed 500M."

32. "Facebook Statistics by Country," www.socialbakers.com.

33. LinkedIn corporate website.

34. Hayley Tsukayama, "Your Facebook Friends Have More Friends than You," *Washington Post*, February 3, 2012.

35. Hay Group, *Stepping into Their Shoes: Engaging the Next Generation in Malaysia*, November 2011.

36. Avelyn Ng, "Work-Life Balance More Important than Salary: Survey," Channelnewsasia.com, November 22, 2011.

37. Jens Hartmann and Andre Tauber, "Warum Großkonzerne in Deutschland Kitas bauen" [Why Large Firms Are Building Kindergartens in Germany], *Die Welt*, January 17, 2013.

38. Hay Group, *Stepping into Their Shoes*.

39. Jeanne Meister, "Job Hopping Is the 'New Normal' for Millennials: Three Ways to Prevent a Human Resource Nightmare," *Forbes*, August 14, 2012.

40. Kelly Services, *Global Workforce Index*, September 2012.

41. Richard L. Florida, *The Rise of the Creative Class and How It's Transforming Work, Leisure, Community and Everyday Life* (Basic Books, 2002).

42. Jamie Peck, "Struggling with the Creative Class," *International Journal of Urban and Regional Research*, December 2005.

43. Commentators have identified Generation Y as being born at various points from the late 1970s through to the early 2000s, but the 1980s and 1990s is the most commonly accepted definition.

44. Hay Group, *Stepping into Their Shoes*.

45. "Retention of Gen Y Is Biggest Concern for Managers," *Executive Grapevine*, December 7, 2012.

46. Sue Honoré and Carina Paine Schofield, *Generation Y and Their Managers Around the World*, Ashridge Business School, November 2012.

47. Tom Newcombe, "Managers Concerned for the Future Because of Gen Y, Says Ashridge," *HR Magazine*, December 3, 2012.

48. Ibid.

49. Hay Group, *Stepping into Their Shoes*.

50. Klaus Werle, "Karriere? Ohne mich!" [Career? Without Me!], *Der Spiegel*, August 27, 2012.

51. Klaus Werle, "Wer will noch Chef werden?" [Who Still Wants to Be Boss?], *manager magazin*, August 24, 2012.

52. Steven B. Wolff, Ruth Wageman, and Mary Fontaine, "The Coming Leadership Gap: An Exploration of Competencies That Will Be in Short Supply," *International Journal of Human Resources Development and Management*, February 2009.

53. Klaus Werle, "Karriere? Ohne mich!"

54. Bettina Dobe, "Ein Jahr Bundesfreiwilligendienst: Wartelisten für die Bewerber" [A Year of the Federal Voluntary Service: Waiting Lists for Applicants], *Frankfurter Allgemeine Zeitung*, July 1, 2012.

55. European Bureau for Conscientious Objection, *Report to the Committee on Civil Liberties, Justice and Home Affairs of the European Parliament*, September 2012.

**Chapter 4**

1. Natasha Wilson, "Swedish 'Nerds' Petition to Get Definition Changed in Dictionary," *Digital Spy*, November 3, 2012.

2. Kathryn Westcott, "Are 'Geek' and 'Nerd' Now Positive Terms?" *BBC News Magazine*, November 16, 2012.

3. ODM Group, "Social Media, How It Impacts Your Business Now," YouTube, May 26, 2011; www.youtube.com/watch?v=ukA2zKGQClk.

4. Infographic Labs, *Facebook 2012*, February 15, 2012; and ODM Group, "Social Media."

5. Rip Empson, "How's Skype Doing at MSFT? Usage Jumps 50%, Users Logged 115B Minutes of Calls Last Quarter," Tech Crunch, July 19, 2012.

6. ODM Group, "Social Media."

7. "Call of Duty®: Black Ops™ Delivers Engaging Online Experience That Connects Millions of Players Everyday," Activision press release, December 24, 2010.

8. Lev Grossman, "Google Wave: What's All the Fuss About?" *Time*, October 19, 2009.

9. Klaus Goldhammer et al., *Mobile Life Report 2012: Mobile Life in the 21st Century, Status Quo and Outlook*, Goldmedia, 2008.

10. Rolf R. Hainich, *The End of Hardware* (Booksurge, 2009).

11. John Palfrey and Urs Gasser, *Born Digital: Understanding the First Generation of Digital Natives* (Basic Books, 2010).

12. ODM Group. "Social Media."

13. Cisco, *Connected World Technology Report*, 2011.

14. Carl Johnson, "The Internet: Can't Live Without It," *Forbes*, November 2, 2011.

15. Cisco, *Connected World Technology.*

16. Antony Mayfield, *Me and My Web Shadow: How to Manage Your Reputation Online* (A&C Black, 2010).

17. Cisco, *Connected World Technology.*

18. Jeffrey Rosen, "The Web Means the End of Forgetting," *New York Times*, July 21, 2010.

19. Mayfield, *Me and My Web Shadow.*

20. Bernhard Warner, "How to be unGoogleable," London *Times*, May 28, 2008.

21. Veit Medick and Severin Weiland, "German Agency to Mine Facebook to Assess Creditworthiness," *Spiegel Online International*, June 7, 2012.

22. Michael Fertik, "Your Future Employer Is Watching You Online, You Should Be Too," *HBR Blog Network*, April 3, 2012.

23. Susan Adams, "More Employers Using Social Media to Hunt for Talent," *Forbes*, July 13, 2011.

24. ODM Group, "Social Media."

25. Chris Anderson, *The Impact of Social Media on Lodging Performance*, Cornell University Center for Hospitality Research, 2012.

26. "Berkeley Economists Study Link Between Online Reviews and Restaurant Bookings," *Review Trackers*, September 6, 2012.

27. CSIMarket, "eBay Inc. Active Users," August 2013.

28. "eBay Inc. Reports Strong Fourth Quarter and Full Year 2011 Results," eBay press release, January 18, 2012.

29. Craigslist website, www.craigslist.org/about/factsheet.

30. Ian Cowie, "Bank Chief Claims Peer-to-Peer Lenders Could Replace Banks," *Daily Telegraph*, December 17, 2012.

31. Ellen Lee, "As Wikipedia Moves to S.F., Founder Discusses Planned Changes," *San Francisco Chronicle*, November 30, 2007.

32. Kickstarter website, www.kickstarter.com.

33. Cowie, "Bank Chief Claims."

34. "Peer-to-Peer Finance Celebrates its 7th Birthday as UK Banks Inflict the Highest Lending Rates in Recorded History," Zopa press release, March 6, 2012.

35. Sharlene Goff, "Peer-to-Peer Lending: Model Takes Off Worldwide," *Financial Times*, June 13, 2012.

36. Patrick Collinson, "Vince Cable Launches £110m Loan Scheme Aimed at Small Firms," *The Guardian*, December 12, 2012.

37. Goff, "Peer-to-Peer Lending."

38. Elaine Moore and Jonathan Moules, "Peer-to-Peer Loans Company Closes," *Financial Times*, December 7, 2011.

39. Margareta Pagano, "Bank Supremo: Peer-to-Peer Lending Is a Good Reason to Be Cheerful," *The Independent*, December 17, 2012.

40. Google Apps Documentation and Support, "Gmail App for Blackberry End of Life announcement," support.google.com/a/bin/answer.py?hl=en-uk&hlrm=en-uk&hlrm=en-uk&hlrm=en&answer=1733075.

41. "American Diversified Holdings Corporation Formally Enters $160 Billion Cloud Computing Industry," American Diversified Holdings press release, June 29, 2012.

42. Holm Friebe and Sascha Lobo, *Wir nennen es Arbeit: Die digitale Boheme oder: Intelligentes Leben jenseits der Festanstellung* [We Call It Work: The Digital Bohemians, or Life Beyond Fixed Employment] (Heyne, 2006).

43. Holm Friebe, "The Digital Bohemians," Goethe Institut, September 2006.

44. Reuven Gorsht, "Unemployed? Buy An iPhone," *Forbes*, January 4, 2013; Benedikt Fuest, "Das virtuelle Büro ist die Basis für die Zukunft" [The Virtual Office Is the Basis for the Future], *Die Welt*, January 19, 2013; and Jessica Leeder, "Virtual Offices Are Altering the Future of Work," *Globe and Mail*, December 28, 2012.

45. Fuest, "Das virtuelle Büro."

46. There are, of course, many individuals in older generations who are extremely competent at using digital technology. However, it is by no means an overgeneralization to suggest that younger generations are as a rule much more comfortable doing so.

47. Shane Hickey and Fiona Ellis, "PricewaterhouseCoopers Staff Brought to Book Over Raunchy Emails," *Belfast Telegraph*, November 10, 2010; and Claire Murphy, "Now KPMG Under Fire as Sexist Email Surfaces," *Evening Herald*, November 11, 2010.

48. Evelyn Rusli, "Unvarnished: A Clean, Well-Lighted Place for Defamation," *Tech Crunch*, March 30, 2010.

49. Rusli, "Unvarnished"; Ki Mae Heussner, "Honestly.com Wants You to Rate Your Co-Workers," ABC News, October 19, 2010; and Marshall Kirkpatrick, "Unvarnished: Is Pete Kazanjy an Evil Genius?" *ReadWrite*, March 30, 2010.

50. Heussner, "Honestly.com Wants You."

51. Ibid.

52. Jason Kincaid, "Cubeduel: Hot or Not Meets LinkedIn. Your Darker Side Will Love It," *Tech Crunch*, January 13, 2011.

53. John Cook, "LinkedIn Shuts Down Cubeduel, the Viral Co-Worker Rating Service," *Puget Sound Business Journal*, January 14, 2011.

54. Michael Arrington, "Reputation Is Dead: It's Time to Overlook Our Indiscretions," *Tech Crunch*, March 28, 2010.

55. Annika Breidthardt, "Annette Schavan Resigns: German Education Minister Quits Amid Plagiarism Scandal," *Huffington Post*, February 9, 2013; "Germany's Education Minister Annette Schavan Quits Over ' Plagiarism' Row," *The Independent*, February 9, 2013; and "German Education Minister Quits Over PhD Plagiarism," *The Guardian*, February 9, 2013.

56. Stephen Evans, "German Minister Annette Schavan Quits Over 'Plagiarism': Analysis," *BBC News*, February 9, 2013.

57. Christoph Amend, "Unter Verdacht" [Under Suspicion], *Die Zeit*, January 31, 2013.

58. John K. Mullen, "Digital Natives Are Slow to Pick up Nonverbal Cues," *Harvard Business Review Blog Network*, March 16, 2012.

59. Adam Hartley, "'Digital Natives' Lack Social Skills and Suffer Increased Attention Deficit Disorder," *TechRadar*, October 28, 2008.

60. Ibid.

61. Mullen, "Digital Natives Are Slow."

62. Steven B. Wolff, Ruth Wageman, and Mary Fontaine, "The Coming Leadership Gap: An Exploration of Competencies That Will Be in Short Supply," *International Journal of Human Resources Development and Management*, February 2009.

63. "Yahoo Acquires Summly App," *Yahoo! Finance*, March 27, 2013; and Heesun Wee, "Meet the 17-Year-Old Who Is Reinventing News," *CNBC.com*, November 16, 2012.

64. Ian Kar, "Summly: 5 Fast Facts You Need to Know," *Heavy.com*, March 27, 2013.

65. Tim Bradshaw, "News App Makes Millionaire of Web Whizz Kid," *Financial Times*, March 25, 2013.

66. Ibid.

67. "Use of Personal Mobile Devices in the Workplace to Double by 2014," *BCS*, August 8, 2012.

68. Shara Tibken, "Danger-to-Go," *Wall Street Journal (Europe Edition)*, September 25, 2011.

69. Cisco, *Connected World Technology*.

70. Ian Cook, *BYOD—Research Findings Released*, CXO Unplugged, November 28, 2012.

71. Greg Ferenstein, "Why Banning Social Media Often Backfires," *Mashable*, April 13, 2010.

72. Sharon Gaudin, "Study: 54 Percent of Companies Ban Facebook, Twitter at Work," *Wired*, September 10, 2009.

73. James Surowiecki, "In Praise of Distraction," *The New Yorker*, April 11, 2011.

74. Adi Gaskell, "Banning Social Media at Work Is Useless," *Technorati*, December 20, 2011.

75. Iain Thompson, "Facebook Ban Could Lead to Staff Exodus," V3.co.uk, June 5, 2008.

76. Oscar Wilde, *The Picture of Dorian Gray* (1890).

## Chapter 5

1. "Population Seven Billion: UN Sets Out Challenges," *BBC News*, October 26, 2011.

2. "U.S. and World Population Clock," U.S. Census Bureau, U.S. Department of Commerce, www.census.gov/popclock/.

3. United Nations Population Division, *World Population Prospects*, 2002 Revision; and "World Population to Reach 10 Billion by 2100 if Fertility in All Countries Converges to Replacement Level," United Nations press release, May 3, 2011.

4. Sarah Harper, *Ageing Societies: Myths, Challenges and Opportunities* (Hodder Arnold, 2006).

5. Sebastian Mallaby, "Japan Should Scare the Eurozone," *Financial Times*, December 11, 2012.

6. "Meet the Most Typical Person on Earth," *The Week*, March 7, 2011.

7. "World's Population to Reach 7 Billion this Month," *Daily Telegraph*, October 17, 2011.

8. "World Population to Reach 10 Billion."

9. United Nations Department of Economic and Social Affairs, International Migration 2006, March 2006. The seventh country was the United States.

10. Joel E. Cohen, B*eyond Population: Everyone Counts in Development*, Center for Global Development, July 2010.

11. Deutsche Stiftung Weltbevölkerung [German World Population Founda-

tion], *Datenreport: Soziale und demographische Daten zur Weltbevölkerung* [Data Report: Social and Demographic Data on the World's Population], 2007.

12. United Nations Population Division, *Replacement Migration: Is It a Solution to Declining and Aging Populations?* 2000.

13. Guan Xiaofeng, "Most People Free to Have More Child [*sic*]," *China Daily*, July 11, 2007.

14. Jeffrey Kluger, "China's One-Child Policy: Curse of the 'Little Emperors,' " *Time*, January 10, 2013.

15. Science magazine podcast, January 11, 2013.

16. Alexa Olesen, "Experts Challenge China's 1-Child Population Claim," Associated Press, October 27, 2011.

17. "400 Million Births Prevented by One-Child Policy," *People's Daily*, October 28, 2011.

18. "China Faces Growing Gender Imbalance," *BBC News*, January 11, 2010.

19. Dominic Bailey, Mick Ruddy, and Marina Shchukina, "Ageing China: Changes and Challenges," *BBC News*, September 20, 2012.

20. Malcolm Moore, "China: The Rise of the 'Precious Snowflakes'," *Daily Telegraph*, January 8, 2012.

21. Kluger, "China's One-Child Policy."

22. It should be noted that some of these traits have specific definitions according to psychologists, i.e., conscientiousness (organized, thorough, detail-oriented), pessimism (anxious, defensive), and neuroticism (anxious, tense).

23. L. Cameron et al., "Little Emperors: Behavioral Impacts of China's One-Child Policy," *Science*, January 10, 2013.

24. "China's One-Child Policy 'Has Created Risk Averse Little Emperors'," *Daily Telegraph*, January 11, 2013.

25. "China Thinktank Urges End of One-Child Policy," *The Guardian*, October 31, 2012; and Tom Phillips, "Chinese Academics Urge End to One-Child Policy," *Daily Telegraph*, July 5, 2012.

26. "China Thinktank Urges End."

27. United Nations, World Population Ageing: 1950-2050, 2002.

28. United Nations, *Population Facts*, April 2012.

29. United Nations, *Population Challenges and Development Goals*, 2005.

30. Alex Spillius and Julian Ryall, "World Faces Ageing Population Time Bomb, Says UN," *Daily Telegraph*, October 1, 2012.

31.   Carl Haub, "World Population Aging: Clocks Illustrate Growth in Population Under Age 5 and Over Age 65," Population Reference Bureau, January 2011.

32.   IMF, *Global Financial Stability Report*, International Monetary Fund, April 2012.

33.   Philippa Roxby, "Is There a Limit to Life Expectancy?" *BBC News*, March 19, 2011.

34.   Ibid.

35.   "Into the Unknown," *The Economist*, November 18, 2010.

36.   Hiroshi Yoshikawa, "Japan's Aging Population and Public Deficits," *East Asia Forum*, June 21, 2012.

37.   "Into the Unknown."

38.   Julian Ryall, "Japan's Population Contracts at Fastest Rate Since at Least 1947," *Daily Telegraph*, January 3, 2012.

39.   "Into the Unknown."

40.   Ibid.

41.   Yoshikawa, "Japan's Aging Population."

42.   "Into the Unknown."

43.   Takashi Oshio and Akiko Sato Oishi, *Social Security and Retirement in Japan: An Evaluation Using Micro-Data*, National Bureau of Economic Research, January 2004.

44.   "Aging Populations in Europe, Japan, Korea, Require Action," *India Times*, March 22, 2000.

45.   OECD, *Factbook 2011–2012: Economic, Environmental and Social Statistics*, 2012.

46.   Richard Cincotta, *Population Aging: A Demographic and Geographic Overview*, National Intelligence Council, Global Trends 2030 website, July 30, 2012.

47.   "World Briefing—Asia: Japan Most Elderly Nation," *New York Times*, July 1, 2006.

48.   Tim Ross, and James Kirkup, "Steve Webb: The Era of Early Retirement Is Over," *Daily Telegraph*, January 9, 2013.

49.   Mallaby, "Japan Should Scare."

50.   Laurence Kotlikoff, "What Neither Candidate Will Admit—Social Security Is Desperately Broke," *Forbes*, July 13, 2012.

51.   William Selway, "U.S. States Pension Fund Deficits Widen by 26%, Pew Center Study Says," *Bloomberg*, April 26, 2011.

52. Ross and Kirkup, "Steve Webb."

53. Hay Group, *The War for Leaders: How to Prepare for Battle*, December 2007.

54. V. Rukmini Rao and Lynette Dumble, "Why the World Is More Dangerous with Fewer Girls," *The Age*, January 17, 2013.

55. Amartya Sen, "More Than 100 Million Women Are Missing," *New York Review of Books*, December 20, 1990.

56. Monica Das Gupta et al., *Why Is Son Preference so Persistent in East and South Asia? A Cross-Country Study of China, India, and the Republic of Korea*, World Bank, January 2003.

57. Monica Das Gupta, "Cultural Versus Biological Factors in Explaining Asia's 'Missing Women': Response to Oster," *Population and Development Review*, June 2006.

58. Rao and Dumble, "Why the World."

59. Das Gupta et al., *Why Is Son Preference.*

60. Rao and Dumble, "Why the World."

61. Ibid.

62. Sen, "More Than 100 Million."

63. Tasneem Siddiqui, "Migration and Gender in Asia," UN Expert Group Meeting on International Migration and Development in Asia and the Pacific, September 19, 2008.

64. *International Migration Report 2009: A Global Assessment*, United Nations Department of Economic and Social Affairs, December 2011.

65. "UNFCCC Executive Secretary Says Significant Funds Needed to Adapt to Climate Change Impacts," United Nations Framework Convention on Climate Change press release, April 6, 2007.

66. Robert O., *Future Trajectories of Migration and Issues Policy Makers Will Face—Migration and Europe*, National Intelligence Council, Global Trends 2030 website, July 9, 2012.

67. Moore's Law is a computing industry axiom stating that the number of transistors on a circuit doubles every two years, effectively doubling computer processing power in that time.

68. Hay Group, *The War for Leaders.*

69. Richard van Noorden, "Global Mobility: Science on the Move," *Nature*, October 17, 2012.

70. Hay Group analysis.

71. Jane Qiu, "China Targets Top Talent from Overseas," *Nature*, January 28, 2009; and van Noorden, "Global Mobility."

72.  Robert O., *Future Trajectories.*

73.  *The MetLife Study of Working Caregivers and Employer Health Care Costs: New Insights and Innovations for Reducing Health Care Costs for Employers,* University of Pittsburgh, Institute on Aging, February 2010.

74.  "Your U.S. Benefits Program: Winning with Wellness," Hewlett Packard brochure, January 2013; and IBM website.

75.  Thomas Öchsner, "Weniger als 200 Deutsche nutzen Pflege-Auszeit" [Less than 200 Germans Use Care Leave], *Süddeutsche Zeitung,* December 28, 2012; and OECD, "Help Wanted? Providing and Paying for Long-Term Care," Organisation for Economic Co-operaton and Development, May 18, 2011.

76.  Sylvia Ann Hewlett and Ripa Rashid, *Winning the War for Talent in Emerging Markets: Why Women Are the Solution* (Harvard Business Press Books, 2011).

77.  Rahim Kanani, "Winning the War for Talent in Emerging Markets: Why Women Are the Solution," *Forbes,* September 6, 2011.

78.  Michael Austin, "India's Missing Women," *The American,* January 10, 2013.

79.  Kanani, "Winning the War."

80.  Ibid.

81.  World Economic Forum, *Corporate Gender Gap Report,* 2010.

82.  Kanani, "Winning the War."

83.  Ibid.

84.  Hewlett and Rashid, *Winning the War.*

85.  Kanani, "Winning the War."

86.  Hewlett and Rashid, *Winning the War.*

87.  Kanani, "Winning the War."

**Chapter 6**

1.  Paul Taylor et al., "Samsung Gets Ticking with Smartwatch Launch." *Financial Times,* September 4, 2013.

2.  Lance Laytner, "Did Steve Jobs Study Star Trek?" *Edit International,* 2011; Michael Cooney, "The Top 10 Real-Life Star Trek Inventions," *Network World,* February 11, 2007; and Reed Farrington, "Treknobabble #50: Top 10 Star Trek Inventions in Use Today," www.filmjunk.com, January 21, 2009.

3.  "Probable Quotes from History," *The MATYC [Mathematics Association of Two-Year Colleges] Journal* 12, no. 3, Fall 1978, p. 189.

4. Vincenzo Balzani, Alberto Credi, and Margherita Venturi, "Molecular Devices and Machines," *Nano Today*, April 2007.

5. K. Eric Drexler, Chris Peterson, and Gayle Pergamit, *Unbounding the Future: The Nanotechnology Revolution* (William Morrow, 1991).

6. Bill Joy, "Why the Future Doesn't Need Us," *Wired*, April 4, 2000.

7. "As Nanotechnology Goes Mainstream, 'Toxic Socks' Raise Concerns; Unknown Risks from Nanosilver Cited," *Science Daily*, April 7, 2008.

8. "Market Research Forecast Tissue Engineering Market at $11 Billion by 2012," Marketresearch.com, February 15, 2012.

9. Manik Surtani, "On Ubiquitous Computing," talk presented at the Institute of Physics conference Physics in Perspective 2012, February 14, 2012.

10. Joy, "Why the Future."

11. Caroline Perry, "What Ultra-Tiny Nanocircuits Can Do," *Harvard Gazette*, February 9, 2011.

12. "Columbia Engineers Prove Graphene Is the Strongest Material," www.columbia.edu, July 21, 2008.

13. Alex Hudson, "Is Graphene a Miracle Material?" *BBC News*, May 21, 2011.

14. "Columbia Engineers Prove."

15. Hudson, "Is Graphene a Miracle."

16. Anna Kurkijärvi, "Hero Material: 10 Fascinating Facts About Graphene," *Conversations by Nokia*, conversations.nokia.com, February 7, 2013.

17. Hudson, "Is Graphene a Miracle."

18. Nidhi Subbaraman, "Flexible Touch Screen Made with Printed Graphene," *MIT Technology Review*, June 21, 2010.

19. "Graphene and Human Brain Project Win Largest Research Excellence Award in History, as Battle for Sustained Science Funding Continues," European Commission press release, January 28, 2013; and Iain Thompson, "Nokia Shares $1.35bn EU Graphene Research Grant," *The Register*, February 1, 2013.

20. Hudson, "Is Graphene a Miracle."

21. Simon Karger, "The Cutting Edge of Surgery," Cambridge Consultants, Autumn 2012.

22. Ray Kurzweil, "Bring on the Nanobots, and We Will Live Long and Prosper," *The Guardian*, November 22, 2007.

23. Anne Trafton, "Turning Off Cancer Genes," *MIT News*, November 16, 2010; and Kurzweil, "Bring on the Nanobots."

24. Andrew Goldman, "Talk: Ray Kurzweil Says We're Going to Live Forever," *New York Times*, January 25, 2013.

25. "Nanotechnology in Food," UnderstandingNano.com.

26. Emily Sohn, "Scorpion Venom Tapped as Pesticide," ABC, January 20, 2010: and Bob Beale, "Funnel Webs Reduce Insecticide Need," ABC, July 7, 2003.

27. Kurzweil, "Bring on the Nanobots."

28. Farhad Manjoo, "The Bully on the Night Stand," *New York Times*, June 27, 2012.

29. Nick Goldman et al., "Towards Practical, High-Capacity, Low-Maintenance Information Storage in Synthesized DNA," *Nature*, May 15, 2012; "Test-Tube Data," *The Economist*, January 26, 2013; and Robert F. Service, "Half a Million DVDs in Your DNA," *Science*, January 23, 2013.

30. "7 Massive Ideas That Could Change the World," *Wired*, January 17, 2013.

31. www.pipistrel.si.

32. Grant Naylor, *Better Than Life* (Penguin, 1991).

33. Steve Connor, "Students Could Face Compulsory Drug Tests as Rising Numbers Turn to 'Cognitive Enhancers' to Boost Concentration and Exam Marks," *The Independent*, November 7, 2012.

34. W. S. Bainbridge, *Converging Technologies (NBIC)*, U.S. National Science Foundation, 2003.

35. Stephen Harris, "Cyborg Pioneer Prof Kevin Warwick," *The Engineer*, October 3, 2011.

36. M. N. Gasson et al., "Invasive Neural Prosthesis for Neural Signal Detection and Nerve Stimulation," *International Journal of Adaptive Control and Signal Processing*, June 2005.

37. University of Reading website, www.reading.ac.uk/.

38. Kevin Warwick et al., "Thought Communication and Control: A First Step Using Radiotelegraphy," *IEE Proceedings Communications*, June 25, 2004.

39. Joy, "Why the Future."

40. CIA, The Darker Bioweapons Future, Central Intelligence Agency, November 3, 2003.

41. K. Eric Drexler, *Engines of Creation: The Coming Era of Nanotechnology* (Anchor Books, 1986); and Joy, "Why the Future."

42. Henry David Thoreau, *Walden* (Ticknor and Fields, 1854).

43. Jeff Klein, "Only Time Will Tell if Nanotechnology Will Be the 'New Asbestos'," *Boulder Business Law Advisor*, March 25, 2011.

44. Steven Vaughan, "Laying Down the Law on Nanotechnology," *The Guardian*, June 11, 2012.

45. Klein, "Only Time Will Tell."

46. James Abbey, "Nanotechnology: Market Growth and Regional Initiatives," *Connexions*, April 11, 2012.

47. Donald Light, "A Scenario: The End of Auto Insurance," *Celent*, May 8, 2012.

48. Lucintel, *Global Motor Vehicle Insurance Industry 2012–2017: Trend, Profit, and Forecast Analysis*, June 2012.

49. Chunka Miu, "Fasten Your Seatbelts: Google's Driverless Car Is Worth Trillions (Part 1)," *Forbes*, January 22, 2013.

50. Jonathan Cohn, "The Robot Will See You Now," *The Atlantic*, March 2013.

51. "DNA Nanorobot Triggers Targeted Therapeutic Responses," *Science Daily*, February 16, 2012.

52. Alice Park, "Top 10 Medical Breakthroughs: 7. Speeding DNA-Based Diagnosis for Newborns," *Time*, December 4, 2012.

53. Matt Ridley, "Editing Our Genes, One Letter at a Time," *Wall Street Journal*, January 11, 2012; and Randall Parker, "New Gene Editing Technique to Revolutionize Gene Therapy?" *Future Pundit*, January 8, 2012.

54. Jeremy J. Song et al., "Regeneration and Experimental Orthotopic Transplantation of a Bioengineered Kidney," *Nature Medicine*, April 14, 2013; and James Gallagher, "Scientists Make 'Laboratory-Grown' Kidney," *BBC News*, April 15, 2013.

55. Masahito Tachibana et al., "Human Embryonic Stem Cells Derived by Somatic Cell Nuclear Transfer," *Cell*, May 15, 2013; and Ian Sample, "Human Embryonic Stem Cells Created from Adult Tissue for First Time," *The Guardian*, May 15, 2013.

56. "The Third Industrial Revolution," *The Economist*, April 21, 2012; Tim Hulse, "Big in 2013: 3D Printing," *BA Business Life*, January 1, 2013; and Alexander Hotz, "3D Printers Shape Up to Lead the Next Technology Gold Rush," *The Guardian*, October 5, 2012.

57. "The Third Industrial Revolution."

58. Spencer Thompson, "3D Printing Is Coming—So Let's Not Strangle the Industry at Birth," *The Guardian*, October 16, 2012; and "The Third Industrial Revolution."

59. "The Third Industrial Revolution"; and Hotz, "3D Printers Shape Up."

60. "The Third Industrial Revolution."

61. Robert A. Guth, "How 3-D Printing Figures to Turn Web Worlds Real," *Wall Street Journal*, December 12, 2007.

62. "The Third Industrial Revolution."

63. Thompson, "3D Printing Is Coming."

64. James Legge, "US Government Orders Cody Wilson and Defense Distributed to Remove Blueprint for 3D-Printed Handgun from the Web," *The Independent*, May 10, 2013.

65. Rosabeth Moss Kanter, "To Create Jobs, Break the ICE—Innovate, Collaborate, Educate," *Huffington Post*, June 24, 2012; and Darren Murph, "Verizon's Innovation Center: Incubating the Next Generation of Connected Devices Keeps the 'Dumb Pipe' Naysayers at Bay," *engadget*, June 3, 2013.

66. IBM, *Leading Through Connections: Insights from the Global Chief Executive Study*, 2012.

67. Hay Group, *Best Companies for Leadership*, 2012.

68. Ariel Schwartz, "The Future of Work: Quantified Employees, Pop-Up Workplaces, and More Telepresence," *Fast Company*, January 23, 2013.

69. Alex McNally, "Nestlé Buys Novartis Medical Nutrition in Long-Awaited Deal," Nutraingredients.com, July 2, 2007.

## Chapter 7

1. This, of course, is true of both publicly listed and private companies. These two types of ownership and their different consequences for leadership are beyond the scope of this book.

2. The degree of variation between local markets will be greater in some sectors than others. It is likely to be felt more keenly in the FMCG area, for example, than in a more platform-based industry such as automotive. But even there, standardized platforms will not help the cause of, say, a German component supplier looking to win business among Chinese OEMs.

3. Maxim Duncan and Clare Jim, "Foxconn China Plant Closed After 2,000 Riot," *Reuters*, September 24, 2012.

4. *New Oxford Dictionary of English* (Oxford University Press, 1998).

5. This positive outcome for younger workers may seem at odds with the current economic climate—particularly in Europe, where youth unemployment has reached all-time highs in several countries. This is a consequence of the financial collapse, which was caused by short-term shock (the credit crisis) in a specific context (banking), or what Nicholas Naseem Taleb termed a "black swan" in his book *Fooled by Randomness* (Random House, 2001). Black swans are distinct from megatrends, which are long-term and pervasive in nature. We might reasonably expect the economies affected by the financial crisis to look very different by 2030.

6. German sociologist Andreas Reckwitz defines a *practice* as "routinized behavior" consisting of several interrelated elements: physical and mental activity, objects and their use, background knowledge and understanding, know-how, states of emotion, and motivational knowledge. See A. Reckwitz, "Toward a Theory of Social Practices: A Development in Culturalist Theorizing," *European Journal of Social Theory*, vol. 5, no. 2, 2002, p. 249.

7. danah m. boyd [*sic*] and Nicole B. Ellison, "Social Network Sites: Definition, History, Scholarship," *Journal of Computer-Mediated Communication*, vol. 13, 2007, pp. 210–230; and Nicole B. Ellison, Charles Steinfield, and Cliff Lampe, "The Benefits of Facebook 'Friends': Social Capital and College Students' Use of Online Social Network Sites," *Journal of Computer-Mediated Communication*, vol. 12, 2007, pp. 1143–1168.

## Chapter 8

1. Kerstin Bund, Uwe Jean Heuser, and Claas Tatje, "Die Super-Männchen. Begabt, bescheiden und effizient: die Konzernlenker von heute sind anders. Sind sie die besseren Chefs?" [The Supermen. Talented, Modest and Efficient. Today's Corporate CEOs Are Different. Are They Better Leaders?], *Zeit Online*, June 28, 2012.

2. "Aktionärswatsche für Schrempp: 'Er ist ein Manager des Misserfolgs' " [A Blow from Shareholders for Schrempp: "He Is a Manager of Failure"], *Spiegel Online*, March 31, 2005.

3. In biology, of course, there are only alpha-males. In leadership terms, however, we can certainly identify a number of women who possess (or possessed) alpha-male type leadership qualities, e.g., former UK Prime Minister Margaret Thatcher. But this style of leadership is a predominantly male approach and displays classic male behavior.

4. Mats Alvesson and Stefan Sveningsson, "The Great Disappearing Act: Difficulties in Doing Leadership," *The Leadership Quarterly*, vol. 14, 2003.

5. William H. Drath and Charles J. Palus, *Making Common Sense*, CCL Report No. 156, 1994. This is a rough summary of their definition, but sufficient for our purposes. The term *social practice* has a long tradition in philosophy and social theory, stemming from different philosophical schools. See Georg Vielmetter, *Die Unbestimmtheit des Sozialen. Zur Philosophie der Sozialwissenschaften* [The Indeterminacy of the Social: On the Philosophy of Social Science], eds. Axel Honneth, Hans Joas, and Claus Offe (Campus Press, 1998). A great overview can be found in Andreas Reckwitz, "Toward a Theory of Social Practices: A Development in Culturalist Theorizing," *European Journal of Social Theory*, vol. 5, no. 2, 2002.

6.  Brigid Carroll, Lester Levy, and David Richmond, "Leadership as Practice: Challenging the Competency Paradigm," *Leadership*, vol. 4, 2008. Another critique of the competency framework can be found in Richard Bolden, "Leadership Competencies: Time to Change the Tune," *Leadership*, vol. 2, 2006.

7.  These are the six styles of leadership identified by Hay Group over decades of research. A great overview of these can be found in Mary Fontaine, Ruth Malloy, and Scott Spreier, "Leadership Run Amok," *Harvard Business Review*, June 2006.

8.  This is not to suggest that these styles are always inappropriate. Effective leadership depends on the context and the situation. When a fire breaks out, we do not expect firefighters to sit down and discuss what to do about it until they agree (participative leadership style). We expect them to shout clear commands (directive leadership style). Similarly, in a business context, directive and pacesetting leadership styles are effective in a crisis or turnaround situation. The issue with the alpha-male leaders is that they overrely on these styles in the long run and that they do not listen to others.

9.  A good overview of post-heroic leadership can be found in Fabian Lotze, *Practical Implications of Post-Heroic Leadership Theories: A Critical Examination*, dissertation, Anglia Ruskin University, September 2011. See also Noshir S. Contractor et al., "The Topology of Collective Leadership," *The Leadership Quarterly*, vol. 23, 2012, pp. 994–1011. Another version of the post-heroic leader is Jim Collins's "Level 5 leader," described as "modest and willful, humble, and fearless"; see Jim Collins, *Good to Great: Why Some Companies Make the Leap … and Others Don't* (Harper Business, 2001). A very early leadership approach that shares some characteristics with the post-heroic leader is Robert Greenleaf's "servant leader": a leader who focuses primarily on the growth and well-being of people and the communities to which he belongs. See Robert K. Greenleaf, *Servant Leadership: A Journey into the Nature of Legitimate Power and Greatness*, 25th Anniversary Edition (Paulist Press, 2002).

10. *New York Times Magazine*, October 28, 1973.

11. Ian Robertson, *The Winner Effect: How Power Affects Your Brain* (Bloomsbury, 2012).

12. Jan-Emmanuel De Neve et al., "Born to Lead? A Twin Design and Genetic Association Study of Leadership Role Occupancy," *The Leadership Quarterly*, vol. 24, 2013, pp. 45–60.

13. Fontaine, Malloy, and Spreier, "Leadership Run Amok."

14. Ruth Malloy, *The Women Executives Study. A Comparative Study of Highly Successful Female Leaders with Their Male and Typical Female Counterparts*, McClelland Center for Innovation and Research, Hay Group, February 2004. See also *Style Matters: Why Women Executives Shouldn't Ignore Their "Feminine Side,"* Hay Group, 2012.

15. Bund, Heuser, and Tatje, "Die Super-Männchen."

16. The iceberg illustration and description of personal characteristics are taken from Hay Group, *The Three Social Motives*, 2000. This paper is based on David C. McClelland, *Motives, Personality, and Society* (Praeger, 1984); and David C. McClelland and D. H. Burnham, "Power Is the Great Motivator," *Harvard Business Review*, vol. 73, no. 1, 1995, pp. 126–139.

17. A motive scoring test, developed by David McClelland, can be used to understand social motives profiles and is available from Hay Group at http://www.haygroup.com/leadershipandtalentondemand/ourproducts/item_details.aspx?itemid=53&type=2&t=1

18. Our work on the competencies of altrocentric leaders draws partly on outstanding empirical research by Signe Spencer, Ruth Malloy, Deb Nunes, and Ruth Wageman for Hay Group on the critical success competencies of CEOs and senior executives. See Hay Group, *CEO Competency Dictionary Version 3.0*, November 2011, and *Executive Competency Dictionary Version 2.0*, November 2011. These capture the unique competencies that contribute to the effectiveness of CEOs and executives.

19. Max Weber's "ideal type" is a hypothetical concept constructed in order to analyze, order, and interpret social reality by highlighting and accentuating crucial aspects of it.

20. Daniel Goleman, *Emotional Intelligence* (Bantam Doubleday Dell, 1996).

21. Rick Lash and Chris Huber, *Leading in a Global Environment: 2010 Best Companies for Leadership Study*, Hay Group, January 25, 2011.

22. Ibid.

23. Stewart Ashley Dutfield, "Leadership and Meaning in Collective Action," *Leadership Review*, vol. 5, Spring 2005, p. 24.

24. "Stephen Elop's Memo in Full," FT.com, February 9, 2011.

25. Susie Cranston and Scott Keller, "Increasing the Meaning Quotient at Work," *McKinsey Quarterly*, January 2013.

26. "Stephen Elop's Memo."

27. Ibid. Elop told his employees: "We've lost market share, we've lost mind share and we've lost time…. I believe at least some of it has been due to our attitude inside Nokia. We poured gasoline on our own burning platform. I believe we have lacked accountability and leadership to align

and direct the company through these disruptive times. We had a series of misses. We haven't been delivering innovation fast enough. We're not collaborating internally." Interestingly, Elop's memo makes reference to only two of the five meaning-making perspectives described by Cranston and Keller: the company perspective (the turnaround story) and the customer perspective (he discusses Nokia's brand perception). It makes no mention of society, teams, or individuals. In this critical phase, he focused on the core: the company and its customers. The other perspectives came later in the meaning-making process.

28.    The process and conditions for creating an effective leadership team are expertly captured in Ruth Wageman et al., *Senior Leadership Teams: What It Takes to Make Them Great* (Harvard Business School Press, 2008). The senior team leadership competency we describe here is based on this book.

# Index